THE
National ⚾ Pastime
A REVIEW OF BASEBALL HISTORY

With great sadness, we run in this issue the late Ralph Horton's final article for SABR, a typically well-researched, clearly written exposition on the Big Four who brought success to Detroit in the 1880s. Ralph's example as an exemplary colleague, researcher, and friend, will stay with us.

SABR members fortunate enough to attend the annual convention in Scottsdale, Arizona this past June had two never-to-be-forgotten thrills: watching José Jimenez pitch the Arizona Diamond Diamondbacks' first no hitter, and listening to Tommy Henrich's marvelous keynote talk at the banquet. Our lead article in this issue is Old Reliable's appreciation of outfield mate Joe DiMaggio Along with the baseball insights, we learn just how quiet and distant the Clipper was, even with longtime teammates.

Chris Lamb writes perceptively about how differently the white and black press covered the first spring training appearances of Jackie Robinson with Montreal. This pairs nicely with Tom Gallagher's piece on the role played in baseball integration by Lester Rodney and the *Daily Worker*.

David Voigt gives us his choice of the twelve key years of baseball's twentieth century—and a little philosophy to boot.

There's plenty more, of course, from Grove to Gumpert, from semipro to the minors to Japanese ball. Jump in!

—*Mark Alvarez*

THE NATIONAL PASTIME (ISSN 0734-6905, ISBN 0-910137-77-3), Number 19. Published by The Society for American Baseball Research, Inc., 812 Huron Rd., Suite 719, Cleveland, OH 44115. Postage paid at Birmingham, AL. Copyright 1999, The Society for American Baseball Research, Inc. All rights reserved. Reproduction in whole or in part without written permission is prohibited. Printed by EBSCO Media, Birmingham, AL.

Editor
Mark Alvarez

Copy Editor
A.D. Suehsdorf

Designated Reader
Dick Thompson

The Society for American Baseball Research

History

The Society for American Baseball Research (SABR) was founded on August 10, 1971, by L. Robert "Bob" Davids and fifteen other baseball researchers at Cooperstown, New York, and now boasts more than 6,500 members worldwide. The Society's objectives are to foster the study of baseball as a significant American institution, to establish an accurate historical account of baseball through the years, to facilitate the dissemination of baseball research information, to stimulate the best interest of baseball as our national pastime, and to cooperate in safeguarding proprietary interests of individual research efforts of members of the Society.

The National Pastime

The Society published its first issue of **The National Pastime** in 1982. The present volume is the nineteenth. Many of the previous volumes are still available for purchase (see inside back cover). The editorial policy is to publish a cross section of research articles by our members which reflect their interest in history, biography, statistics and other aspects of baseball not previously published.

Interested in Joining the Society?

SABR membership is open to all those interested in baseball research, statistics or history. The 1999 membership dues are $50 US, $60 Canada & Mexico and $65 overseas (US funds only) and are based on the calendar year. Students and Seniors can join for $30 ($40 in Canada & Mexico and $45 overseas) Members receive the **Baseball Research Journal**, **The National Pastime**, *The SABR Bulletin*, a Membership Directory and other special publications. To join SABR, send the appropriate amount and your name and address to the address below . Feel free to contact SABR for more information at the address below as well.

SABR
Dept. TNP
812 Huron Rd E #719
Cleveland, OH 44115
216-575-0500
www.sabr.org
info @ sabr. org

The Last Yankee

Tom Henrich
with Richard Nikas

Looking around the Yankee clubhouse after my recall from Newark in 1937, I knew the men who filled it shared a common sense of purpose—to win. Only one of these men, though, would be a Yankee with me throughout my entire career: "the great DiMaggio." We played together in the outfield that season and were joined in 1939 by Charlie Keller to make up what many people say is the greatest offensive outfield in baseball history. As is if that didn't put me close enough to Joe, we hit back-to-back in the Yankee batting order, with me third and Joe fourth.

I was his teammate longer than anyone else, so maybe I am in the best position to appreciate him. Joe was without a doubt the greatest baseball player that I ever saw. I think he was the greatest baseball player of all time, with the possible exception of Babe Ruth who might rate higher because of his ability as a pitcher. I'm sure Joe would have broken the Babe's records for home runs if he had played in any park other than Yankee Stadium. A righthanded batter in a park built to order for lefties, Joe hit a ton of balls that died in "Death Valley," that deep, deep area in left center field. In any other park those shots would have fallen beyond the fence for home runs.

Joe's burning desire to win and his corresponding fear of failure were the forces that drove him. His attitude was that the best way for his team to succeed was for him to succeed. Of course, he, and we, did. He was the most valuable player that I ever saw on a diamond. If I had to pick one player from history to start a team with, Joe would be the man.

When we played Bob Feller you could see the veins sticking out of Joe's neck. He was determined that he was not going to look bad against the best. Fans remember how graceful he was, running around the bases, playing the outfield with ease, and making the toughest catches look easy. But Joe was a fierce competitor. He always had strawberries on his legs from sliding into the bases so hard. They stayed with him, because he continued to slide on them every day. Joe would go into the clubhouse after a game and say to the trainer, "Fix 'em up, Doc." The next day he would be back out there sliding hard with strawberries on both legs.

Joe led by example. He was always at his best under pressure, getting the hit to win the game or making the catch to save it, taking an extra base as a runner or cutting down opposing runners with his strong, accurate throwing arm. It has often been said that he never threw to the wrong base. It's true. Playing next to him all those years, I can tell you: he never did.

We never collided in the outfield—never even came close. If I called for a fly ball, Joe would let me take it. If I didn't call for it, my responsibility was simply to get out of the way and let Joe take it.

In Yankee Stadium I saw him get a hit to left that looked like a double, but the left fielder got to the ball quickly, released it in a hurry, and made an exceptionally strong throw to second base. Joe was running hard

Tom Henrich *played right field and first base for the New York Yankees from 1937 to 1942 and 1946 to 1950. With Joe DiMaggio and Charlie Keller he was part of one of the game's great outfields. "Old Reliable," who has always preferred "Tom" to "Tommy," soldiers on in Prescott, Arizona, with his wife Eileen.* **Richard Nikas** *is an admiralty lawyer practicing in Long Beach, California. He is a SABR member and a pitcher for the Greek National Baseball Team which will compete in the 2004 Olympic Games in Athens.*

from the start, but when he saw what a good play the left fielder had made, he somehow found even more speed and made it to second safely. I was sitting next to Bill Dickey in the Yankee dugout when it happened. Bill said to the rest of us, "You know something? That guy can run as fast as he has to."

The early days—Joe never knew how much I admired him. He was a loner to us on the team as much as he was a loner to the general public. Lefty Gomez was the one he enjoyed. They shared an apartment in Manhattan and eventually roomed together on the road. Before that, I was Lefty's roommate on trips for three years, yet even then I hardly ever saw Joe. Lefty saw him almost every day and night both at home and on the road, but the rest of us didn't.

Joe and I were Yankees together from 1937 through 1950, with the same three years—'43, '44, and '45—out for military service during the war. In our eleven years together, the Yankees were in the World Series eight times and we won seven. Our only loss came to the Cardinals in '42, two months after I joined the Coast Guard for basic training. Eventually they started calling me "Old Reliable," and Joe was "the Yankee Clipper." To me, he was the Yankees, period.

Joe was a star from the very beginning. In 1936, he made an immediate contribution to the Yankees' success both on the field and at the gate. As a rookie he hit .323 with twenty-nine home runs and 125 runs batted in. In '37 he did even better, with a .346 average, 167 RBIs, and a major-league-leading forty-six home runs and 151 runs scored. In the '36 World Series, he hit .346 against the Giants. In '37, when we beat the Giants again, he drove in two runs with a bases loaded single to help us win the first game, and hit a home run to help us win the final game.

At the beginning of the 1938 season we knew we had a chance to win the World Series three years in a row. But while we were at spring training in St. Petersburg, Joe was in San Francisco holding out for more money. The Yankee management felt Joe wasn't worth as much as the rest of the world thought he was. When he returned for the money that he was originally offered, Joe was booed in every American League park. The country was still dealing with the Great Depression, and the fans had trouble relating to a baseball player who held out when many people were unable to find work at all. Heck, even many of his teammates had trouble understanding how anyone not named Gehrig could ask for that much money.

He never said anything to his teammates about how he felt about all the boos. On the field, Joe handled it well, as he always did when the public put pressure on him. He hit .324, with thirty-two home runs, and 140 runs batted in. After his first three seasons, "the great DiMaggio" had 107 home runs and 432 runs batted in.

He was twenty-three years old.

The next year, 1939, DiMaggio was in our lineup on Opening Day for the first time in his career. He didn't stay there long. A few games later, he tore muscles in his right leg above the ankle while making a sharp turn. He was out of our lineup for thirty-five games. When he came back, he hit so well that he was batting .409 with only three weeks left to go in the season. Then a nerve in his eyelid began giving him trouble and made him blink. A hitter who blinks is no hitter at all, and Joe wasn't. His average dropped twenty-eight points, which still topped both leagues. He was fourth in the league with thirty home runs and second in runs batted in. In recognition of his success, the Baseball Writers' Association of America selected him the Most Valuable Player of the American League.

The best center fielder in baseball—As always, Joe won games for us with his glove as well as his bat. He was the best center fielder in baseball. In '39 I saw him make the greatest catch that I have ever seen. You can talk about Willie Mays in the 1954 World Series, or name any other catch you like, but to me the one that Joe made off Hank Greenberg at Yankee Stadium in 1939 was tops.

I was playing in right field and Joe was in center when Greenberg hit a long fly ball into the monuments that used to be in play in deep center field. DiMag was off at the crack of the bat, maybe even a split second before. He set sail for the outfield wall with his back to the plate, flying over the grass and not looking back until he was almost out of room. Then he leaped, reached up, and caught the ball in the middle of an acrobatic turn. He banged into the wall but held onto the ball.

It was not only the greatest catch that any of us ever saw, it was also the only time that I ever saw Joe make a mistake in eleven years as his teammate. As soon as the play was over, he started to trot off the field, but his catch was only the second out. Earl Averill had already rounded second and was headed for third when Joe made the catch. Joe's hesitation before he realized it was only the second out gave Averill the chance to make it all the way back to first.

Any man who plays center field in the major leagues for thirteen years is entitled to one momentary lapse, especially one that never resulted in a run. That was the only one that I ever saw Joe make, and no one else ever saw him make another one, either.

That World Series in 1939 was our first without Lou Gehrig. The final game against the Reds was a strange one. After nine innings we were tied, 4-4. In the tenth, the wheels fells off the wagon for Cincinnati. Frank Crosetti led off the inning with a walk, and was advanced on a sacrifice bunt by Red Rolfe. Keller reached base on an error by Billy Myers, the shortstop, which allowed Crosetti to reach third. DiMaggio then singled to right, scoring Frankie. The right fielder let the ball roll through his legs, and Keller scored by sliding into Ernie Lombardi. When DiMaggio saw the big catcher on the ground, he just kept coming, and scored as Ernie, who'd really been stunned by the collision, tried to put the tag on him. It was vintage DiMaggio: speedy, aggressive, and heads-up.

The Streak—Of all the seasons, however, 1941 was one to remember. I played next to Joe for every game of his streak and can appreciate it for what it was— magic. It started on the May 15 when our record was 14-15. We had never been in that position before, so we knew something had to be done. Joe was the one who actually did it. He kept on hitting, and he hit the ball hard, even the outs.

We were just glad to be winning again. We weren't excited until well into the streak. The game that I remember most was number thirty-eight at Yankee Stadium. We were facing Elden Auker and the St. Louis Browns. By the bottom of the eighth, Joe was hitless and we were up, 3-1. He was scheduled to bat fourth, so he might not get up at all.

Johnny Sturm popped up to start the inning off, but Rolfe saved the day by drawing a walk. I was up next. I owned Auker, hitting him better than anyone else in the league. The problem was that I hit him so hard that I might hit a sharp grounder that would be perfect for a double play that would end the inning.

I asked for time and walked over to the dugout to ask manager Joe McCarthy for permission to bunt. I knew that if Joe got a chance to bat, Auker had too much class to walk him. McCarthy thought about it for three seconds and said, "That's all right." I laid a bunt down the third base line and was thrown out at first. With Rolfe now at second Joe hit the first pitch into left center for a double. The streak went on.

Joe broke the modern record of hitting in forty-one consecutive games during the first half of a double-header in Washington. Between games, an overly fanatical Yankee rooter swiped Joe's bat. Nobody knew it had happened until I stepped into the batter's box early in the second game. As my left heel dug into the dirt I heard DiMag yelling at me, "Hey Tom. You have my bat." I asked for time and walked toward Joe to show him my bat. It was a DiMaggio model, but it was my bat. We realized that somebody had stolen his bat.

When he batted that inning using another bat he lined out to right center. As we trotted out to the outfield moments later, Joe said, "If that was with my bat it would have been in there." He looked worried, which made me worried. In the dugout the next inning I told him to use my bat. After all, it was a Louisville Slugger D29 model just like his. Joe refused at first, because he didn't want to crack it. After another line out, though,

he grabbed my bat and smacked a single in the seventh to set the modern record.

After we returned to New York for a series against Boston, some friends of Joe's found the guilty kid in Newark and impressed upon him how important the bat was to DiMaggio. With the bat back, the streak went on. Joe's attitude never changed. He handled everything that came his way and he carried the rest of us along for the ride. We were in first place as the streak grew into the forties. Even when it ended, he was hitting the ball hard. It took those two spectacular plays by Ken Keltner and another by Lou Boudreau to hold him hitless during game fifty-seven in Cleveland.

With all the attention focused on Joe, the rest of us were able to just go out and play. We hit home runs in twenty-five consecutive games, for a major league record that still stands. More important, we won forty-two out of the fifty-six games during the streak. We finished with 101 wins and beat the Dodgers that year in the first installment of what would become a great World Series rivalry.

Changes—The next year, 1942, was my last for the duration of World War II. I was drafted by the Coast Guard and began training before the end of the season. Joe continued to play that year, but we lost to the Cardinals in an upset. Joe was called up in 1943, and when we returned things weren't the same. After thirty-five games of that 1946 season, McCarthy was gone. The front office said he was fired, McCarthy said he quit. All of us were in a state of shock. DiMaggio probably took it worst of all. He failed to hit .300 and was in a funk the whole year.

Under Bucky Harris, 1947 was a better year. Joe won his third MVP trophy after hitting twenty home runs and batting .315. Once again, we beat the Dodgers in the World Series. This was the Series of the famous Al Gionfriddo catch off Joe. In the sixth inning of the sixth game we were down, 8-5, when Joe hit a long fly to left center. Gionfriddo, who had just entered the game, took off after the ball and hauled it in at the bullpen fence along the outfield wall.

Many people call it one of the greatest catches ever, but it should have been an easy play. As he ran back to the fence, Gionfriddo actually ran too far and had to pivot back to make the grab. It was a great catch after some not-so-great positioning. As the ball was caught, Joe was rounding second. He pulled up and kicked at the infield dirt, sending up a little cloud of dust. Many people have noted how rare that little display was. They're right. It was the only time during all of our years together that I ever saw Joe express any emotion on the field. He never said anything about it to me, either, in keeping with the DiMaggio that said nothing, ever.

The last Yankee—In 1949, Joe returned from injury to lead us back to the World Series against the Dodgers, again. That year we played under Casey Stengel who was as far a cry from Joe McCarthy as you could ever imagine. Joe never said much about Casey but we all knew that DiMaggio was a McCarthy man. I was too. The two of them, DiMaggio and McCarthy, had a mutual respect that went beyond the Yankees.

Once, Tex Hughson of the Red Sox stuck a fast ball in DiMaggio's ribs during a game in Boston. McCarthy, who was the skipper of the Red Sox by then, looked at his bench and said, "Look at that guy. He won't even rub it." Joe never did. McCarthy wanted his Red Sox to act like Joe DiMaggio. Easier said than done.

After that 1949 season our time together drew short. Joe had a great year in 1950 even as my playing time decreased due to an old injury to my left knee. That year still bothers me. Just before the World Series I was informed by General Manager George Weiss that I would be left off the roster for the Fall Classic. My only consolation came from DiMaggio. The evening before the first game of the series Joe was with Toots Shor in the cocktail lounge of the Warwick Hotel. Talking about the series, Joe told Toots, "I'd rather lose with Tom than win without him." Atta boy, Joe.

The Yankees went on to win that World Series without me and would continue to have great success under Stengel. Maybe Joe and I made a difference to that next generation of Yankees. We used to tell young players with us for the first time, "Go out there like a Yankee." Well, the Great Yankees are all gone: Gehrig, Ruth, Mantle, and DiMaggio. To my mind, Joe was the last Yankee—the last one of us who you could look at and recognize as a Yankee ballplayer. He was a remarkable player, and that is how I am sure he would want to be remembered. It is the only thing that I think about when Joe crosses my mind—he was simply the best that I ever saw play the game.

The day Joe DiMaggio wore a Red Sox uniform

At the end of the 1946 regular season, the Dodgers and Cardinals entered a three-game playoff to break their 96-58, 154-game tie to determine the National League champion. Their American League rivals, the Boston Red Sox, had clinched early and while waiting for their World Series opponent to be decided, engaged a group of hastily assembled American League All Stars in a three-game set to keep tuned. The Bosox won two of the three, but in cold weather before crowds of only 2,000 fans. The cold weather is blamed for pitch Mickey Haefner's inability to break off a curve ball that instead smashed into Ted Williams' right elbow. For several days afterward, the Thumper was unable to follow through even in practice swings. (See "The Curse of Mickey Haefner," by Phil Bergen in TNP 17.)

The All Star lineup featured Hank Greenberg, Hal Newhouser, Eddie Lopat, Luke Appling, Cecil Travis, and the Yankee Clipper, Joe DiMaggio. Either Joe forgot to bring his uniform up from the Bronx or it got lost, but Joltin' Joe had to borrow a Red Sox road suit, playing center field against his kid brother, Dominic, who wore a real Red Sox uniform. The pinstripes were delivered for the next day's game. Later rumors of a DiMaggio-for-Williams trade might have gotten their start here.

—Fr. Gerry Beirne

Baseball's First Full Century: A Fin de Siècle Survey

David Q. Voigt

'Tis a pity to have to delay addressing the important topic of major league baseball's twentieth century highlights because of a continuing debate over when the present century begins or ends. Echoing the broader national debate over the exact date of the new century's onset, some SABR "statistophiles" urge our organization to accept Jan. 1, 2001, as the proper onset date for the new millennium. Like latter-day Pythagoreans, many ascribe a kind of mystical significance to their choice of the year 2001, arguing with the same cocksure certainty that some attach to arcane baseball factoids.

In challenging their position, this writer sides with the "populist" position that accepts the year 2000 as the onset date for both the new century and the new millennium. I side with the vast majority of Americans who plan to celebrate the big event at 11:59 PM, on Dec. 31, 1999. And why not? To most Americans the number 2000 not only looks more symmetrical, but it also has a decisive ring to it! And lending support for the choice of 2000 is the much ballyhooed fear of the "millennium bug"—a menacing computer glitch that threatens to shut down some major computer systems on Jan. 1, 2000!

Granted that the threat of a "millennial bug" is frightening, it seems to me that more to be feared is the "itch for certainty" that seems to motivate the zealots as they try to impose their onset date of 2001 on the populace. What these proponents fail to see is that any act of numbering is an arbitrary human decision. That "what most people wish will be," or that "the folkways can

make anything right" are persuasive truisms that latter-day Pythagoreans ought to ponder lest they run afoul of what the philosopher A. N. Whitehead called "the fallacy of misplaced concreteness."

The need to avoid the pitfall of "misplaced concreteness" was eloquently sounded years ago by the late anthropologist Gordon Childe. Writing in *Man Makes Himself*, Childe warned his readers not to treat with certainty any dates that are applied to events like the onset of the Old or the New Stone Ages. As Childe wryly warned, "It must not be imagined that at a given moment in the world's history a trumpet was blown in heaven and every hunter from China to Peru thereupon flung aside his weapons and traps and started planting grains and breeding pigs, sheep, or turkeys."

Let the 2001 zealots with their itch for certainty and "misplaced concreteness" chew on that quote! Then, as a face-saving bit of advice why shouldn't the zealots simply celebrate both New Years—that of 2000 and 2001. Such was Stephen J. Gould's suggestion, which included his hope that the extra intake of celebratory libations might cool their itch for certainty.

Transitions—Major league baseball carried a lot of nineteenth century baggage into the present century. It was already a thirty-year-old enterprise that had seen much change. But the rules had settled down, the familiar 60'6" pitching distance was set, and so seasonal records have been fully comparable for over a century.

The National League was in business in 1900, but it wasn't doing all that well at the gate. Club owners decided to cut back from twelve clubs to eight, a wise move, but one that emboldened Western League presi-

Historian **David Q. Voigt** *is a professor at Albright College.*

dent Ban Johnson to sign surplus NL players, to occupy some vacated territories, and to declare his newly christened American League a major league in 1901.

The NL owners did not yield their monopoly gracefully. Over the next two seasons a baseball war raged, with the AL scoring turnstile victories with the help of over a hundred NL players who were supported by their Players Protective Association in choosing to join AL teams for higher pay. Thus strengthened, Johnson forced the NL to the bargaining table, where the two sides agreed on the National Agreement of 1903. By and large, peace has reigned ever since.

As imperatives shaped in the last century affected the game in 1900, over the next ninety-nine years powerful external forces constantly altered the staging of major league games. Wars, Depression, booms, social changes, and technology have all had powerful effects.

In the 1940s, major league baseball finally abandoned its traditional policy of institutionalized white supremacy. Over the next decades, African-Americans, Hispanics, and Asians would make their mark on the game.

Beginning in the 1950s teams began to leave their original cities to follow the growing American population west. Expansion began in the 1960s, gradually building the major leagues from sixteen teams to thirty.

By 1970, revenues from TV and concession sales made a myth of the old adage, so true in 1900, that "at the gate is baseball's fate."

In light of all these changes and transitions, here are my choices for the dozen most auspicious years in major league baseball's first full century.

1. 1903—The National Agreement between the NL and AL restores the dual major league system.

World Series competition revived with Boston AL winning the first modern contest. By winning four of the first six World Series, the NL takes an early lead. However, beginning in 1910 the AL takes eight of the next ten (the best decade performance of the century). Thereafter the AL bests its NL rivals in every decade except 1960-69. As of 1998, AL had won fifty-five World Series clashes to thirty-nine for the NL.

2. 1908—The Fred Merkle "bonehead" episode underscores the uncertainty factor in baseball. Merkle's failure to touch second base in a crucial late-season game results in the game being ruled no contest. When the surging Chicago Cubs force a tie at season's end, the Merkle game is replayed. The Cubs win it and go on to win their second World Series in a row—and their last of the century.

This year sees publication of baseball's enduring hymn, "Take Me Out to the Ball Game."

And in the wake of this season, baseball's first modern ballpark building boom begins—the first of three such building booms of the century.

3. 1919—The infamous Black Sox Scandal. Revelations of this thrown World Series reverberate in 1920 and lead to the ouster of eight crooked Chicago players and to the installation of Judge Landis as commissioner. Although legendary as the symbolic purifier of major league baseball, Landis was mostly a front man for owners. This was true of all subsequent commissioners.

4. 1927—Babe Ruth's apotheosis as the greatest hero in twentieth century sports. His sixty homers epitomized the enduring "big bang" style of play. The Yankees' second World Series victory establishes the dominance that saw Yankee teams rack up thirty-five AL pennants and twenty-four World Series titles through 1998.

5. 1941—A storied season for the AL. Coming on the eve of America's entry into World War II, its highlights feature Joe DiMaggio's fifty-six-game hitting streak; Ted Williams's .406 batting and his dramatic homer that won the All-Star Game; "Lefty" Grove's final season of a career that saw him notch 300 pitching wins, and Dodger catcher Mickey Owen's missed third strike which helped the Yankees rally to win Game 4 and go on to notch another World Series win.

6. 1947—Major league baseball's long era of institutionalized white supremacy cracked when Dodger Jackie Robinson became the first African-American in this century to play in the majors. Larry Doby integrates the AL when he joins the Cleveland team. Subsequently, black players like all-time homer champ Hank Aaron became outstanding stars as would other minorities, including Hispanics and Asian players.

7. 1953—The Yankees became the only major league baseball team to win five consecutive World Series titles.

8. 1957—By quitting New York City for Los Angeles and San Francisco, the NL Dodgers and Giants hasten the coming Expansion Era. By 1962 each league would field ten teams, thus ending major league baseball's fifty-year format of eight teams per league.

9. 1969—From an unwieldy ten-team format in each league, major league baseball expanded to twelve teams in each league, east and west divisions, and a tier of playoffs to determine the champion of each league.

The majors go international, with an NL club in Montreal.

By 1995, with twenty-eight teams and each league deployed in three divisions, a third tier of playoffs would be held with a "wild card" winner in each league competing with divisional winners to determine the two teams in each league that would battle for league championship honors. And by 1998, with thirty teams in major league baseball (sixteen in the NL and fourteen in the AL), a team moved from one major league to the other for the first time in this century when the AL Milwaukee team joined the NL.

In 1969 the "Miracle" New York Mets became the first expansion team to win a World Championship by downing the favored AL Orioles in five games.

10. 1973—The AL unilaterally adopted the Designated Hitter Rule, enabling AL hitters to top NL hitters in seasonal batting averages. However, even after twenty-six years, many still seek to overturn this rule.

11. 1981—This year saw the great players' strike. Led by director Marvin Miller of the powerful Major League Players Association, the strike gutted the middle of the playing season of a third of the scheduled games. The strike ended with the players successfully defending hard-won rights of free agency. When the strike ended, a split season format was staged (the first since 1892), with winners of the first half of the interrupted season vying with second-half winners to determine the eventual champions of each league.

Continuing labor strife over "Basic Agreement" labor contracts precipitated another major strike as the owners attempted to cap soaring salaries. Extending into the 1995 season, the struggle forced cancellation of the 1994 World Series (the first time it wasn't played since 1904). Hostilities ended with the antagonists agreeing to a "luxury tax" on teams with high payrolls, but with no cap on rising salaries.

The spiralling salary trend, which saw average seasonal salaries of $27,325 in 1968 climb to $1,324,503 in 1997, testifies to the success of the Players Association under Miller and Don Fehr. In October, 1998 Mets' catcher Mike Piazza briefly became the reigning player plutocrat by inking a seven-year contract worth $91 million.

12. 1998—Dazzling performances on major league diamonds helped dispel much fan outrage engendered by the strike of 1994-95. In the NL the awesome homer duel between Mark McGwire of the Cardinals and Sammy Sosa of the Cubs captivated fans who followed the blow-by-blow assault that ended with McGwire slugging seventy homers and Sosa poling sixty-six. The fusillades blew away Roger Maris's thirty-seven-year-old seasonal mark of sixty-one.

In the AL Oriole shortstop Cal Ripken ended his skein of consecutive games played at 2,632 games, having eclipsed Lou Gehrig's mark of 2,130. But it was the 1998 Yankees who enthralled fans by posting an AL seasonal record of 114-48 and following that feat with an 11-2 post season record that included a sweep of the NL champion San Diego Padres. In winning their twenty-fourth World Series title, the Yankee seasonal total of 125-50 set a record.

The greatest team of the century?—This is an absurd question to ask inasmuch as any attempt at answering it invokes the fallacy of "misplaced concreteness." But the question of which club fielded the greatest teams is quite another matter. The answer is obvious—the New York Yankees stand supreme as the dominant organization of the century. By winning twenty-four of the ninety-four World Series encounters (nearly one of every four) played through 1998, and thirty-five (or better than one of every three) AL championships, the Yankee teams established a breathtaking legacy of dominance. But the imminent dawning of a new century and millennium at least affords all downtrodden rivals a clean slate for the future.

Wally Yonamine

Frank Ardolino

Some athletes achieve greatness not just through their ability and accomplishments on the field, but through unique achievements. By this definition, Wally Yonamine has achieved a sports career that may never be matched. He is the only athlete to have played professional football and to have been elected to the Japanese Baseball Hall of Fame. Yonamine is a quintessential Hawaiian hero who used his physical gifts and his racial background to create a forty-year career as a player, coach, manager, and executive.

In 1908, Yonamine's father, Matsai, then seventeen, left Okinawa to work on a sugar plantation in Hawaii. Japanese emigration to the Hawaiian sugar and pineapple plantations had begun in 1868 when the *Gannon Mono*, or the "first-year men," arrived from Yokohama. These immigrants were followed by successive waves of Issei Japanese with the result that by 1924 they constituted over forty percent of the population of Hawaii.

Matsai Yonamine was sent to Maui to work for Pioneer Mill on the Olowalu Plantation. He soon married, and he and his wife Kikue struggled to raise their family, which eventually included eight children. Wally, their third child, was born on June 24, 1925, and he became interested in baseball at an early age, serving as a bat boy for Pioneer Mill. He watched his idol and Hawaiian legend Ishiro "Iron" Maehara—who later scouted for the Dodgers and signed pitcher Sid Fernandez—play for the Puueneno plantation team. Yonamine soon was playing for the Olowalu team, and as a sophomore at Lahainaluna School, the oldest public school west of the Rockies, he led the football team to the island championship.

After his junior year, he went to Oahu and decided to attend Farrington High School. Playing right halfback, he led the football team to an unbeaten season and its first Interscholastic League championship in 1944. In the championship game, he scored all of his team's points in the 14-6 victory. Father Bray, the renowned coach of Iolani School, made the comment that Yonamine was "like a man playing among boys." Yonamine also received a new first name at Farrington. Up to this time, he had used his Japanese name "Kaname," but an equipment manager began calling him "Wallace," which was quickly shortened to "Wally" and subsequently became his legal name.

Pro football—In 1946, after he served a year in the Army at Schofield Barracks on Oahu, where he played football for the champion base team, Yonamine joined the Lei Alums, a semipro football team that was the class of the Hawaii Senior League in the 1940's. During a mainland tour, the team travelled to Portland University, which it beat badly, with Wally scoring forty of its sixty points. Unknown to him, a scout for the San Francisco 49ers, then of the All-American Football Conference, was in the stands and offered him a two-year contract at $7,000 per year. Although Yonamine had already been offered a football scholarship by Ohio State, he decided to play for the 49ers. He made the thirty-three man squad and played in spots during the 1947 season against such teams as the Cleveland Browns (who won the title), the New York Yankees, the Chicago Rockets, and the Brooklyn Dodgers .

Frank Ardolino *is a professor of English at the University of Hawaii, where he teaches Shakespeare and modern drama.*

During the off-season, Yonamine returned to Hawaii and played baseball for the Asahis, the most famous team in Hawaiian amateur baseball history. The team, which was founded in 1905 and survived for seventy-five years, was composed of the best players from the Americans of Japanese Ancestry senior league (AJAL). During World War II, the Asahis were forced to change their name—which meant "Rising Sun"—to the Athletics because of anti-Japanese sentiment. After the war, when Yonamine played for them, their name and reputation were restored. In 1948, before he was to report to the 49ers, Wally suffered a wrist injury in an Asahi game. Unable to play football in 1948, he signed with the San Francisco Seals of the Pacific Coast League, who were managed by Lefty O'Doul. Yonamine was assigned to their Salt Lake City affiliate in the Class C Pioneer League, where he batted .335 in 1950 and played the outfield with another star athlete from Hawaii, Herman Wedemeyer. "Squirmin' Herman" was a first-team football All-American at St. Mary's College in 1945, and, after two seasons in professional football, he signed with Salt Lake City and joined Yonamine in the outfield. Wedemeyer was to enjoy even more fame as a regular on TV's "Hawaii Five-O," appearing in more than three-hundred episodes as Duke Lukela, with the redoubtable "McGarrett," Jack Lord.

To Japan—After the 1950 season, O'Doul, whose team trained on Maui, advised Wally to play baseball in Japan, where league officials were looking for Nisei players. Wally had suffered a football injury to his shoulder which left him unable to make a full throw, and he felt he would never make the American major leagues. Taking O'Doul's advice, he signed with the Yomiuri Giants in 1951 to play center field and lead off.

From the outset, Yonamine encountered culture shock at many levels. He did not know the language, did not like raw fish, and the travel was third class all the way. More important, he was not prepared for the fans' hostile reaction to him. He was seen by many Japanese as a traitor to war-time Japan.

Compounding the problem, Yonamine was determined to play the game aggressively. According to Robert Whiting in his study of Japanese baseball, *The Chrysanthemum and the Bat*, Wally was the Asian Jackie Robinson, who was reviled both as a Nisei and for his overly aggressive American style of play. The 5'9" 165-pounder used his football prowess in hard slides to knock down pivotmen on double play attempts. In his first time at bat, he was asked to lay down a sacrifice bunt. After fouling one off, he bunted one down the third base line, but instead of trotting to first in the accepted Japanese style, he ran as hard as he could and beat it out, causing a storm of controversy. The fans' opposition to Wally grew in intensity. Once, in Hiroshima, three gangsters took exception to his daring play and attempted to get to him, but he was protected by his teammates.

His style gradually became more accepted, as fans and other players realized that it brought success. His teammate Sadaharu Oh, the all-time home run leader in Japanese baseball, has said that Wally taught him how to slide to avoid tags and how to steal bases, even though he was slow. Yonamine had a stellar ten-year career with the Giants, winning three batting titles and an MVP award. He was an All Star seven times and helped his team win eight pennants and five championships. Through his accomplished and aggressive style, Wally changed the way Japanese baseball was played.

After being released by the Giants in 1961, Wally played two years for the Chinuichi Dragons and then coached for nine years. In 1972, he became the third foreigner to manage. Two years later he was voted manager of the year when he led the Dragons to the league championship, ending the Giants' skein of nine straight Central League titles. After his managing and coaching career ended in 1989, Yonamine became an advisor to Shigheo Nagashima, the Giants' general manager, and was responsible for signing American players. In 1994, Wally Yonamine was inducted into the Japanese Hall of Fame with his great teammate Sadaharu Oh.

During his "retirement," Wally continued to serve baseball. In 1998, Governor Ben Cayetano of Hawaii appointed him his liaison to help persuade Japanese teams to conduct part of their spring training in Hawaii. Yonamine also established in his name a foundation to support high school baseball in Hawaii through athletic and academic financial awards and grants. On June 9, 1998, he was awarded Japan's Imperial Order of the Sacred Treasure, Gold Rays with Rosette, in recognition of outstanding service and achievement in strengthening bonds of friendship between Hawaii and Japan.

Lou Pierotti's Clowns

Jeff Laing

One early spring afternoon, a work acquaintance began waxing nostalgic about the five-man softball team he watched weekends at Bomber Field in Los Alamos, New Mexico. It had been years since I heard such spontaneous and joyous enthusiasm for any sport. No soapboxing about player salaries and court cases, no pillorying of owners' arrogance and stupidity, no haranguing about umpires' hubris. Just my colleague's fond memories of the past and his continuing love for baseball. He left me with a tantalizing final thought: "I don't even know if Lou Pierotti is still alive." He is and I, too, became a eager convert to the story of "Lou Pierotti's Clowns."

The Funny Man—On a messy, snowy mid-autumn Los Alamos day, I met a well-groomed, handsome man of medium build and height who looked two decades younger than his seventy-seven years. Lou Pierotti then transported me to a sports paradise beyond economics and self-interest.

Lou Pierotti was a baseball prodigy who played a few games for the Balboa Brewers while he was stationed in Panama in 1944-45. Professional baseball in Panama in the 1940s was a hard-nosed game that paid by piecework—four dollars for a home run, three for a triple, two for a double, one for a single, and one for every point above .250 at the end of the year. But it still was competitive baseball. Lou had a firm offer for the 1945-46 season in Panama, but he was being mustered out of the service, and with the demands of a young, growing family he returned to New Mexico. Back in the States,

Lou turned down a final professional temptation. He was offered a contract to play C ball for Pine Bluff, Arkansas. Firmly ensconced in the young Los Alamos community, Pierotti became a successful businessman, owning first a soda shop and then a floral shop. Lou insists that the Clowns owe a debt of gratitude to his wife Lee, who ran the business(es) while he played ball.

Pierotti has always felt compelled to give something back. He has set fund-raising records for Los Alamos Kiwanis and United Way of Los Alamos in this his fiftieth consecutive year of charitable work. If Lou's passion was sports—he has played for national titles in five separate sports—his life's work has been helping others.

Having fun and raising funds—Presaging the era of mascots and promotions, Lou decided in 1953 to spur charitable fund-raising by organizing a five-man softball team that combined family entertainment and superior ball playing

But why a clown team? Some former teammates say that Lou had dressed as a girl to play in a comedy game in his hometown of Walsenberg, Colorado, but this tale is evidently apocryphal. The shy Lou does not disagree with those who say he started the team because he was a frustrated actor. He more readily agrees that he has always been a fan of the circus.

Winning 177 of 200 games over the twenty-five-year life of the club, the Clowns were one heck of a team, but their most amazing accomplishment was never accepting a penny, not even for expenses, for their work. "Lou Pierotti's Clowns" were literally the "Goodwill Ambassadors of Los Alamos."

Jeff Laing *is is a Santa Fe, New Mexico, professor and writer who is still in denial that Ernie Banks never played in the World Series.*

The Clowns before

local Washington Generals. There were entertainment bits, but games were on the level and often hard-fought. Speed-demon second baseman Jim Higgins remembers that the Clowns were successful because they clowned mostly on defense while Bun struck everyone out. Lou was the catalyst for the acts and Jim remembers that even the inmates at the state pen, who didn't like to lose, responded to Lou's gambits by riding their own side.

Lou modeled his acts directly on those he'd seen in the circus. The Clowns introduced to the diamond such acts as pitching blindfolded, leaving the field, hitting the string and mush ball(s), lying in front of the pitcher, kneeling to hit, and using the big bat that was actually a lightweight one. And from the beginning, the Clowns were a family affair with Lou breaking in two of his young sons as batboys, bench players, and, of course, clowns.

He is proud that his team influenced others. The famous touring team the "Queen and Her Maids" (whom the Clowns easily handled) went on to create their own clowning strategies after their frustrating experiences with the Clowns.

As long as it was a charity affair, the Clowns accepted all comers, wandering far afield in the Inter-Mountain Range states. However, most of the games were played in New Mexico against such colorful teams as the Tierra Amarilla Bombers, the Los Alamos *Monitor* Newshounds, the Kirtland Air Force Base Flyers, the Santa Fe Penitentiary Rocks,

The dominant pitcher—Their lineup was filled with intelligent, exceptionally gifted athletes. However, the acknowledged superstar was a tall Irishman, Bun Ryan, who was a dominating, nearly unhittable pitcher. Ryan is especially proud of his seven appearances in the nine-man World Softball Tournament 1954-1960.

After winning decorations for World War II service in the field artillery in New Guinea and the Philippines, Bun appreciates the delicious irony of living in the bomb-making city that he is certain saved his life in the Pacific. Bun moved from Taos to Los Alamos to accept a position at the National Laboratory. A Leadville, Colorado, native, Bun became a force in Los Alamos politics, often fighting the quixotic fight of a Democratic liberal in a fiercely conservative Republican county. He has received an appropriate reward for his public service: a local softball field is now "Bun Ryan Field."

Firing smoke and possessing pinpoint control, Bun allowed his teammates the opportunity to clown. But Bun played it straight and hard, never employing illegal pitches as did megastar Eddie Feigner of the "King and His Court" fame.

Clowning and winning—Wearing expensive theatrical makeup and sporting first-class uniforms, the Clowns never played the Harlem Globetrotters to the

... and after.

Frank's Bar and Grill, and the Los Alamos National Laboratory Theoretical Division Thinkers.

The Clowns had their share of luck and misfortune on the diamond. They won a 2-1 victory over state champs Durango, Colorado, on a miracle play: Ted Godwin went to catch a pop fly behind his back, the ball hit his right wrist, popped over his shoulder into his mitt to end the game. The crowd went wild, believing that this was all part of the act. In contrast, the Clowns' most disappointing loss, 3-2 to the Carlsbad, New Mexico Potashes, was decided by an infielder who tried to duplicate Godwin's play and dropped the ball for two unearned runs.

Off the diamond, no Clown ever sustained a major injury. And with all their travel, they never had a car accident, breakdown, or even a flat tire. All the Clowns believed their good luck was "the good lord looking after us."

The Clowns had little trouble with their opponents, who tolerated their shenanigans. However, Bun remembers head clown Lou razzing a young kid in Chama, New Mexico, "Don't feel bad, big boy. He strikes out good hitters." When Bun hit the batter with the next pitch, he had to duck a flying bat.

It was often with their teammates that the Clowns had the most fun. In one game, Bun's catcher Bill Cramer called for only the riser and the fastball. Called out to the mound, Bill confessed to why he didn't call for the drop. "I forgot my cup, Bun." Bun won that day with only two-thirds of his arsenal.

The Clowns had a distinct psychological advantage over their opponents when playing a team for the first time. Equally important, they had no easy outs in their lineup. But his fellow Clowns argue that Lou was their secret weapon with his foghorn, drill sergeant's voice.

Memories—The no-nonsense Bun is stingy with his praise, but he does have plaudits for certain colleagues. Bun believes that Henry Filip was the best athlete to ever perform for the Clowns. That Bun would so praise a catcher is extraordinary considering

The Clowns at work and play.

his usual view of them: "I wore out more catchers than socks." He also praises another catcher, Noe Lujan, for "loving the charity part of the games." Finally, Bun praises Lou's son Michael, who in his preteen years filled in capably when the team was caught short.

As a seven-year old batboy, substitute first baseman, and occasional pinch hitter, Michael Pierotti was, in turn, fascinated with Bun who "could hold court on religion for two hours and then shift gears and go out and pitch another gem." Michael points out that Los Alamos, a small town of young families, had few television sets and little cheap family entertainment to compete with the Clowns. But he remembers that the spirit that animated Lou Pierotti's Clowns was simple: "They had to help others."

The Clowns' diffident first baseman Verdie Raper argues that Lou, Bun, and a good catcher were the keys to the team's extraordinary success. Verdie's daughter, Trina Cron, has wonderful memories of going with her father to "Lou's Soda Shop" before games and of watching the Clowns put on their makeup on Lou's porch, becoming "their real selves." She also remembers Lou's constant chatter and Jim Higgins' incredible speed afoot. But her fondest memory is of her father's signature trick, "the fat bat." Verdie would struggle to swing a gargantuan bat that tiny batboy Michael Pierotti would then carry off easily over his shoulder.

A 1989 reunion of the Clowns underscores a tempus fugit reality: the original trick ended with Verdie being carried off the field by two teammates. At the reunion, a heavier Verdie could not be budged by his struggling colleagues.

Trina was proud that the Clowns played before sellout crowds even when the community knew the tricks as well as the players did.

Catcher Henry Filip played a hundred games for the Clowns over ten years, during which the team went 86-14. A gymnast who entertained the crowds with flips and hand-walking, he could also steal pitches from lunging batters. Off the diamond, he was a physicist who worked on Fermi's pile and was an early member of the Los Alamos National Laboratory.

Hal Aden, Bun's successor after the Clowns' mainstay lost a few feet off his fastball, played the last twenty-five games of the team's existence without losing a game. In the seventies, Hal's softball career took off when he hurled for the dominant New Mexico team of the decade, the Albuquerque Roadrunners. Beginning in 1971, the Roadrunners won five consecutive state tourneys. As with Bun before him, Hal played at the highest levels of his sport in the International Softball Congress Tournaments.

Hal has special affection for the Clowns. At first Bun and Lou had to persuade the serious young pitcher that he'd be invigorated by playing for them. And he was. Besides, Hal remembers that he wanted "to give something back" and the Clowns gave him the chance to do so.

Impact—Lou Pierotti's Clowns had a major social impact on the communities in northern New Mexico. They played the Albuquerque Dukes three times, tying two and winning the finale. More important, they drew 1,800 fans when the then-Cincinnati farm club was drawing only 500 at the gate. Now one of the more successful minor league teams in professional baseball, the Dukes were given a boost by the Clowns' appearances, which helped establish the fan base for the Albuquerque organization. The Clowns did more than help other sports teams. They played in the state penitentiary against inmate teams. These games were so positively received by all that forward-thinking Superintendent of Prisons Alex Rodriquez allowed the Rocks to play the Clowns at Los Alamos's Bomber Field. This was the first time in state history that maximum security prisoners were permitted out to interact with nonprisoners.

The Clowns even had a brush with national fame. They appeared in the inaugural August 16, 1954 edition of *Sports Illustrated*. Anticipating the infamous *SI* jinx, Lou Pierotti's Clowns lost their first game ever on the day the photographer appeared.

The communities of Northern New Mexico benefited wanderfully from the magic spun by the team. Lou and Bun agree that Lou Gehrig was their role model, and they like to think that the Gehrig heritage has found eloquent expression in the careers of Lou Pierotti's Clowns.

All-time "Lou Pierotti's Clowns" Roster
Hal Aden, John Alexander, Doug Anderson, Jim Bond, Bill Cramer, Stan Ewing, Henry Filip, Walt Garcia, Ted Godwin, Jim Higgins, Tony Kimer, Goofy Lujan, Noe Lujan, Tommy Marshall, Bruce Martinez, Steve Mims, Gay Obrink, Jim Pappen, Virgil Parker, Lou Pierotti, Mike Pierotti, Verdie Raper, Walt Rich, Dale Ripley, Buddy Robertson, Bobbie Robinson, Ernie Roth, Lou Speers, Mel Trampe.

Jim Higgins scoring at the New Mexixco pen.

One-Arm Daily

Frank Vaccaro

On May 9, 1998, Cubs rookie Kerry Wood joined multiple Cy Young award winner Roger Clemens as the only pitchers to strike out twenty batters in a nine inning game. It was Wood's fifth career start. A hundred and fifteen years ago, on July 7, 1884, another Chicago pitcher, Hugh Daily was the first to set this remarkable record. But a dropped third strike and the ad-hoc scoring of the period combined to deny Daily his rightful place alongside the two twentieth-century hurlers.

Daily was a mean, tall, mutton-chopped, stringbean of a man, known throughout his career as "One-Armed" Daily. In a childhood accident while playing with a loaded pistol he blew most of his left hand away. A hollowed out leather covering with thin padding was strapped to his sensitive stump wrist and helped him field balls. With his good hand, Daily rolled the ball on his stump pad in small circles as each batter got set to swing.

He threw sidearm and pitched with his back foot planted, so he held runners on base well and was unaffected by the many changes in pitching rules during the decade of the eighties. His fastball and drop ball were both considered top-notch. But he was "useless out of the box," as the Brooklyn *Eagle* once wrote. "He can neither bat nor field...and is a poor base runner." He swung a toothpick bat with one hand and somehow managed to hit .157 over his career.

"The usual display of temper" became the catch phrase used by many newspapers to describe a Daily start—with good reason. Daily may have been the most frustrated pitcher in baseball history. In an era when pitching changes could only be made by switching the pitcher with another position player, Daily's handicap forced him to complete over ninety-six percent of his starts. Only injury could take him out. A one-handed, gloveless fielder was out of the question.

Forced to finish games when he had "no stuff" or when he had "lost his head," Daily's reputation as a foul mouthed embarrassment grew. On May 11, 1880, while pitching for Horace Phillips' Baltimore National Association team, Daily so shocked the home crowd by his tantrums during a 20-9 loss to Albany that he was kicked off the team. So much for his professional debut. Early in 1886, the Washington *Post* blamed Daily for the team's poor start and announced his retirement in the headline of the game report. "It will probably be gratifying to the friends of the Nationals to know," the *Post* wrote, "that Hugh Daily pitched his last game for the Washington team yesterday." In 1906, Hugh Fullerton, on the cusp of national fame as a baseball writer, wrote that in one game Daily repeatedly called to his catcher, Tom Deasly [Deasly never played on any of Daily's teams. Fullerton probably meant Tom Dolan, who caught Daily at Buffalo], to slow down his return throws to the mound because his stump was tender. "Arch 'em, Tom! Arch 'em!" Daily yelled, acording to Fullerton. But the catcher kept throwing hard until Daily called him out for a conference on the mound. As the receiver approached, Daily knocked him down with his stump arm. "Now will you arch 'em?" he reportedly said.

Frank Vaccaro *lives in New York. He has done most of his baseball research since the majors adopted the wild card format. "For me," he says, "it's like opening day comes in October."*

Hugh "One-Arm" Daily

Almost in Cleveland—The turning point of Daily's career came on August 25, 1883, when he wasn't even pitching. Stout Jim McCormick limped off the field in the fifth inning in Detroit, probably due to a recurring ankle injury that would keep him out for the rest of the season. Cleveland was in first place by two games and McCormick made up the other half of the team's two-man rotation.

Daily pitched his heart out. He started three games in five days and saved a fourth before teenager Will Sawyer could meet the team in Chicago. (Sawyer's parents hadn't let him go on road trips.) Sawyer lost to Fred Goldsmith, 9-1, and Daily lost to Larry Corcoran, 21-7. Daily needed to beat Pud Galvin twice in two days for Cleveland to stay in first place. He split. When seventeen-year-old rookie outfielder Charlie Cady pitched and lost to Galvin, 13-1, on September 8, Cleveland was in fourth place. Boston, Chicago, and Providence had all rushed past. Rainouts gave Daily six days rest, then he beat last place Philadelphia twice in two days, one of them a 1-0 no-hitter. But Cleveland's season was over and Daily was made the scapegoat. He finished with a 23-14 record in 1883, but went 5-6 at the end of the season. Cleveland manager Frank Bancroft didn't help the team any by scheduling fifty exhibition games.

The atmosphere in the Cleveland clubhouse after the collapse was awful. Five players jumped their contracts and joined the upstart Union Association. Daily and soft-handed second baseman Fred Dunlap were the first to leave, Daily signing with the Chicago Unions and Dunlap with St. Louis. On August 8, 1884, McCormick, shortstop Jack Glasscock, and catcher "Fatty" Briody signed with the Cincinnati Unions. Thirty minutes before an exhibition game in Grand Rapids, Michigan, the three told Cleveland manager Charlie Hackett of the deal and demanded $25 each to play. Hackett talked them down to $10 and the game was played. Briody played with his $1,000 signing bonus stuffed into his stockings. After the game Hackett swiped three players from Grand Rapids and that team, leading the Northwest League, was forced to disband. Eight days later the entire Northwest League collapsed.

Moving to the Unions—The surly Daily was the franchise player for the Chicago Unions. His twenty-strikeout performance followed a tough two weeks. The 5-0 victory over Boston actually broke a personal eight-game losing streak. Boston slugger Ed Crane got the only hit off Daily that day: a two-out sixth-inning triple to left center. Two other batters reached on infield errors and Walt Hackett reached on a "balk"—a call by ump Pat Dutton after warnings that Daily released a pitch over his shoulder. Like Kerry Wood, Daily's pitching line should read:

                9   1   0   0   20   0.

Clemens never walked anybody either, but gave up three and four hits, respectively, in his twenty-K gems on April 29, 1986, and September 18, 1996. Stormin' Gorman Thomas hit a seventh-inning solo home run to spoil Clemens' shutout in the '86 game.

Daily's one-hitter was the first of two consecutive one-hitters he would pitch, a feat you can find in the record books. The second one came again in Boston three days later, and he pitched four for the year. What the record books won't tell you is that his other two one-hitters were also back-to-back, May 14 and 18. These games, and three huge wins in late August, were the highlights of Daily's year. He finished the season 28-28, a record blighted by the losing streak, when he was forced to start nine of eleven straight games. Those June innings took their toll. Against Philadelphia, the basement team that was then 10-34, he threw a five-hitter with ten strikeouts but lost, 7-2, his seventh straight loss. Two days later, on the fourth of July, after watching a 5-1 lead evaporate in the sixth, he started pacing around the mound cursing and refusing to pitch. Captain Joe Ellick, in a moment of sublime cruelty, switched Daily to second base. One-handed and gloveless, Daily actually made one fine stop. His twenty-strikeout game came in his next start.

The Game—The game has always been listed in the record books as a nineteen-strikeout performance. With two outs in the bottom of the fifth, Daily's catcher Bill Krieg dropped a third strike, allowing Pat Scanlon to scamper to first. Krieg recovered the ball in time for a play, but threw wild. The official scorer could have followed the rulebook to the letter, in the manner that would be universally adopted later that decade: "An assist should be given the pitcher when a batsman fails to hit the ball on the third strike...even if the player

who should complete the play fails." Unfortunately for Daily, the scorer that day charged an error to Krieg, no assist to Daily, and no strikeout.

Scoring was a mess in the 1880s. Boston's Joe Hornung had a unique play in which he stayed in the batter's box after hitting a double play ground ball, thereby "creating" no force at second base. In the 1870s, rule changes made strikeouts a play in which each strikeout victim had to be thrown out at first, whether or not the catcher caught strike three cleanly. This is the origin of the pitcher's assist on a strikeout. Eventually, most batters refused to run a humiliating footrace to first base against the arm of a professional catcher, and, some historians believe catchers instead threw the ball around the horn for the putout at first. For cocky fielding teams without gloves, it was a titillating display. One miscue and the batter would break for first. This requirement of batters was lifted prior to 1884, but to this day, catchers snap the ball to third base after strike three.

In 1884, as now, the pitcher's assist could be coupled with either a strikeout or with a dropped third strike, even if the runner reached first base safely. But there was no provision for coupling a pitcher's assist with an error. The scorer in Daily's case selected the error alone. *Sporting Life*, the finest baseball weekly of the time, seems to have scored an error on the throw, and a passed ball. The Boston *Morning Journal* scored a passed ball only. Neither scored a strikeout.

The question of crediting Daily with twenty strikeouts that day is vexing. *Total Baseball* says "there can be no statute of limitations on historical error; the researcher and historian must go where the evidence leads them." The question is, is there evidence that Daily's feat was recognized in his time as a twenty-strikeout performance?

The answer is yes, and the answer comes from the Boston *Morning Journal*, a paper with a baseball column written for the aficionados of the sport. The headline the next day read 'ONE-ARMED' DAILY STRIKES OUT 20, despite the fact that Daily was a member of the opposition. The subhead, DAILY PROVES A TERROR TO BOSTON AND BREAKS THE PITCHER'S RECORD, refers to the record of nineteen strikeouts set by Charlie Sweeney just a month earlier. The second sentence of the game report says "nineteen had been put out...and the twentieth had a life on a missed third strike." That batter, Scanlon, fresh up from "amateur" ball in Atlanta, was in the third day of a week-long major league career. The *Journal* actually outlines the number of times each batter struck out. "The strike-outs were: Slattery (4), Irwin (3), Butler (3), McKeever (3), Crane (2), Scanlan (2 and a missed third strike), Hackett and Burke. Murnane alone escaped." Not a very fearsome bunch. Five of the players had careers of less than 140 games. Tim Murnane was the manager and had to come out of five years of retirement to play. For four Boston players, 1884 was only a cup of coffee, and Sam Crane, despite his golden arm, would be the starter at the Polo Grounds' off-season "toboggan run" by 1887.

Daily's pitching record in baseball record books show him splitting time later that season with Pittsburgh and Washington of the Union Association. Those weren't trades. On August 1, the Chicago Unions found themselves locked out of their "Union Grounds" ballpark at Wabash Avenue and 39th Street. Owner Al Henderson was pocketing the rent money. A long road trip let the team find another field in time for its next scheduled home game, August 25. Unfortunately for Chicago fans the field was in Pittsburgh.

Henderson would disband his Pittsburgh franchise within four weeks, but not until the team finished a mid-September series in Baltimore, against a team owned by Al's brother Willie. After Al announced Pittsburgh would disband, the two siblings pitted their teams against each other on September 19 in a tryout for the nine Baltimore positions. The teams played a somber eleven-inning scoreless tie, and Daily was one of the dozen cut. Then Henderson backed out of paying Daily his lucrative salary, insisting the contract was with "Chicago" and was signed by "President." No name, just the word in script. But

public support was on Daily's side, and Henderson coughed up the dough in October. Daily's two starts with Washington were also tryouts before that team went on its season-ending trip. Daily was cut again. Daily finished the year with 483 strikeouts, not counting the extra whiff, despite missing the last month of play. On October 16, three days before the end of the long Union Association season, Willie Henderson liquidated his Baltimore franchise as well, the final stake into the heart of Henry Lucas, the iconoclastic founder, president, and owner of the Union Association.

On August 21, 1887, Daily, making a comeback bid with Cleveland of the American Association, lost 7-5 to New York's Ed Cushman in the first legal Sunday game in Cleveland history. (Municipal authorities, however, closed that loophole the next day.) Two thousand fans attended, but Daily's fastball was gone, and he relied on a slow curve. *The Sporting News* wrote: "One-armed Daily is still a great pitcher… never loses his head at critical stages…always smiling, always cool and self-possessed." It would be Daily's last game, although he pitched semipro ball in Pennsylvania for several years. But no greater contrast to his debut could have been imagined.

Sources:

Sporting Life, Philadelphia, PA., 1883: May 27, July 8, August 13, and August 20. 1884: January 9, July 16, August 20, September 24, and October 8.

The Sporting News, St. Louis, MO., 1887: January 29, July 2, July 9, July 25, August 27, and September 3.

Boston *Morning Journal*, Boston, MA., 1884: July 8, August 9, August 14, September 22, and October 8.

Clipper, New York City, NY., 1884: September 27, and October 4.

Baltimore *Sun*, Baltimore, MD., 1880: May 12.

Milwaukee *Daily Journal*, Milwaukee, WI., 1884: August 15, 1892: July 13.

St. Louis *Post Dispatch*, St. Louis, MO., 1885: June 8.

Washington Post, Washington, DC., 1886: May 23.

Brooklyn *Eagle*, Brooklyn, NY., 1887: August 3.

Chicago *Daily Tribune*, Chicago, IL., 1906: April 8.

Constitution and Playing Rules of the National League of Professional Base Ball Clubs, A. G. Spalding & Bro., Chicago, IL., 1877, 1879-1887.

Constitution and Playing Rules of the National Base Ball Association, Louis H. Mahn, Jamaica Plains, MA., 1880.

Constitution and Playing Rules of the Eastern League of Professional Base Ball Clubs, A. G. Spalding, Chicago, IL., 1886.

Nineteenth Century Stars, Society for American Baseball Research, Kansas City, MO., 1989.

The Sporting News, Complete Baseball Record Book, St. Louis, MO., 1996.

Total Baseball V, Viking, New York, NY., 1997.

March 17, 1946

Chris Lamb

Sportswriters and photographers joined the Brooklyn Dodgers and their AAA team, the Montreal Royals, in the dugout and on the field as the players warmed up before their spring training game at City Island Ballpark in Daytona Beach, Florida, on March 17, 1946. Black journalists were restricted to the segregated section of the field, down the right field line. Billy Rowe, a photographer with the Pittsburgh *Courier*, struggled to get a photograph of his friend, Jackie Robinson, who was scheduled to be in the lineup for Montreal.

Brooklyn manager Leo Durocher spotted Rowe in the stands and motioned him to the field. "You can't get any pictures from way back there! Come into the dugout!" Durocher said. As Rowe remembered later, he began to walk across the field when someone in the bleachers yelled, "Get that nigger out of there!" Rowe froze. He didn't know whether to continue or go back to the segregated stands.

Durocher motioned him to keep walking—and Rowe continued. The Brooklyn manager then went to ballpark officials and said that if the fan who called Rowe the racial epithet was not removed, there would be no game. In a few minutes, a man was escorted from the ballpark. "I don't know if it was the right guy or not, but they made somebody leave," Rowe remembered with a laugh.[1]

Brooklyn won, 7-2, yet the day was Robinson's. To *Courier* sports editor Wendell Smith, the world seemed to begin the moment Robinson took the field.

"Six thousand eyes were glued on the mercury-footed infielder each time he came to bat," Smith wrote. "His performance with the willow failed to provide any thrills, but, nevertheless, his vicious swings and air of confidence as he faced real major league pitching for the first time, won the admiration of a crowd that seemed to sense the historical significance of the occasion.[2]

Robinson went hitless and played just five innings at second. But Smith saw something that wasn't in the box score. Robinson had just become the first black ballplayer in the twentieth century to take the field with whites in an organized, professional baseball game. In a month, he made his regular season debut with Montreal. And a year later, in April, 1947, he broke major league baseball's color barrier. "Baseball's great experiment," as author Jules Tygiel called the integration of the national pastime, got its first real test on March 17, 1946.

This was a turning point for baseball and for Robinson, who had struggled offensively and defensively through the first two weeks of spring training. But he had more on his mind that day than a sore arm and a weak bat. He doubted whether Daytona Beach officials would let him take the field. If that happened, it would represent a significant failure of the experiment. All the same, the white press paid remarkably little attention to the drama unfolding on the field.

The integration of baseball was a different story for the black press. In contrast to what was reported in white newspapers, black weeklies gave Robinson's first game more attention, stressed its historical importance, and mentioned that the ballplayer was cheered by all spectators, black and white.

Chris Lamb *is an assistant professor of Media Studies at the College of Charleston in Charleston, South Carolina. He is writing a book about baseball's first integrated spring training.*

Things were changing, but America was still a segregated society in the mid-1940s. Integration was a touchy subject on the sports pages. Some white sportswriters believed in segregation. Others knew the subject made their editors and readers uncomfortable. As a result they kept it at a distance. In contrast, the story affected black sportswriters, like Smith and Rowe, personally. This was especially true for Smith, who had campaigned for the integration of baseball columns for nearly a decade.

During spring training, Brooklyn president Branch Rickey paid Smith and Rowe to act as chauffeurs, confidants, and father confessors to Robinson and Johnny Wright, a second black prospect with Montreal whom Rickey signed so Robinson wouldn't be alone.

Smith and Rowe had the inside story of baseball's first integrated spring training. They knew about Rickey's meetings with Daytona Beach officials. And they knew that there were a lot of people who wanted to keep sport and society segregated. Smith admitted later that he didn't write about certain incidents for fear of jeopardizing the integration of baseball.[3]

Different reactions—When Rickey signed Robinson for Montreal on October 23, 1945, white sportswriters and their editors didn't treat the event as a big story. *The Sporting News* downplayed it by doubting whether Robinson was good enough to play in the majors.[4] By comparison, the news hit black newspapers "like a bombshell."[5] Smith called the signing of Robinson "the most American and democratic step baseball has made in 25 years."[6] Writing in *The Crisis*, Dan Burley called Robinson a "symbol of hope for millions of colored people in the country."[7]

Robinson's troubles with Jim Crow began during his trip from his home in California to spring training in Florida. Robinson and his wife, Rachel, were twice bumped from planes—first in New Orleans and then in Pensacola, Florida—and had to spend an exhausting and humiliating sixteen hours making the final leg of the trip in the back of a bus. They were prohibited from eating in restaurants and staying in hotels. By the time they arrived in Daytona Beach, Robinson, furious, wanted to quit and return to California.[8]

In their reporting of the story, black newspapers wanted to convey to their readers the cruelties and ironies of segregation.[9] The Chicago *Defender*, whose sports editor, "Fay" Young, had frequently written about the need for integration, said that Robinson had been bumped from an airplane in Pensacola with two other passengers "because the plane could not refuel with the weight of the three people aboard."[10] Smith wrote that the Robinsons had to sit in the back of a bumpy bus from Pensacola to Daytona Beach, "in accordance with the jim-crow laws in Dear Ole Dixie."[11]

Daytona Beach didn't have room for the scores of ballplayers returning from the war, hoping to win a spot on one of the teams in the Brooklyn organization. Rickey moved the Montreal team forty miles away to Sanford. This turned out to be a costly mistake.

The New York city dailies left their top sportswriters in Daytona Beach to cover the Dodgers and relied on secondary writers, stringers, or wire service accounts to cover what black sportswriter Sam Lacy called "the Jackie Robinson beat."[12] Florida papers used brief wire service accounts or said nothing.[13]

Smith, Lacy, Young, and other black sportswriters became emotionally involved in the story. Smith praised the ballplayers for "their determined bid for sports immortality."[14] According to Lacy, Robinson wasn't just playing for himself, he was playing for something bigger. "It is easy to see why I felt a lump in my throat each time a ball was hit in his direction those first few days; why I experienced a sort of emptiness whenever he took a swing in batting practice," he wrote.[15] None of this emotion was found in white newspapers.

The first day of practice at Sanford was uneventful. But after the second day, a delegation of Sanford citizens told Montreal officials that they wouldn't permit blacks and whites to play on the same field.[16] Montreal began training the next day at Kelly Field in the segregated section of Daytona Beach. Robinson and Wright lived with black families a few blocks away. Their white teammates stayed in a hotel on the banks of the Halifax River, several miles distant.

Robinson could feel the pressure. During the first couple weeks of practice, he struggled. He wasn't hitting and, to make things worse, he'd hurt his arm and couldn't make the throw across the infield. He wasn't the only one concerned. So was Rickey, who had risked a lot by challenging baseball's color ban.

Given the reaction in Sanford, Rowe, Smith, Robinson, and others wondered if Daytona Beach would prohibit the black ballplayers from taking the field. There were rumors that city officials were putting pressure on Rickey to remove Robinson from the lineup.[17] As Robinson later learned, the reverse was true: Rickey had been pressuring Daytona Beach.

"He had done a fantastic job of persuading, bullying, lecturing, and pulling strings behind the scenes," Robinson wrote in his autobiography, *I Never Had It Made*.[18] Brooklyn team officials had secured the promises of the mayor and city manager that Robinson and Wright would be permitted to play, not just in practices but in games.

But nobody really knew what would happen when Robinson took the field. Unlike the embarrassment in Sanford, if something happened on this day it probably couldn't be kept out of the newspapers. For this game, the New York sportswriters who covered the Dodgers and the wire services joined the black reporters on the so-called "Jackie Robinson beat." Rickey, of all people, wasn't there. He wouldn't make an exception to his rule against attending Sunday games.[19]

The local newspaper barely mentioned Robinson in its story the morning of the game. Daytona Beach *Sunday News-Journal* sports editor Bernard Kahn wrote that he didn't know whether Robinson would play or not. He quoted Montreal manager Clay Hopper as saying: "I don't know if Robinson will play or not. But he'll accompany the Montreal squad."[20]

The New York *Times*, however, reported that Robinson would play against Brooklyn that afternoon. From the reception given the ballplayer, sportswriter Roscoe McGowen said Montreal could predict how he would be treated in minor league ballparks that summer. He wrote that the crowd was expected to include many Northern tourists, who would be sympathetic toward Robinson. "But," he wrote, "one citizen voiced the view that there might be some native Southerners who would boo him."

The weather was threatening in the morning but cleared up for the 3 PM game. A crowd of about four thousand filled the ballpark in downtown Daytona Beach. The segregated section filled beyond its capacity and many black spectators had to stand beyond the rightfield foul line.

The game—Montreal didn't score in the top of the first inning. In the bottom of the first, Brooklyn's Dixie Walker hit a bases-loaded triple. After a half inning, Brooklyn led, 4-0.[21]

When Robinson came to bat for the first time in the second inning, he expected to be booed. "This is where you're going to get it," he told himself as he walked to the plate. Instead, to his surprise, he said he received applause from both white and black fans.[22] He remembered hearing one drawling Southern voice: "Come on, black boy! You can make the grade!" And he also heard someone else yell: "They're giving you a chance—now come on and do something about it!" In his first at bat, he fouled out.[23]

He played five innings at second before being removed to rest his shoulder. He went hitless in three at-bats, fouling out twice. In the sixth inning, he reached base on a fielder's choice, stole second, and scored a run. In the field, he made no errors.

The coverage—The score was overshadowed by Robinson's appearance. Jack Smith of the New York *Daily News* reported that Robinson made history by becoming the first black to play against a major league team in a regularly scheduled spring training game.[24] Harold Burr of the Brooklyn *Eagle* wrote that Robinson was on the spot "when he shuffled out to cover second base for the Montreal Royals."[25] The story said that Robinson was booed mildly by the white fans after each

of his foul outs.[26] Burr also wrote the account of the game in *The Sporting News*.

The Sporting News continue to express its attitude on integration by burying the history-making, three-paragraph item toward the back of the issue.[27] Author Mark Ribowsky has written that J.G. Taylor Spink, the longtime editor of *The Sporting News*, reflected the voice of conservative reactionaries who wanted to keep the sport segregated.[28]

The New York *Times* provided an unemotional account of the game, saying simply that Robinson played five innings, had two chances in the field, had no hits in three trips to the plate, stole a base, and scored a run. The article noted that the historic game was "seemingly taken in stride by a majority of the 4,000 spectators," nearly 1,000 of whom were black.[29]

The Daytona Beach newspapers continued to hold the story at arm's length. The *Morning Journal* said nothing about it. In the *Evening News*, Robinson wasn't mentioned until the third paragraph of the six-paragraph story. The game shared the page with two longer stories, one on the city's Class D minor league team and another longer story on a pair of Swedish milers.[30] Other Florida newspapers published short wire-service accounts or said nothing.

Robinson didn't impress anyone with his hitting, putting only one ball in fair territory in three at-bats. The Brooklyn *Eagle* wrote that the nervous Robinson struggled against the curves thrown by the Brooklyn pitcher.[31] *Daily Mirror* sportswriter Gus Steiger wrote: "At this stage he is a soft touch for such a pitch. Many a rookie before him has been curved into oblivion, indicating an arduous road ahead."[32]

Robinson's hitting problems continued to discourage him, but he was encouraged by the crowd's reaction, especially after what had happened in Sanford. He later called the game a turning point. "I didn't get a single hit that day, nor did we win the ball game; but when I got home, I felt as though I, personally, had won some kind of victory," he told Wendell Smith a few years later. "I had a new opinion of the people in the town. I knew, of course, that everybody wasn't pulling for me to make good, but I was sure now that the whole world wasn't lined up against me. When I went to sleep, the applause was still ringing in my ears."[33]

Smith also was encouraged. In the next issue of the *Courier*, he called the response of the Southern fans the most gratifying part of the day. "It definitely proved that baseball fans, whether in the North or South, appreciate talent and will not hesitate to give credit where credit is due," he wrote.[34]

The mere fact that Robinson took the field represented progress, and Smith tried to capture that. Smith wrote that there had been a considerable amount of doubt whether Robinson would be allowed to play, but no objections actually were raised. According to Smith, "the most talked about player in baseball today played five innings and was given a rousing reception when he stepped to the plate in the second inning."[35]

The game was at least a couple days old before the black weeklies reported it to their readers. In contrast to what was reported in white newspapers, black weeklies mentioned that Robinson was cheered by all spectators, black and white. They also stressed the game's historical importance. They gave the story bigger play than daily newspapers, usually including photographs of Robinson.

The Atlanta *Daily World*, using an American Negro Press account, told its readers that "all southern precedents were shattered" when Montreal's Robinson played in a game against Brooklyn.[36] The *People's Voice* of New York said Robinson became the first black athlete to play against a major league team in a regularly scheduled spring training game. It added that the ballplayer was cheered by fans of both races.[37]

In addition, the Washington *Afro-American* said that Robinson was applauded during each trip to the plate, which the newspaper interpreted as a good sign that he would be well-received in the International League.[38] The Norfolk *Journal-Guide* reported that it had been predicted that Robinson would be booed by white Southerners, but this didn't happen.[39]

The future—During the spring, the Robinson story remained little more than a minor human interest story to the mainstream press. By comparison, it was clearly the big story in the black press. History has proven the black press was right.[40] No sports story has had greater ramifications on society than Robinson's breaking of the national pastime's color ban.

As it turned out, Daytona Beach was the only city to permit Robinson and Wright to play in games during the spring training of 1946. Florida cities, such as Jacksonville, DeLand, Sanford, and other Southern cities like Richmond and Savannah, refused to let blacks and whites share the same field in their ballparks.[41]

By the end of spring training, Robinson found his hitting stroke and his throwing arm had healed. When Montreal began its regular season, he was the team's starting second baseman. He led the International League in hitting during the 1946 season. Johnny Wright would be released by Montreal after pitching poorly and would return to the Negro Leagues.

Most baseball fans remember Robinson for what he did in April, 1947, not March, 1946. But the earlier date is an important one in the story of the integration of baseball. The city of Daytona Beach hasn't forgotten. There is a monument to Robinson outside the ballpark where he played his first game. The facility is now called Jackie Robinson Stadium.

Notes:

1. Telephone interview with Billy Rowe, March 10, 1993.

2. Pittsburgh *Courier*, March 23, 1946.

3. Ibid., April 13, 1946.

4. *Sporting News*, November 1, 1945.

5. Bill Weaver, "The Black Press and the Assault on Professional Baseball's `Color Line,' October, 1945-April, 1947," *Phylon* 40 (Winter 1979), p. 305.

6. Pittsburgh *Courier*, November 3, 1945.

7. Dan Burley, "What's Ahead for Robinson?" *The Crisis*, December, 1945, p. 364.

8. Telephone interview with Billy Rowe, March 10, 1993. See, Chris Lamb, " `I Never Want to Take Another Trip Like This One': Jackie Robinson's Journey to Integrate Baseball," *Journal of Sport History* 24 (Summer 1997), pp. 177-191.

9. See, Chris Lamb and Glen Bleske, "Democracy on the Field: The Black Press Takes on White Baseball," *Journalism History* 24 (Summer 1998), p. 54.

10. Chicago *Defender*, March 9, 1946.

11. Pittsburgh *Courier*, March 9, 1946.

12. Telephone interview with Sam Lacy, February 17, 1995.

13. Lamb and Bleske, p. 54.

14. Pittsburgh *Courier*, March 16, 1946.

15. Washington *Afro-American*, March 16, 1946.

16. Jackie Robinson and Wendell Smith, *My Own Story* (New York: Greenburg Publishers, 1948), p. 27.

17. Ibid., p. 78.

18. Jackie Robinson and Alfred Duckett, *I Never Had It Made* (Hopewell, N.J.:

Ecco Press, 1995), p. 46.

19. *New York Times*, March 17, 1946.

20. Daytona Beach *Sunday News-Journal*, March 17, 1946.

21. *New York Times*, March 18, 1946.

22. Robinson and Smith, p. 78.

23. Robinson and Smith, p. 78.

24. New York *Daily News*, March 18, 1946.

25. Brooklyn *Eagle*, March 18, 1946.

26. Ibid.

27. *Sporting News*, March 21, 1946.

28. Mark Ribowsky, *A Complete History of the Negro Leagues* (New York: Birch Lane Press, 1995), p. 253.

29. *New York Times*, March 18, 1946.

30. Daytona Beach *Evening News*, March 18, 1946.

31. Brooklyn *Eagle*, March 18, 1946.

32. *Daily Mirror*, March 18, 1946.

33. Robinson and Smith, p. 79.

34. Pittsburgh *Courier*, March 18, 1946.

35. Ibid.

36. Atlanta *Daily World*, March 20, 1946.

37. *People's Voice*, March 23, 1946.

38. Washington *Afro-American*, March 23, 1946.

39. Norfolk *Journal and Guide*, March 23, 1946.

40. Lamb and Bleske, p. 58.

41. Ibid, p. 57.

The King of Coolie Hats

Andy McCue

Wander up to a souvenir stand as new as the team-run boutiques at Kauffman Stadium or as old as the family businesses that line the streets around Fenway Park and you will find the same merchandise. The logos will change, and the colors, but the same array of caps, jackets, bobble-head dolls, plastic batting helmets, lighters, packs of baseball cards, sun visors, miniature bats, and pennants will decorate the display cases.

The sizes of these businesses are testimony to a man named Danny Goodman. Their sameness is not, for Danny Goodman taught major league baseball the value of souvenirs without losing the ideas of team, ballpark, and city.

In 1962, Goodman was working for the Los Angeles Dodgers. In early August, with the Dodgers enjoying a five-and-a-half-game lead over San Francisco, the team traveled to Candlestick Park. Giants manager Alvin Dark, anxious to slow Maury Wills and the other Dodger base-stealers, ordered groundskeeper Matty Schwab to water down the basepaths. The Dodgers protested, the umpires ordered Schwab to drain the wetlands, and the groundskeeper cleverly made it worse. Dodger broadcaster Vin Scully labeled Dark the "Swamp Fox," after Revolutionary War guerilla leader Frances Marion. Los Angeles reporters rehashed the tale endlessly.

Goodman's natural response was different. Three weeks later, when the Giants showed up for a four-

game series beginning with one on a Labor Day afternoon, he sold Dodger fans 3,000 duck calls at $1.50 apiece.[1]

Four years earlier, when the Dodgers were new to Los Angeles, fans with bugles had risen in the stands, playing a six-note refrain that had elicited the call of "Charge!" at University of Southern California football games in for years. Dodger fans responded. Over the next winter, Goodman found a man to make foot-long brass bugles that came with instructions on how to play those six notes. He sold them for $1.[2]

Apprenticeship—Goodman was quick on his feet because he'd worked in burlesque houses and ballparks since the 1920s, forsaking an education and becoming famous for his attacks on the English language. Goodman was "an off-the-field syntactical equivalent of Yogi Berra," said Los Angeles *Times* columnist Jim Murray. "I may not be the best talker, or the best educated man in this room, but at least I'm illiterate," Goodman responded.[3]

Over time, Goodman came to accept the entertainment industry's belief that all publicity was good and the impact of the stories he told reporters was far more important than the accuracy of the details.

At different times, he told different reporters that he'd dropped out of school and started working when he was eleven, or twelve, or fourteen, or seventeen.[4] Born in Milwaukee on May 17, 1912, Goodman lost his father at the age of eleven. He was already a paper boy, but became a vendor for the Jacobs Brothers, who served burlesque houses, theaters, and the American Association's Borchert Field. Within a few years, he

Andy McCue *is a 1991 SABR Macmillan Award winner for his* fiction bibliography, Baseball by the Books. *He is working on a biography of Walter O'Malley. His father refused to buy him a duck call or a trumpet.*

Danny Goodman

was a full-time employee.

While he was still in his teens, he was sent around the country by the Jacobs Brothers to handle their various operations. In the late 1920s, he was in Baltimore running the Jacobs' concessions for Jack Dunn's International League Orioles. By the early 1930s, he'd been moved to Newark of the same league, where he worked for George Weiss. But he handled any assignment—race track, theater, or stadium—that the Jacobs Brothers needed.

In 1934, Jacobs Brothers moved all their top operators to Detroit for the World Series. Goodman was given charge of the bleachers and was doing a tremendous business in pies. The business picked up even more in the seventh game. After St. Louis outfielder Joe Medwick spiked Detroit third baseman Marv Owen in the sixth inning, the Tiger fans, already upset that the home team was losing badly, showered

Medwick with pies and other trash when he took the field. Eventually, baseball commissioner Kenesaw Mountain Landis made his well-known decision ordering Medwick out of the game. He also made a less well-known decision, ordering Goodman to stop selling pies.[5]

Goodman learned all the tricks. In those days, vendors turned in their unsold merchandise at the end of the game and were refunded what they'd paid the concessionaire. As part of his education, Goodman found that drink salesmen filled empty bottles with coffee and turned them back. Ice cream vendors put wood blocks in empty cartons. One hot dog vendor painted his forefinger with iodine, slipped it into the bun, let the customer see it and then pulled the reddened finger back. When the customer complained there was no frank, the vendor suggested the customer had dropped it.[6]

One day the Jewish Goodman caught the unmistakable fragrance of kosher hot dogs, which Jacobs Brothers didn't sell. He found a vendor who was bringing his own supplies to the park.[7]

Soon he started making up tricks of his own. In Reading, he found the customers wouldn't pay a nickel to rent seat cushions. So, he had the seats hosed down.[8] He claimed to be the first to sell hats and pennants.[9] And, Chuck Stevens, who played for the Hollywood Stars, says Goodman came up with the idea of dragging the infield between innings during the years Jack Salveson pitched for the Stars. Salveson, a fast worker with excellent control, tended to pitch short games and Goodman needed the extra time to sell food and souvenirs.[10]

To Tinseltown—Jacobs Brothers moved Danny Goodman to Hollywood for the 1939 baseball season and the opening of Gilmore Field. It was a match made in heaven. A number of real Hollywood stars (Gary Cooper, George Raft, Robert Taylor, Cecil B. DeMille, Barbara Stanwyck, Bing Crosby, and William Powell among others) owned stock in the team.[11] Bob Cobb, owner of the Brown Derby restaurants, was the principal owner and convinced Goodman to expand the Gilmore menu to a higher class of food. Soon, Goodman said, they were back to hot dogs and hamburgers because that's what George Raft and the others wanted when they showed up.[12] "We've experimented with dozens of chef's specials, but they've all been a flop in the pan," Goodman explained.[13]

Gilmore Field became known as a place where starlets could get their pictures taken. Danny Goodman was only too happy to pose them holding the newest of his souvenirs. He could always get entertainment industry friends to pitch in on his promotions. When he introduced the toy trumpets to the Coliseum, for example, he brought the great jazz trumpeter Ziggy

Elman along to ham it up with the merchandise.[14]

Danny Goodman lived in Beverly Hills 90210 before it *was* 90210. He was an early riser who was usually in the office before six. He spent his morning on the phone, doing meetings, setting up business. He'd have a long lunch at a very public restaurant or club, always ready to talk, tell stories, and buy drinks for reporters. He'd take a midafternoon nap, go to the ballpark or another public dinner, and be in bed by ten or so.[17]

He was always willing to buy a drink, give a gift or do a favor, especially for a reporter or somebody from the movies or television. Through the 1950s, he was the only non-entertainment industry figure who'd been the subject of a Friars' Club roast, an honor he received in 1953[18]. Ronald Reagan acted as "roastmaster," with Jack Benny, Phil Silvers, George Burns, Chico Marx, and others pitching in. He was also honored with similar dinners by the Leukemia Foundation of California and the Westwood Shrine Club.[19] He did a lot of volunteer work, serving on the Friars' board of directors for thirty-two years, and organizing benefit dinners for other clubs. "I've been the chairman of six Fred Haney dinners alone," he once joked.[20] He also helped organize dinners for Ty Cobb, Stan Musial, Casey Stengel, Maury Wills, Vin Scully, Lefty O'Doul, Leo Durocher, Sandy Koufax, and a host of Hollywood types and other celebrities. "You want celebrities for this event?" he asked one group, "I'll get you celebrities you never even heard of."[21]

The Dodgers—The Dodgers arrived with a full crew from Brooklyn and the Coliseum's concessions' contract locked up by rival ABC Vending Co., which had handled the Coliseum for years.[22] Goodman's position became uncertain. He loved the Hollywood life, but Jacobs Brothers (by then known as Sportservice, Inc.) had no work for him there.

Bob Hunter, who covered the Dodgers for the Los Angeles *Examiner*, later told how he kept urging Walter O'Malley to meet Goodman. Eventually, Hunter picked up the phone in O'Malley's Statler Hotel office and made the call himself, shoving the phone into O'Malley's hand. It was a shove O'Malley would never regret. Goodman served as vice president/advertising for twenty-five years, handling novelties and selling the advertising for the yearbook and programs. Hunter said afterward O'Malley told him, "That was a great thing you did that day."[23]

Danny Goodman was always looking for new ideas. He first saw bobble-head dolls when a Japanese manufacturer brought them to him in 1958.[24] They became a staple, first for the Dodgers and then everywhere. He came out with plastic bats in 1958 as well, and his supplier had to go to double shifts by the item's second month.[25] When the Dodgers opened in the Coliseum,

Goodman offered a dozen brands of hats, from Tyroleans with a feather to sun visors. The roofless Coliseum, baking in the Southern California sun, proved an excellent place to sell woven straw coolie hats ($1.50), and Goodman gave them a larger and larger role. Even Walter O'Malley bought one, but refused to have his picture taken wearing it. [26]

With two months left in the 1958 season, Goodman's novelty operations had contributed over $200,000 to the team's profits. [27] By the end of the season, Goodman reported, Dodger fans had bought more souvenirs than all other major league teams combined. [28] And that was just at the ballpark. He had also persuaded Sears and local department store chains to carry the Dodger merchandise. [29] With a year's experience, Goodman rolled out an even more lavish array for the Coliseum's fifteen novelty booths in 1959. There were twelve hat styles, and thirty-three other items from bolo ties to pillow cases to complete child-sized uniforms. [30] There were aprons emblazoned: "To Heck with Housework, let's go to the ball game."[31]

But selling souvenirs was not always a sure thing. In 1962, with the Dodgers enjoying a four-and-a-half game lead on the Giants with a week to go, Goodman ordered 10,000 seat cushions and 20,000 drinking glasses labeled "Dodgers vs. Yankees, 1962." The Giants caught the Dodgers and Goodman had a large supply of gifts he could give to people who showed up in his office. [32]

Even the bugles didn't work out too well. They shattered when dropped by kids, and adults had a distressing tendency to expect them to work well. O'Malley made him discontinue the line. [33]

Goodman also played a strong role in the growing list of giveaway days that the Dodgers pioneered during the 1960s. There were Pennant Days and Cap Nights, Team Picture Days and Ball Nights. Eventually, there were Helmet Weekends, with plastic batting helmets given out Friday, Saturday, and Sunday. By the time of Goodman's death in 1983, there seemed to be a giveaway or a special event every game.

Intrigued, other major league teams began to push their souvenir sales. By the early 1970s, Danny Goodman had to reduce his boast. Now, he said, the Dodgers sold more souvenirs than the entire National Football League combined. By then, the Dodgers were drawing an average of two million fans a year and they would average thirty cents apiece on souvenirs. That was $600,000 a year, most of it profit. [34]

"Baseball," he said, "is the best sport for selling novelties."[35]

Notes

1. Plaut, David. *Chasing October: The Dodgers-Giants Pennant Race of 1962.* South Bend, In: Diamond Communications, 1994. Pp. 144-5.

2. *The Sporting News* (hereafter TSN), March 25, 1959, p. 12.

3. Los Angeles *Times* (hereafter LAT), August 29, 1971, Sect. D, p. 1.

4. Bob Hunter in TSN, Oct. 27, 1962, p. 9. Ned Cronin in the Los Angeles *Daily News*, September 4, 1947, p. 34, Vincent Flaherty column from Los Angeles *Examiner* in *Sporting News* files, marked February 1956, Frank Finch in TSN, May 14, 1958, p. 13. Goodman also reported that he went to work for the Stars in 1937, 1938, and 1939 in different interviews, but since all the interviews tied his start to the opening of Gilmore Field, it seems safe to place it in 1939, the date the park did open.

5. TSN, October 27, 1962, p. 9.

6. Los Angeles *Daily News*, April 4, 1951, p. 31.

7. TSN, May 14, 1958, p. 13.

8. Los Angeles *Daily News*, Sept. 4, 1947, op. cit. and TSN, October 27, 1962, op. cit.

9. *Los Angeles Major League Baseball News*, April 15, 1963, p. 7 (Saying he started in 1940 in Hollywood) and LAT, August 29, 1971, op. cit. (where he says it was 1931 in Newark).

10. Interview, Chuck Stevens, May 17, 1997. Also, ibid. This claim is open to question. Jon Light's *Cultural Encyclopedia of Baseball* (Jefferson, NC: McFarland, 1997), p. 308, says the custom of dragging the infield was invented by the Cincinnati Reds between 1949 and 1951. Cincinnati general manager Gabe Paul is quoted as saying the custom led to greater concession sales. Interestingly, Salveson pitched for the Stars from 1949 to 1951, the same time period. Stevens played for the Stars from 1948 to 1954.

11. Beverage, Richard. *Hollywood Stars: Baseball in Movieland, 1926-1957.* Placentia, CA: Deacon Press, 1984, p. 99.

12. LAT, July 11, 1957.

13. LAT, August 29, 1971, op. cit.

14. TSN, August 26, 1959, p. 15.

15. Los Angeles *Daily News*, Sept. 4, 1947, op. cit.

16. Clipping from TSN Danny Goodman file, Vincent Flaherty column dated Feb. 1956, also LAT, Oct. 24, 1957, Pt. IV, p. 5.

17. LAT, August 29, 1971, op. cit.

18. TSN, May 14, 1958, p. 13.

19. ibid.

20. ibid. Also, LAT, June 17, 1983, Pt. III, p. 11.

21. LAT, August 29, 1971, op. cit.

22. LAT, Feb. 6, 1958, Pt. IV, p. 3.

23. TSN, October 27, 1962, p. 9.

24. LAT, August 29, 1971, op. cit.

25. LAT, May 30, 1958, Pt. IV, p. 3.

26. After the first nine home games, Goodman said he'd sold 5,000 coolie hats. LAT, April 29, 1958, Pt. V, p. 2.

27. TSN, August 6, 1958.

28. TSN, January 14, 1959, p. 13.

29. LAT, April 7, 1960, Pt. IV, p. 3.

30. LAT, March 10, 1959, Pt. IV, p. 5. and TSN, March 25, 1959, p. 12.

31. LAT, August 26, 1963, Pt. C, p. 2.

32. Los Angeles *Herald Examiner*, September 27, 1963, Pt. D, p. 1.

33. LAT, May 11, 1971, Pt. III, p. 1.

34. LAT, August 29, 1971, op. cit.

35. Ibid.

Robin Roberts, (Blue) Rock of Ages

Al Cartwright

In March, 1948, Robin Roberts, a twenty-one-year-old picher at Michigan State signed for what then was an obscenely generous bonus of $25,000, and reported to the Phillies' spring camp in Clearwater, Florida. His mental and physical command of the art of pitching was so outstandingly evident during the weeks of training heavy thought was given to his going north and starting the season with the big club. Manager Ben Chapman even told the big rookie, "You're the best pitcher I've got."

But just before the club broke camp, the Philadelphia brass decided that Roberts should be tested in the minors. Public relations director Babe Alexander broke the news to the somewhat stunned righthander over a Clearwater milkshake.

And so on April 16, Roberts got off the train not at Thirtieth Street in Philadelphia, but in Sumter, South Carolina, the camp of the Wilmington (Delaware) Blue Rocks and also the site of the world's largest squab farm. He reported to manager Jack Sanford who, trivia buffs may not recall, was Chapman's brother-in-law.

Two weeks later, Roberts, as advertised, was preparing to pitch the Rocks' opening game of the Class B Inter-State League's 1948 season in Wilmington Park.

April 29

His debut took a while. The game was rained out the first night and chilled out the second. Finally, the Blue Rocks took the field against the Harrisburg Senators.

Roberts and the Blue Rocks then took the Senators, 19-1.

Robin was hot on a cold night. He struck out eight of the first ten batters and a total of seventeen, and pitched a five-hitter. He didn't have to be nearly that effective after the Rocks scored a run in the first inning and ten in the second, but that's baseball. He had the Senators shut out until the ninth, when their run was batted in by Ed Musial (Stan's brother).

Les Bell, the Harrisburg manager, was postgame livid. He accused Phillies owner Bob Carpenter of trying to break up the league by unleashing Roberts in Class B.

They could all say they were in the Wilmington lineup The Night That Roberts Broke In: catcher Jack Werner, infielders Joe O'Connell, Rudy Rufer, Don Hasenmayer, and Mike Goliat, outfielders Jack Lorenz, Frank Whalen and Barney Lutz. Werner and Goliat hit home runs.

				R	H	E
Harrisburg	000	000	001	1	5	7
Wilmington	1(10)2	200	13x	19	15	2

Winning pitcher, Roberts (1-0). Strikeouts 17. Walks 1.

May 4

Robin's second start also was postponed by rain. The next night, he continued to send fright waves through the league by shutting out visiting Trenton, 2-0, on four hits, striking out fourteen. The Rocks won it for him with their two runs in the eighth, driven in by Goliat and Lorenz.

Al Cartwright *is a retired newspaperman of fifty years service who is a National Headliners Club winner as the nation's outstanding sports columnist. He lives in Wilmington, Delaware.*

					R	H	E
Trenton	000	000	000		0	4	0
Wilmington	000	000	02x		2	7	0

Winning pitcher, Roberts (2-0). Strikeouts 14. Walks 1.

May 8

Now it was Lancaster's turn to come to Wilmington Park and see, or try to see, the Phillies' second annual Wilmington pitching phenom, the first having been Curt Simmons. Roberts produced a four-hitter, struck out a dozen and the Rocks won another, 8-3. They scored four in the first inning, two on a triple by Lutz. Robin shut out the Red Roses until the ninth. Lorenz had a five-for-five night.

					R	H	E
Lancaster	000	000	003		3	4	1
Wilmington	400	010	21x		8	18	0

Winning pitcher, Roberts (3-0). Strikeouts 12. Walks 2.

May 14

Roberts' very first road show, at Hagerstown. Make it a one-hitter, even though Robin spent a lot of time waiting for his pals to stop scoring runs. The score was 23-1. Twelve more strikeouts. Hagerstown's playing manager, Pep Rambert, got his club's only hit and drove in the run with it. Hasenmayer led the Blue Rocks' feast with seven—of their twenty-seven—hits in seven at bats. Roberts' catcher, Ed Oswald, was five-for-seven.

					R	H	E
Wilmington	004	251	803		23	27	2
Hagerstown	000	100	000		1	1	2

Winning pitcher, Roberts (4-0). Strikeouts 12. Walks 1.

May 18

This was a major-league pitching duel in Class B. The Blue Rocks and York played to a fifteen-inning, 2-2 tie at Wilmington Park, with Roberts and the Eastern Shore's Joe Muir both going the long distance. The league's curfew (no inning to start after 11:50 p.m.) stopped it. York loaded the bases on Roberts in the second inning with nobody out, so he struck out the next three. Trailing 2-1 in the ninth, the Rocks tied it when Goliat tripled and scored on a wild pitch. Robin had sixteen strikeouts.

						R	H	E
York	000	000	020	000	000	2	8	2
Wilmington	000	100	001	000	000	2	8	2

Roberts: Strikeouts 16. Walks 3.

May 23

They don't make them like him anymore. After a three-day rest following that marathon, Roberts came

back in the seven-inning half of a home doubleheader and turned back Hagerstown, 6-2, on five hits. Time of game: 1:15. Roberts now had five wins, all complete games, and a fifteen-inning no-decision, and was striking them out at fifteen-plus per game.

				R	H	E
Hagerstown	000	001	1	2	5	1
Wilmington	010	23x	6	10	1

Seven-inning game.

Winning pitcher: Roberts (5-0). Strikeouts 8. Walks 2.

May 27

Now he's mortal. Two firsts for Robin Roberts: first time not completing a game, first defeat. The visiting Sunbury club did it to him, 9-7, with two big innings. Robin couldn't hold a 5-3 lead and was yanked with two out in a six-run sixth after giving up six hits and an unlikely seven walks. All the walks came in two innings, and six became runs. Manager Jack Sanford also left in the sixth, tossed out by umpire Tom Murphy and his stopwatch for too impolitely objecting to a pitch call.

					R	H	E
Sunbury	030	006	000		9	9	1
Wilmington	002	300	200		7	5	2

Losing pitcher: Roberts (5-1). Strikeouts 5. Walks 7.

June 1

In the seven-inning opener of a home doubleheader, Roberts bounced back and tamed Trenton, 5-1, on a three-hitter and a no-walker. The Giants didn't get their first hit until the fifth inning. Shortstop Rufer gave him spectacular support and Goliat tripled to stretch a hitting streak to sixteen games. As expected from anyone from Springfield, Illinois, Robin said thanks.

				R	H	E
Trenton	000	001	0	1	3	2
Wilmington	100	130	x	5	5	1

Seven-inning game.

Winning pitcher: Roberts (6-1). Strikeouts 6. Walks 0.

June 5

Turning it all on before a season-high crowd of 3,620, Roberts equaled the league strikeout record of eighteen as he beat Trenton for the third time, 4-1. A Bridgeport, Connecticut, pitcher, Jimmy Wallace, had set the mark vs. Reading in 1941. The Giants actually took a 1-0 lead into the bottom of the fifth, but that's when the Rocks scored their four. Jesse Levan went three-for-three at the plate. After facing Roberts in twenty-five innings, Trenton had two runs, eleven hits and—what else?—three losses.

					R	H	E
Trenton	000	100	000		1	4	1
Wilmington	000	040	00x		4	10	2

Winning pitcher: Roberts (7-1). Strikeouts 18. Walks 2.

June 10

Host Harrisburg managed to get ten hits and five walks off the league's premier pitcher, but Roberts shut out the Senators after the third as the Rocks rallied to win, 6-3, in a scheduled seven-inning game that went nine. Now Wilmington was in first place. Goliat doubled and Hasenmayer singled to tie the score, 3-3 in the ninth, and Lorenz then homered to break it. Chalk up No. 8 for Robbie.

					R	H	E
Wilmington	010	001	103		6	13	2
Harrisburg	030	000	000		3	10	2

Winning pitcher: Roberts (8-1). Strikeouts 7. Walks 5.

June 13

This was to be his finishing touch in Wilmington. Roberts' five- hitter in a seven-inning game defeated York, 5-2, raising his record to a glossy 9-1. Whalen went three-for-three, half of the Blue Rocks hits.

The Wilmington lineup had Ed Oswald catching; Don Hasenmayer, Rudy Rufer, Charlie Dykes (Jimmy's son) and Mike Goliat in the infield, and Jesse Levan, Frank Whalen, and Jack Lorenz in the outfield.

This was the day that Georgia schoolboy pitcher Hugh Frank Radcliffe and his $40,000 bonus joined the Blue Rocks. He was billed as a maybe Robin Roberts. It never happened.

Robin won this one with only two days of rest. It was

suspected that the Phillies wanted a fast final tune-up from him.

				R	H	E
York	001	001	0	2	5	1
Wilmington	001	301	x	5	6	0

Winning pitcher: Roberts (9-1). Strikeouts 6. Walks 2.

June 17

Inevitability struck. Phillies owner Bob Carpenter, who had watched all of Roberts' starts in his home-town ball park, announced that the team was calling up the pride of its farm system. The next night, Robin Roberts started against the second-place Pittsburgh Pirates at Connie Mack Stadium. Now he was facing Ralph Kiner instead of Pep Rambert. He lost, 2-0, but it was a nifty loss, a complete-game five-hitter.

Roberts had left Wilmington with the Blue Rocks in first place by three games. The Phillies sent down Steve Ridzik from Toronto to replace him. Sort of.

Robin took with him to Philadelphia a pen and pencil set his Blue Rocks teammates had given him as a surprise farewell present.

June 23

Robin Roberts was to win 286 games in the major leagues, and this was the first. A short week out of the Inter-State League, he beat the Cincinnati Reds in Philadelphia, 3-2, giving up seven hits and striking out nine. He weathered home runs by Hank Sauer and Danny Litwhiler. Wilmington was far, far away.

Fifty years later—to the day—Roberts returned to Wilmington to become the first inductee in the Blue Rocks Hall of Fame.

Robin Roberts' Official Blue Rocks Statistics

G	CG	W	L	PCT.	IP	H	R	ER	BB	SO	ERA
11	10	9	1	.900	96	55	25	22	27	121	2.06

The Day the Phillies Came of Age

C. Paul Rogers III

The 1949 Philadelphia Phillies began the year with no particular expectations. They had limped into sixth place the year before, a scant two games out of the cellar. The 1949 club had a few veterans, most of whom, like Hank Borowy, Eddie Miller, Bill Nicholson, and Schoolboy Rowe, seemed to be past their prime. The bulk of the team, however, consisted of largely untested kids, whom Phillies' president Bob Carpenter had aggressively signed out of high school and college. Bonus babies Robin Roberts, Richie Ashburn, and Curt Simmons, among others, had gotten their major league baptism the previous year under the patient, watchful eye of Eddie Sawyer.

In late July, 1948, former college professor Sawyer, without any big league experience, had taken over from interim manager Dusty Cooke, who had replaced volatile Ben Chapman. Sawyer had nurtured many of the young Phillies while managing the Eastern League Utica Blue Sox, then the Phillies' top farm club, from 1945 through 1947. In 1948, he played the youngsters the last two months of the season and the Phillies finished twenty-two games under .500, twenty-five-and-a-half games behind the pennant-winning Boston Braves.

The 1949 Phillies seemed to start where they left off the year before, losing eight of their first eleven games. They soon made some progress, however, and the team began June 2 in sixth place with a 19-21 won-loss record, only four-and-a-half games behind the league-leading Braves. Nonetheless, even with their improved

C. Paul Rogers, III *is the co-author with boyhood hero Robin Roberts of* The Whiz Kids and the 1950 Pennant. *He teaches law at Southern Methodist University in Dallas.*

play, there was little to suggest what was about to unfold. The club had shown little of the form that in 1950 would propel it into national prominence as the National League pennant-winning Whiz Kids.

The fifth-place Cincinnati Reds were in town for a four-game series. The Phillies had beaten the Reds, 4-3, in ten innings the previous evening and now were only one game behind the Reds in the standings.

The June 2 ballgame was a tight pitchers' duel for seven-and-a-half innings between two southpaws, the Phils' twenty-year-old phenom Curt Simmons, and the Reds' crafty veteran Ken Raffensberger. Phillies catcher Andy Seminick slugged a second inning home run for a 1-0 lead, but the Reds bunched four hits for two runs and a 2-1 lead in the top of the fifth. The Phillies tied it in the sixth on a bunt single by Granny Hamner, a two-out walk to Seminick, and a base hit by Stan Hollmig to drive in Hamner.

The Reds again took the lead in the seventh with doubles by Ray Mueller and Raffensberger. Going into the bottom of the eighth Raffensberger had allowed only four hits and two runs, and appeared to be on the way to a 3-2 victory.

Del Ennis changed that on Raffensberger's first pitch with a screaming line drive into the left field stands. Andy Seminick boomed the next pitch over the roof of the left field stands for one of the longest home runs ever hit at Shibe Park. Raffensberger was through for the day. His two eighth-inning pitches had resulted in two home runs and he left the mound suddenly down, 4-3.

Reds manager Bucky Walters brought in Jess Dobernic. Hollmig lined to shortstop Virgil Stallcup for the first out. Willie "Puddin' Head" Jones followed with the third homer of the inning into the left field stands to make the score to 5-3. Eddie Miller popped up for the second out, but Schoolboy Rowe, pitching in relief of Simmons and known as an excellent hitter, belted the fourth circuit blast of the inning into the upper deck in left to send Dobernic to the showers.

Walters next tried southpaw Kent Peterson, who responded by walking Ashburn. Shortstop Hamner followed by sending a blast high off the left field wall, missing a home run by less than a foot. He ended up with a double, sending Ashburn to third. Although Eddie Waitkus grounded to third baseman Bobby Adams, the inning stayed alive when first baseman Ted Kluszewski dropped the throw to first. Ashburn scored on the error to run the score to 7-3.

With runners on the corners, Ennis, batting for the second time in the inning, singled to center for his second hit of the frame, driving in Hamner. Seminick was next. He clubbed the team's fifth home run of the inning well over the fence in left, driving in three runs, extending the score to 11-3. The blast was his third of the game, and he became the first player since Joe DiMaggio in 1936 to hit two homers in an inning.

Walters refused to change pitchers again, and Peterson plunked Hollmig with a pitch, sending him to first. Jones then missed his second home run of the inning by two or three inches, ripping a shot off the very top of the wall in left and winding up at third with a triple. Hollmig scored, but Miller mercifully struck out to end the inning. What had started as a pitchers' duel was now 12-3.

Seminick's streak—For the inning the Phillies had belted a total of five home runs to tie a major league record.[1] While five home runs in one inning is quite an accomplishment (it annually gets a mention in the agate type in many newspapers' "This Day in Baseball" column), the Phils were a total of about fifteen inches from clubbing seven. Hamner's blast had missed by less than a foot and Jones' second shot by only a few inches.

In that single inning the Phillies had scored ten runs on eight hits, including five home runs, a triple, a double, and a single. Their twenty-six total bases established a modern major league record and their seven extra-base hits tied the major league standard for an inning. Altogether they set or tied nine National League or major league records.

Andy Seminick, the only surviving member of the June 2 home run brigade, remembers the day well: "I hit a home run off Ken Raffensberger in the second inning but he was pitching a fine ballgame. Then Del Ennis hit a home run on the first pitch of the eighth inning to tie the score and I hit the very next pitch over the roof in left field. Raffensberger always tried to throw me a slider over the outside part of the plate, but he got it in too far, right in my wheelhouse, and I really smoked it. It was one of the hardest balls I ever hit.

"Raffensberger was my former roommate when he was with the Phils. We came up together in 1943. But after he was traded to the Reds, I always had good luck against him. He didn't like pitching against me at all. Del Ennis and I, our bats were jumping when he pitched against us.

"Then later in the inning I came up again after we batted around. Another lefthander, Kent Peterson, was pitching by then and I worked the count to 3-2 and hit another home run into the left field stands. I remember that Eddie Miller was upset about making the second and third outs of the inning and said, 'Hey, maybe I ought to go on home and not come out here.'

"If Willie Jones had run hard all the way on his triple he might have had an inside-the-park home run, which would have been his second homer of the inning, too. The ball caromed off the top of the wall way back to the infield and Willie sort of coasted into third, standing up.

"After the game there was a lot of celebrating in the clubhouse, like we won the pennant. The sportswriters all came in taking pictures of the four of us and Eddie Sawyer. Bob Carpenter, our president, came into the clubhouse and said he had never been so excited. A lot of people hadn't seen that kind of hitting, with everyone popping the ball out of the ballpark.

"The next day I had a congratulatory telegram pinned to my locker from our owner, Mr. Carpenter [Bob Carpenter's father]. He had not been feeling too well and our hitting really picked him up."

That fabulous inning was a turning point for the Phillies. Led by the robust hitting of Andy Seminick, the Phillies won twelve of seventeen to shoot into third place in the National League. Seminick, then a twenty-eight-year-old veteran, had lost his starting catching job in spring training to rookie Stan Lopata after hitting only .225 the previous year. In fact, Seminick thought he was going to be traded. By the end of April. However, Sawyer reinserted him in the starting lineup after the team's slow start.

Seminick's clutch hitting had begun on Memorial Day when he hit a long sacrifice fly to drive in the winning run in the tenth inning of the second game of a doubleheader with the Boston Braves. On May 31, he hit a homer and a double to drive in three runs in a 7-6 loss to the Braves. The next day, in the first game of the series against the Reds, he again drove home the winning run in the Phillies' ten-inning victory with another long sacrifice fly to left.

The day after his three-home-run, five-RBI outburst in the record setting June 2 game, Seminick drove in two runs, including the winning run, with a scorching two-out double in a 3-1 Phillies victory over Cincinnati. On June 4 he did it again, smashing a seventh-inning home run against Bob Rush of the Cubs for the only run in a taut 1-0 Phillies win over Chicago. It was his fourth circuit clout in three days. For the week Seminick slugged five homers in six games and drove in thirteen runs. He drove in the winning run in all five Phillies victories for the week.

But he was still not done. On June 7 against the Pirates, he keyed a three-run game-tying rally in the eighth inning with a timely single. Then in the ninth, he smashed a line drive to right to drive in the winning run in a seesaw 6-5 game. Two days later he set up the winning tally in a marathon eighteen-inning game with the Pirates, sending the eventual winning run to third with a ringing double which bounced against the left field fence.

After a couple of relatively quiet games, Seminick broke loose again on June 12, smashing three home runs in a doubleheader split with the Cardinals. For the two games he was seven-for-eight, with seven runs batted in. His second homer of the day, a three-run shot in the third inning of the second game off Gerry Staley, provided Robin Roberts with the winning runs in an 8-3 triumph.

He clubbed yet another homer in his next game as the Phillies opened a road trip with a 9-2 pounding of the Cubs in Chicago. It came in the sixth inning with two men on and was hit so far over the left center field wall that Cubs' left fielder Harry Walker and center fielder Andy Pafko never moved from their respective positions. That was the night that Eddie Waitkus was shot and almost killed by a deranged female admirer in the Edgewater Beach Hotel. (While the Phillies did slump shortly thereafter, they defeated the Cubs in a doubleheader the next day, 4-1 and 3-0, to move into a third-place tie with the defending champion Braves.)

In fourteen games, Seminick had blasted nine home runs and had driven in twenty-five runs. He had produced in the clutch as well, driving in the winning run in seven Phillies wins in a slightly more than two week span.

The Phillies would rarely be out of the first division for the rest of the year. Although they slumped in July, they caught fire again in August, sweeping the pennant-bound Brooklyn Dodgers at Ebbets Field. But

Andy Seminick

catapulted by their record-setting power outburst on June 2 and by Andy Seminick's memorable clutch-hitting streak, the Phillies finished 1949 in third place, ahead of the defending champion Braves. It was the team's highest finish since 1917.

The next year the Phillies would be dubbed the Whiz Kids would win the pennant. Players like Roberts, Ashburn, Ennis, Simmons, Dick Sisler, Hamner, Jones, Bubba Church, and 1950 MVP Jim Konstanty would forever be associated with that memorable ballclub. But it was on June 2, 1949 that the young Phillies, led by Andy Seminick, began showing they were for real.

Notes:

1. On June 6, 1939, the New York Giants hit five home runs in the fourth inning of a game against the Reds (Harry Danning, Frank Demaree, Burgess Whitehead, Manny Salvo, and Joe Moore. Pitcher Salvo's homer was the only one he hit in the big leagues.) The 1961 San Francisco Giants (Orlando Cepeda, Felipe Alou, Jim Davenport, Willie Mays, John Orsino) and the 1966 Minnesota Twins (Rich Rollins, Zoilo Versalles, Tony Oliva, Don Mincher, Harmon Killebrew) subsequently tied the record.

The Big Four Come to Detroit

Ralph Horton

On September 17, 1885, the owners of the Buffalo Bisons of the National League shocked the baseball world by selling their entire team to the Detroit Wolverines. Detroit was in its fifth year in the League and had never been in contention. Frederick K. Stearns, a wholesale druggist who was a Detroit director (and later club president), was determined to change that. From their first year in the league in 1881, the Wolverines had only three solid performers—center fielder Ned Hanlon, an outstanding fielder and team leader although only an average hitter; Charlie Bennett, generally regarded as one of the top catchers of the nineteenth century, and George Wood, a good hitting outfielder.

In 1884 Detroit had finished dead last with only twenty-eight wins, but during the second half of the 1885 season prospects began looking up. Young pitchers Charles (Lady) Baldwin and Charlie Getzien started winning and would account for more than half of Buffalo's forty-one wins, giving promise of a solid pitching staff for 1886. In mid-season, Bill Watkins replaced Charlie Morton as manager. Also joining the Wolverines in mid-year was Big Sam Thompson, a six-foot-two slugging outfielder destined for the Hall of Fame, who had started his professional career only a year earlier, playing for $2.50 a game for Evansville of the Northwestern League.

*The late **Ralph Horton** was for many years one of SABR's key players and strong supports. Researcher, writer, publisher, and friend, Ralph will be sorely missed by the organization and by hundreds of its members, whose lives he touched directly through his personal kindness and indirectly through his work.*

Big Four II—Even with Hanlon, Bennett, Wood, Thompson, and the two young hurlers, Stearns realized he needed three or four more established players to bring a pennant to Detroit. He set his sights on the Big Four of Buffalo—first baseman and premier slugger Dan Brouthers; hard-hitting second baseman-outfielder Hardie Richardson; versatile shortstop-catcher Jack Rowe, and veteran third baseman James (Deacon) White. One of the quartet, White, had been a member of the original Big Four, along with Al Spalding, Ross Barnes, and Cal McVey, when Chicago owner William Hulbert raided the Boston team late in the 1875 season to give the White Stockings a strong entry in the new National League he was planning. Before the end of the 1885 season, Stearns reviewed his plans with the other directors and received the blessing of president Joseph Marsh to go ahead.

Stearns decided to take the direct approach, and immediately went to Buffalo. The Bisons were losing money. They need an attendance of 800 a game to break even but were bringing in only 500. There were rumors that the team might disband, and Stearns envisioned picking up the Big Four for Detroit for the balance of 1885 and also for 1886. Buffalo chose to hold together until the end of the season but Stearns, with the assistance of Detroit center fielder and captain Ned Hanlon, who was a close friend of Brouthers, received verbal agreement from the Big Four to join the Wolverines for 1886.

In early September Detroit went to Buffalo for a series with the Bisons. Stearns, with several other Detroit officials, accompanied the team. He signed the Big Four to contracts for 1886 at figures well above their Buffalo salaries. Brouthers and Richardson would receive $4,000 each, and White and Rowe $3,500. Stearns, manager Watkins, and captain Hanlon were confident that the acquisition of the Big Four would help Detroit attract one or two other big stars for 1886 and make the Wolverines an instant pennant contender. The most prominent name mentioned was that of St. Louis second baseman Fred Dunlap. Rumors also named two Providence stars, pitcher Charles "Old Hoss" Radbourn and outfielder Paul Hines.

On September 15, two days before the sale, Buffalo defeated Philadelphia, 7-3. Buffalo's seventh season in the National League was coming to a close, and this contest proved to be the team's final victory. The Phillies won the final two games of the series.

After the game Stearns made his offer to buy the Big Four. Buffalo management was interested, but suggested that Detroit buy the entire franchise, digging Buffalo out of debt. For $7,000, the deal was completed later that night.

The fuss—It had been common knowledge that Buffalo was in financial trouble, but the baseball world was stunned by the unprecedented transaction. A number of clubs (particularly Boston) were known to be interested in acquiring one or more of the Big Four for 1886, and Detroit's bold stroke caught most baseball men by surprise. A. G. Spalding, president of the Chicago White Stockings, was probably not one of this group. His team had dominated the National League during the 1880s, and he had expressed concern about the lack of competition from the other teams. Some observers now charged him with being involved behind the scenes to help create a worthy opponent—and good gates—for his White Stockings.

The provisions set down in a secret meeting of committees of the National League and American Association held in Saratoga, New York, a month earlier had given the baseball fraternity a false sense of security. The conferees then had drawn up rules setting salary limits for 1886 and outlining certain restrictions involving the transfer of players. One of these stated that no team could negotiate with new players for 1886 prior to October 20, 1885. It was apparent that the Detroit club had decided to ignore that agreement. Management wanted a winner and was prepared to employ whatever means necessary.

The terms of the sale provided that Buffalo was to pay all its debts, but that Detroit would be responsible for salaries and expenses for the balance of the 1885 season. President Josiah Jewett of Buffalo announced that Detroit would assume control of the Bisons after the game with Philadelphia on Saturday, September 19, and that the new owners had agreed that Buffalo would finish the League season, but had made no commitment for 1886.

It was expected that the Big Four would play their last game for Buffalo against Philadelphia on Saturday, then join Detroit for a game against Philadelphia on Monday (there was no Sunday baseball in the National League). But now that the deal had been announced, Detroit decided that it wanted the Big Four in the lineup immediately, and won its point by paying an additional $100 for the early release of the four Buffalo stars. On Friday manager Watkins entrained for Detroit with Brouthers, Richardson, Rowe, and White.

After their arrival in Detroit, it was announced that the four players had signed contracts for the balance of the season and would be reserved for the 1886 season (actually the players had agreed to finish the season under the terms of their contracts with Buffalo). In explaining the acquisitions, Detroit management pointed out that the group of four wanted to continue to play together and that this could be done only in Detroit as no other team had room for all of them. It was announced that the four would play in Saturday's game against New York—Brouthers at first in place of McQuery, Richardson at second instead of Crane, Rowe at shortstop for Manning, and White at third base replacing Donnelly.

New York was in the midst of a great pennant fight with Chicago, and was not pleased with the prospect of taking on a Detroit team that was much tougher than the one they had already beaten in two of the first three games of the current series. New York president John Day recognized the purchase as a clever move on the part of Detroit, but would have preferred it had taken place earlier. Without the new men, Detroit had lost three out of four to Chicago in late August to give Spalding's team a half-game lead over the Giants going into the September stretch drive.

Day advised manager Jim Mutrie not to take the field if Detroit fielded the new players, or to play the game under protest. Looking ahead, however, both Day and Mutrie must have been pleased with the prospect of a five-game series with weakened Buffalo beginning on Monday. The series was scheduled for Buffalo, but the Giants hoped to get the games transferred to New York for a consideration of $1,500.

Temporary setback—Meanwhile, protests from around the country were coming into the office of NL president Nick Young, some calling for the expulsion of Detroit from the league. Young ruled that the Big Four were still members of the Buffalo team and ordered umpire Bob Ferguson to forfeit the game if they took the field for Detroit on Saturday. Detroit was forced to play with its regular team, and was defeated, 6-5, by the Giants on a two-run rally in the ninth.

After Young voided their sale, the Big Four refused to play out the season with the Bisons. They did return to Buffalo briefly, but then scattered—Brouthers to

Chicago, White to his farm in Corning, New York, Rowe to Colorado, and Richardson on a hunting expedition. They announced they would put themselves on the market after October 20. A week later they announced they would play for Detroit in 1886.

With neither the Big Four nor any replacements from Detroit, the Bisons were forced to finish the season with a makeshift team. They lost their remaining fourteen games, many by lopsided scores: 12-2, 10-0, 17-2, 15-1, 13-2, and 18-0. They were shut out four times and scored an average of less than two runs per game. The last four games of the season were unique in that they consisted of two doubleheaders against Providence (October 7 and October 10) in which Frederick "Dupee" Shaw hurled four complete game victories for Providence, including a 4-0 no-hitter. It should be pointed out that three of the games were five innings and one six innings. The games of October 7 were played in Buffalo, but the games of October 10, while scheduled for Buffalo, were played in Elmira. The losing pitcher in all four games was Pete Conway.

As soon as Detroit closed its season with a 3-2 win over Boston and a sixth place finish (forty-four games out), captain Ned Hanlon entrained for St. Louis to make an effort to sign Fred Dunlap. Dunlap was a sure-handed fielder (even without a glove) and a strong hitter. The incentives for Dunlap were an increase in salary and an opportunity to join the Big Four on what was certain to be one of the standout teams in the National League. Hanlon was unsuccessful, perhaps because rumors were circulating that the Big Four were to be broken up. The word was that Brouthers was headed for Chicago to replace Anson, who would retire, and Richardson would go to the Philadelphia Athletics in the American Association.

On October 18 the National League and the American Association held a joint meeting in New York and confirmed the Saratoga agreement of August. The maximum salary for 1886 (destined to be ignored) was to be $2,000 and the minimum $1,000. It was also agreed that a player released by a club could go only to another club in the same circuit unless no one claimed him within ten days.

After the meeting the Big Four were still listed as the property of Buffalo, and Dunlap, who was not getting along with Henry Lucas, owner of the St. Louis club, was rumored to be headed for Chicago. The league called another meeting for mid-November. Buffalo was represented by Stearns, also a director of Detroit. Details of the meeting were not made public, but the "inside" story as reported by *Sporting Life*, was that Detroit would retain the Big Four but would surrender the Buffalo franchise to the league.

By now it was generally accepted that the Big Four would play with Detroit in 1886. Arthur Soden, who had coveted at least one of the stars for Boston, gave up and bought out the Providence Grays, primarily to obtain pitcher Radbourn and catcher Daily.

In early January the Big Four were listed as being under contract to Detroit. Also in January, Washington was formally admitted to the league, and a month later Kansas City was added as the eighth team. The new entries replaced Buffalo and Providence.

The first season—On April 30, 1886, the Detroit Wolverines, under new president Fred Stearns, opened the season in St. Louis against the Maroons. With the addition of the Big Four Detroit was one of the favorites to win the league championship, and 5,000 fans turned out to see the home nine take a 9-2 drubbing. The Big Four manned the infield—Brouthers at first base, batting second; Richardson at second base, hitting third; Rowe at shortstop in the fifth slot; and White at third base, following Rowe. They were joined by Ned Hanlon, leading off and playing center field; cleanup hitter Sam Thompson in right field; Charlie Bennett, the "perfect" catcher; left fielder Jimmy Manning, and pitcher Charles (Lady) Baldwin whose opening day win was the first of his forty-two victories for the year. It was only one game, but the Big Four gave every indication that Detroit had made a master stroke. Rowe and White had three hits each, and Brouthers and Richardson chipped in with one apiece.

Detroit went on to win twenty of twenty-four games in May, but that put them only one game ahead of defending champion Chicago. The Wolverines continued their strong play through July, ending the month with a record of 55-14 (.797) and a four-and-a-half game lead over Chicago. A poor August (10-13), put them two-and-a-half games back entering September.

In an effort to bolster the team for the stretch run, the Wolverines finally got Dunlap in August, purchasing him from St. Louis in time for the stretch run for $4,700—a steep price in those days. Dunlap took over at second base, and Richardson moved to left field, replacing Manning. The Wolverines won twenty-two of their last thirty-one games but the poor August cost them the pennant. They finished 87-36 (.707), two-and-a-half games behind Chicago.

Brouthers (.370) and Richardson (.351) finished among the top five hitters in the League, while Rowe batted .303 and White .288. Brouthers led in doubles and slugging percentage, and tied Richardson for the home run lead, while Richardson led in hits. Baldwin won forty-two games and Getzien thirty. When these two tired in August, rookie Bill Smith and Pete Conway, obtained from Kansas City, helped out.

A pennant—The Wolverines got off to another fast start in 1887 and led all the way, winning the pennant with a record of 79-45 (.637), three-and-a-half games ahead of Philadelphia and six-and-a-half games in front of Chicago. They went on to beat the strong St. Louis Browns, American Association pennant winners, in the World Series, ten games to five.

Brouthers' batting mark dropped to .338, but he led the league in runs scored, doubles and on base percentage. Richardson hit .328, Rowe .318 and White .303. Thompson was the big gun, leading the league in batting, slugging, hits, triples, and runs batted in. Getzien led the pitchers with twenty-nine wins. Baldwin, who won only thirteen games during the regular season, won four of Detroit's victories over St. Louis in the World Series.

After a poor start in 1888, the Wolverines got hot in June and July and entered August in a tie for first place with New York. The season went down the drain in August again, with a sixteen-game losing streak. The slump continued in September, and the Wolverines finished fifth.

Injuries killed Detroit's pennant hopes. Both Richardson and Thompson played less than half the scheduled games, and Rowe missed more than twenty games. The averages of the Big Four all dropped, with Brouthers hitting .307, Richardson .289, Rowe .277, and White .298. Conway led the pitchers with thirty wins. Attendance fell off. The team with one of the highest payrolls in the league lost money. Manager Watkins was replaced by Bob Leadly in late August, and Stearns gave up the presidency to Charles W. Smith, co-owner of a shoe company. After the season, Smith, Stearns and the other Detroit directors decided to sell off their stars and end their city's eight-year stay in the National League.

Breaking up the Big Four—Brouthers, Richardson, Rowe and White played together for eight years—five in Buffalo and three in Detroit. During that time Brouthers hit .345, Richardson .312, White .299 and Rowe .298. By the end of the 1888 season Brouthers had the highest career National League average, and the other three were all in the top ten. Brouthers was also the career home run leader.

With the end of the Detroit franchise the Big Four split up. Brouthers and Richardson went to Boston where they played in the National League in 1889, the Players' League in 1890, and the American Association in 1891, helping their PL and AA teams to pennants. Richardson wound up his career with Washington and New York in 1892. Brouthers played five more years—with Brooklyn, Baltimore, Louisville, and Philadelphia—ending his major league career in 1896 (except for two games with the New York Giants in 1904). After leaving Philadelphia, he hit .415 for Springfield in the Eastern League in 1897 and also batted .373 in 1904 for Poughkeepsie in the Hudson River League, winning his final batting title at the age of forty-six. z played two more years and then spent many years with the New York Giants as a scout, watchman and press box attendent. Rowe and White finished their careers together, with Pittsburgh in the National League in 1889 and Buffalo in the Players' League in 1890.

Rowe died at the age of fifty-three in 1911, but the other three all lived long lives. Richardson was seventy-five when he died in 1931. Brouthers passed away a year later at seventy-four, and White lived until 1939, when he died at ninety-one.

Brouthers, the top National League hitter (and slugger) of the nineteenth century, was elected to the Hall of Fame in 1945. White, who had five outstanding years in the National Association prior to the start of the National League, is certainly more deserving than many who are in the Hall.

It is now more than 100 years since the Big Four played their last game together, but in all that time only one quartet of position players has played together longer. Steve Garvey, Davey Lopes, Bill Russell, and Ron Cey covered the infield for the Los Angeles Dodgers 1972-81.

The Mysterious Case of Dick Brookins

Bill Kirwin

*And, after all, what is a lie? 'Tis but
The truth in masquerade.*
—Byron

Dick Brookins may have been the first black player to play in organized baseball in this century. Preceding Jackie Robinson by forty years, the five foot, nine inch infielder evaded expulsion for more than four years. Initially treated as a white, he averted detection while playing in remote northern Class D leagues from 1906-1910. This Missourian was able to step over baseball's color line until he crossed the Canadian border to play in the Western Canada League in 1910. How did he manage to play several years without official detection, and why was he banned from playing ball in a country that had no legal basis for doing so?

There have been a few black ballplayers who have attempted to "pass" as something other than white. John McGraw tried to pass off Charlie Grant as a "full blooded Cherokee." Jimmy Claxton, a Canadian-born pitcher, was on the Oakland Oaks roster for a week in 1916. And Bill Thompson played a season for Bellows Falls in the Class D Twin State League in 1911.[1] However, Dick Brookins was able to play at least 281 games in three different minor leagues over four seasons before being forced to leave the game.

The *Reach Baseball Guide* mentions that the eight team Western Canada League[2] "fell into difficulties" in 1910 and did not enjoy a successful season especially in

Dick Brookins with Fargo

Medicine Hat, Alberta, and Regina, Saskatchewan.[3] The *Reach Guide* goes on to list the accomplishments of all the players in the Western Canada League for the 1910 season—everyone, that is, except Dick Brookins. His name is absent from league totals, his playing records expunged in a final indignity—a denial of his existence.

Brookins, a third baseman for the Regina club, was expelled by league president C. J. Eckstorm when it was "discovered" that he was not a Native American but was "colored." That is the rudimentary story. But a small group of baseball scholars over the past few years has been working on piecing together a more comprehensive understanding of the brief career of Richard Brookins.[4]

Bill Kirwin *is a professor emeritus at the University of Calgary and is the founder and editor of* NINE: A Journal of Baseball History and Social Policy Perspectives.

Almost half of Brookins' official playing time was with the Green Bay Colts (aka Orphans) in the Wisconsin State League in 1906 and 1907 . He concluded the 1907 campaign with forty-eight games with the Houghton Giants in the Northern Copper League, batting above .300 for the first and only time in his career.(.306). In 1908, he played sixty-five games with the last place Fargo Browns of the Northern League. Inexplicably, there is no record of his playing in 1909. His formal record ended in 1910 when he played twenty games for the Regina Bonepilers.[5]

Brookins' lifetime career batting average of .249 suggests that he was a journeyman player at best. Like any journeyman, he occasionally enjoyed a good day. On April 25, 1910, in a spring training game in La Crosse, Wisconsin (Regina's spring training site), he got three hits, stole two bases, and made two sensational stops, thereby becoming the team's regular third baseman. On opening day, he batted third, went 0-for-3, and committed three errors.[6] By the time he played his last official game he was batting .223.

So there was nothing in particular on the playing field to draw any attention to Dick Brookins, except perhaps the color of his skin. But neither the picture in the 1907 *Guide*,[7] nor the portraits that appeared in the Fargo *Forum and Daily Republic* on June 8, 1910, and the Regina *Leader* that same year tell us much about his race. David Zang reminds us that "...some blacks...made cosmetic attempts to mute their African features," and that a mulatto like Brookins must have faced a life of deceit, both personal and societal.[8] He may have altered his appearance for more than baseball. Perhaps he enjoyed the envy of middle-class blacks who at the time held light complexion to be meritorious.[9]

Nearly 20,000 black slaves fled to Ontario via the underground railroad before the end of the Civil War. They enjoyed nominal rights, but occupied the lower echelons of society. Before 1908, the Canadian prairies had a negligible black population. This abruptly changed between 1908 and 1911, when a thousand blacks migrated from Oklahoma to homestead remote areas of central Alberta. Many had previously migrated from former slave states in the futile hope that they might find freedom in Oklahoma. They were quickly disillusioned and responded to Canadian government advertisements directed at American farmers living in the Midwest and Southwest to settle the Canadian prairies.

There were no legal reasons for emigrant blacks to be denied admittance to Canada if they were healthy and in possession of $300.[10] However, Canadian newspaper editors, along with the Edmonton and Calgary Board of Trade, and women's organizations such as The Imperial Order of the Daughters of the Empire(IODE) railed against black immigration on the grounds that Canada would be importing racial problems from south of the border.[11] A plan was devised dispatching Canadian immigration agents to Oklahoma to persuade blacks living there that the Canadian winters were too difficult for them to adapt to—exactly the opposite argument used on whites, who were told that Canadian winters were healthy and invigorating. One of the half-million white immigrant arrivals from the United States was WCL president C.J. Eckstorm, from Minnesota.[12]

The thousand Oklahoma blacks who had already settled in Alberta were neither harmed nor prevented from living in four isolated communities within a hundred-mile radius of Edmonton.[13] They were easy to ignore. Fear of further black incursions were rampant in Western Canada in 1910 though, and this no doubt contributed to the plight of Brookins.

1906-1907—Richard C. Brookins was born in St. Louis in July, 1879, to Harry W. and Luisa Brookins. The St. Louis census of 1900 lists the Brookins family as white. The city directory lists the occupation of the twenty- two-year-old Richard as "Coal." This listing is repeated annually until 1911, the year *after* he was booted out of organized baseball, when the directory lists his occupation as "Baseball."[14]

Aside from this basic information, we know nothing of Brookins' life until 1906, when he was nearly twenty-seven years old.[15] It wouldn't be unreasonable to speculate that he played for a St. Louis city league team.[16] There is no indication how or why he ended up in Green Bay. His career there was unremarkable. He played a complete season in 1906, batting .226 in 458 at-bats.

The Green Bay *Gazette* sports pages mention his name nearly thirty times during the 1906 season, from a headline, BROOKINS' HOME RUN IS GAME'S FEATURE,[17] to the more mundane information that the runner scored "on a hit by 'Dick' Brookins" or that he "ate up a screaming line drive" while playing third, or that "Brooky" slammed one over the infield.[18] Never was there any mention of his race or color.

The Gazette treated Brookins' teammate Wilson Charles differently. It rarely let an opportunity pass to inform its readers that Charles was an "Indian" or that he was "Dusky," or that "Chief Charles" had performed heroically.[19] As the fourth-place[20] Green Bay team concluded the season, the *Gazette* informed its readers that Charles was off to Carlisle College to play football at the famous Indian school. The same reporter told of Dick Brookins returning to work in the coal business with his brother, and that Brookins should be expected to be "called up."[21]

In 1907, despite the prediction that Brookins would be elevated to a higher classification, he returned to Green Bay, informing a reporter that he had been working out with one of the local teams at home.[22]

The *Gazette* mentioned the color characteristics of shortstop "Dusty" Miller, and noted that "Ninham, the Nebraska Indian twirler," had reported.[23] But the only comments about Brookins had to do with baseball. His teammate and future 1910 manager was second baseman "Roxey" Walters, the very man who would later vouch for Brookins ethnicity and would "never play a negro."[24]

If Brookins was "passing," he might have been nervous when Green Bay scheduled an exhibition against the Chicago Colored Gophers.[25] The Gophers featured pitcher Will Horn, formerly of the Chicago Unions, the Philadelphia Giants, and the Chicago Leland Giants. But the game was cancelled because of rain that was plaguing spring training.

Green Bay *was* able to get in an exhibition series against the Houghton Giants of the Northern-Copper League. Green Bay swept the doubleheader from its Class D rivals, winning the second game, 2-1, when Brookins was hit by a pitch with the bases loaded in the bottom of the final inning. Brookins would be traded to the Houghton team in the middle of season.

Green Bay opened the season in Freeport, Illinois, winning one of three games with Dusty Miller playing shortstop and Ninham—"descendant of Hiawatha and running mate to 'Chief' Charles"[26]—handling much of the pitching. By the time the team arrived for the home opener, Dusty was no longer the team's shortstop.

Newspaper reports merely stated that Walters was now playing the position and that Miller had been moved to left field. Within a few days Miller's name disappears from the roster without explanation. On June 5, 1907, the *Gazette* reported that Brookins would be "sent out to the outer gardens [left field]. 'Dick' certainly has not played the game he did last year around the third sack and the management thinks a change is expedient."[27] A shake-up of the team was apparent, but Brookins was soon back at third for a few games, batting in the ninth slot rather than his customary third or fourth position.

By the middle of June, Brookins had played his last game for Green Bay. His batting average had improved to .260, but his play at third base had evidently been poor. Not once in the season and a half that Brookins played in Green Bay did the newspapers ever mention anything about his racial background.

The Houghton Giants must have rememberd something they liked about Brookins. They offered him a contract, and he was playing in the Michigan Upper Peninsula town in early July. The Hancock *Evening Journal* reported rather dryly on July 10 that "Brookins, the new Houghton shortstop, recently acquired from Green Bay, performed in a satisfactory manner and made a very favorable impression on the audience." He went 2-for-3, scoring one run in a 9-1 vic-

tory over Calumet.[28] The report failed to mention the error he committed, but did comment the following day about one of two errors he committed during that game.[29]

Brookins was soon playing shortstop and third base, receiving such rave reviews that the local newspapers expected him to be called up at the end of the season.[30] He blossomed into one of the team's best hitters, managing a .306 batting average in 199 at-bats with sixteen doubles, three triples and a home run in forty-eight games. His lone home run was overshadowed by the news that fans would soon be able to see "Baseball by Electricity"—telegraph recreations.[31] This promising recovery from first-half disappointment enabled Brookins to look forward to a better opportunity in 1908. Again, there was no mention in the Northern-Copper League press of his race.

"Where there's smoke there must be fire"—The 1908 season found Brookins playing for the weak Fargo Browns of the four-team Northern League. Hampered by an apparent knee injury, he played sporadically. On June 24, came a thunderbolt. The Hannibal (Missouri) *Courier Post* reported "that the playing of Brookins, a negro, with the Fargo team, is causing trouble in the Northern League. Fargo says Brookins will be retained, and the other clubs say he must be fired. Where there is smoke there must be fire"[32]

Ironically, this report occurred shortly after Brookins was the first player of the year to hit a ball over the right field fence in Fargo. This feat, the Fargo *Forum and Republican* reported, "wins him some local prizes for the performance."[33] The Fargo newspaper chose to ignore the claim that Brookins was a Negro, stating only that "The Minneapolis *Tribune* says there is a row over Fargo playing Brookins. The sporting writer evidently got a bum steer."[34]

It is tempting to regard the knee injury as a ruse. Brookins did play sporadically and was even called upon to pitch in Duluth.[35] But the newspaper reports often mentioned his ailing knee. His picture appeared in the June 8 edition of the *Forum*, which gave little cause for those concerned with racial purity to be alarmed.[36] When the official batting averages were released a few days later, his .261 average was eleventh best in the league and second best on the Fargo team.[37] He was able to play in sixty-five of his team's seventy-nine games when on August 13 the league folded.[38] So the question needs to be asked: Was he really injured or was the "injury" a convenient way to get around unspoken sanctions that one or more teams in the league may have unofficially and unilaterally enforced?

The 1909 Hiatus—There is no record of Brookins playing in organized ball in 1909. This may have been because of the charge made in the Hannibal newspaper, but it is important to remember that he was about to be thirty years old and that in the previous three years had produced, overall, only modest results. This season also saw a dramatic drop in the number of Class D leagues, from twenty-two to sixteen, and teams, from 126 to 100. Brookins simply may not have been good enough to play professional baseball in 1909.

"That nigger"—Perhaps sensing that a game in Lethbridge was to be his last in the WCL, Dick Brookins had a very good day on May 31, 1910. He went 2-for-4, scored two runs, and threw out three, to help boost the visiting Regina Bonepilers, then in fifth place, over the sixth-place Lethbridge Miners, 8-3. Adding insult to injury for the Lethbridge team was the fact that Regina's left fielder that day, Chesty Cox, had the previous day been fired as the playing manager of the Lethbridge team. Cox knocked in two of the Bonepilers' runs.

Before his firing, Cox had tried to engineer an under-the-table deal with Regina's manager, Roxey Walters. He released his first baseman, Ohayer, in the hope that both he and Ohayer would then sign on with Regina. This infuriated Lethbridge team official Benton Hatch, who in a meeting with Walters demanded that Ohayer be turned back to his club. Walters refused, and Hatch, in a mean-spirited reprisal, said he would see that "that nigger did not play anymore."[39] Brookins was in the room[40] and a newspaper report states that "there was pretty near a trip through the window for Mr. Hatch but he apologized for his remark."[41]Apology or not, Lethbridge protested the next day to league president and Lethbridge resident C.J. Eckstorm. The result was that Brookins was banned from organized baseball.

Eckstorm first cabled National Association secretary J. H. Farrell in Albany, New York, undoubtably seeking a ruling or advice. Farrell tossed the ball back in Eckstorm's lap: "...it is an affair involving two clubs and should be settled by league president," he wrote[42] Eckstorm then declared Brookins ineligible to play. Regina, in protest, refused to play its next opponent, Medicine Hat, without Brookins, and forfeited the game. [43]

Regina team president J.W. Smith, who claimed that Brookins was of Native-American ancestry,[44] rushed off to Lethbridge to have a meeting with Eckstorm, and demanded to know the wording of the letter sent by the league president and what steps Eckstorm took in determining the status of Brookins. Eckstorm stonewalled the Regina president, refusing to answer any questions, stating only that he had deliberated for a long time and that he would look further into the matter. In a momentary lapse of his silent defense, the WCL president told Smith "...there is just one man you can blame for this...Roxey Walters."[45]

Walters, who had played with both Brookins and Ohayer in Green Bay, gave a caustic interview to the *Albertan*, saying that Eckstorm was, "No good, incompetent, and spiteful." Walters claimed he would never play 'a negro or any (player with) negro blood in his veins." He claimed that Brookins' mother was French and his father Puerto Rican.

The article describes Brookins as not having "a kinky hair on his head, his nose is well formed, his lips ordinary and his shins are not touchy as with the negro race."[46] The writer claimed that the Regina third baseman had signed affidavits from a member of "the U.S. legislature," a Roman Catholic priest, and school teachers.

Prior to 1910 ¡¡°here had never been a mention in the press of Brookins being an Indian. Walters claimed he was of Puerto Rican and French ancestry. And only the 1908 report in the Hannibal paper raised the possibility that he was black. Yet a 1910 preseason report claims that "Brookins, the Indian, has been the sensation in the field."[47] The *Albertan* called Brookins a "dusky gent,"[48] and wrote that the Medicine Hat team believed that his "duskiness was caused by colored blood and the color line is drawn in all Organized Ball."[49]

The *Albertan* reminded its readers that the Regina players "maintain that Brookins is not a negro, but one of the first settlers, being one of the noble red men."[50] The Regina *Leader* concluded that "his Indian birth was established and he was perfectly eligible to play."[51] The sporting editor of The *Leader* took it upon himself to conduct an investigation of the status of Brookins, writing to J. M. Cummings of *The Sporting News*. Cummings replied that he in turn had corresponded with the National Association and that organization found nothing to be concerned about and "the matter will be strictly up to the Western Canada League for adjudication."[52]

The Winnipeg *Free Press* thought that Eckstorm should be the one losing his job and not Brookins.[53] It was clear that Brookins was being hurt as a part of the fallout from the Walters-Cox deal. The Regina team insisted that it would play Brookins when it returned to the Saskatchewan capital.

But Dick Brookins disappeared from the records of organized baseball.

The final scene of this drama took place in Medicine Hat on June 2, the next stop on the Regina club schedule. President Eckstorm ordered umpire Wheeler to forfeit the game to Medicine Hat and fine the Regina team $50 if Brookins was included in the lineup.[54] Regina attempted to field its team with Brookins in the starting lineup, whereupon the umpire declared the game a forfeit. Almost immediately, Regina team president and former mayor J.W. Smith rushed off to Lethbridge to confront Eckstorm. Smith demanded to know how Eckstorm came to his decision especially when it was known the National Association would not stand in Brookins way. Smith had the correspondence from J. M. Cummings of the *The Sporting News* . Surely a letter from "the Bible of Baseball" declaring that no action had ever been taken against Brookins would be enough to declare him "safe," as the Edmonton *Bulletin* declared.[55] Yet the last sentence in Cummings' letter is a rather strange non sequitur: " If the National commission has never barred Brookins for alleged negro blood, and even though the American Association may have done so as a family matter, the matter will be strictly up to the Western Canada League for adjudcation [sic]."

What did the American Association have to do with this? Did Eckstorm suggest that the A.A. had made a ruling?[56] Was the WCL president engaging in a bit of obfuscation himself? Was this a coded message? Do the right thing in the interests of baseball? Whatever it may have meant, Eckstorm held fast despite the ridicule heaped upon him by the press, especially in Winnipeg, Calgary, Edmonton, and—of course—Regina.

The Regina *Leader* satirically poked fun at Eckstorm suggesting that "...the recent visit of the comet [Halley's] is responsible for Eck's peculiar attitude."[57] In the meantime Brookins returned to Regina, prompting the *Leader* to report "...any hope of playing him in the near future...has been abandoned...(t)he Indian has accepted the situation in the stoical manner natural to his race."[58]

The Regina manager made noises about playing Brookins at home, saying "If the other teams in the league don't want to play against him, well they needn't."[59] But the weak franchise was already in financial trouble and could ill afford the fines and loss of revenue that such a noble gesture would provoke. Within two weeks the "Brookins" case disappeared from the sporting pages.

Regina president Smith regretted "that a clean and gentlemanly player like Brookins should be put out of the game."[60] The Winnipeg *Free Press* echoed Smith, protesting that "the ban on the best third baseman in the league and one of the most gentlemanly players that has ever appeared in a uniform in the Western Canada League"[61] should never had happened. The Regina *Leader* said that Brookins did "not receive anything like a square deal, nor the faintest suspicion of British Justice."[62]

C.J. Eckstorm suspended Roxey Walters for the comments that he made in the *Albertan* about the league president.[63] The dispirited team, realizing a stand was futile, lost forty-five of its next sixty games, went into receivership, and was disbanded before the season closed.[64]

On June 10, 1910, the official statistics of the WCL were released. In twenty games, Brookins had a .223 batting average and had made nine errors at third base.[65] The following year when the annual *Reach Baseball Guide* was released, Brookins did not appear. He had been erased.

Notes:

1. See *Northern California Baseball History*, Society for American Baseball Research, Cleveland, OH, 1998, Steven Lavoie, "Oakland Pitcher Broke the Color Line in 1916 Game," p. 11. Also see *The Cultural Encyclopedia of Baseball* by Jonathan Fraser Light, McFarland, 1997, p. 374. Thompson did not attempt to deceive anyone. Refer also Seamus Kearney's "Bill Thompson, Pioneer" in *The National Pastime: A Review of Baseball History*, Number 16(Cleveland: SABR, 1996), pp. 67-68.

2. *The Encyclopedia of Minor League Baseball* states that the WCL was a Class D League whereas the Reach Guide claimed it was Class C. According to Article VII of the National Agreement, the WCL would be regarded as Class D.

3. *Reach Official American League Guide*, 1911, p. 395.

4. Bob Davids, Phil Dixon, David Kemp, Ray Nemec, Tom Newgard, Fr. Bill Sherman, an unpublished paper, "Richard (Dick) Brookins: The First African American in Organized Baseball During the 20th Century." Thanks to David Kemp for sending this paper to me. It shall be referred to hereafter as Davids, et. al. Many people have assisted in the research of this paper including Larry Gerlach, David Mills, Bob Klein, Ray Nemec, Steve Gietschier, Bob Davids, and especially Owen Ricker.

5. Ibid. The unique team name is derived from the original name of the settlement: Regina Pile O' Bones, meaning those of slaughtered buffalo.

6. Regina *Morning Leader*, April 26 and May 4, 1910.

7. *The Spalding Guide* of 1907, p. 276. The picture is of the 1906 Green Bay Colts.

8. David W. Zang, *Fleet Walker's Divided Heart*, (Lincoln, NB: University of Nebraska, 1995), pp. 91- 95. Zang discusses a variety of skin whiteners of the day; e.g. "Black-No-More," "Dr. Read's Magic Flesh Bleach." Concurrently, Zang stressed the ability of the camera through lighting, angles, etc. to alter the appearance of the subject, citing the well-known picture of the last black player to play major league ball in the nineteenth century, Fleetwood Walker in the Oberlin College baseball team photo of 1881 and the "doctored"1883 photo of Walker when he played for Toledo.

9. Leon F. Litwack in *America's Black Past*. Harper & Row, (New York) 1970, p.156.

10. Robin W. Winks, *The Blacks in Canada: A History*, McGill-Queens University Press (Montreal) and Yale University Press (New Haven and London), 1972, p. 308. For a fuller understanding of the situation also see *Peoples of Alberta: Portraits of Cultural Diversity* edited by Howard and Tamara Palmer, Western Producer Prairie Books(Saskatoon, SK) 1985.

11. The French-speaking village of Morinville, outside of Edmonton, petitioned the Canadian Prime Minister: "We submit that the advent of such negroes as are now here was most unfortunate for the country, and that further arrivals in large numbers would be disastrous...It is a matter of common knowledge that it has been proven in the United States that negroes and whites cannot live in proximity without the occurrence of revolting lawlessness and the development of bitter race hatred..." H. and T. Palmer *Peoples of Alberta*, pp.371-2.

12. Lethbridge *Herald*, Oct. 5, 1914.

13. The largest of these communities Amber Valley became well known in the province for its all-black baseball teams.

14. Owen Ricker's research found that Brookins was listed in the city directory as "Coal" 1901-03, "Express" 1907, "Coal" 1909-1910, "Baseball" 1911, "Machinist" 1921, "Assembler" 1922.

15. The author attempted in 1997 to contact all those in Missouri with the surname Brookins in an effort to see if they were related or knew of Richard "Dick" Brookins, a minor league baseball player. No mention of his skin color was indicated in the letter of inquiry. No one responded.

16. The black press in St. Louis was non-existent at that time. A thorough search of St. Louis papers by researcher E. Louise King failed to uncover anything more about Brookins. Several telephone conversations Fall 1997.

17. Green Bay *Gazette*, Green Bay, WI, July 24, 1906.

18. Ibid., June 18, 1906 and August 27, 1906

19. See for example the July 11 and 16 editions of the *Gazette*. Similarly in 1906 the Green Bay *Advocate* mentioned his name at least twenty-six times in its game reports (which were shorter by about half than those that appeared in the *Gazette*). The *Advocate* was less prone to use colorful racial adjectives than was the *Gazette*; however it occasionally permitted itself to report such things as "Chief Charles was on the warpath…he carried home the scalps of the LaCrosse players." Never was there any mention about the racial status of Brookins in the *Advocate*.

20. Twenty-one games behind pennant winning La Crosse. The Green Bay Colts finished fourth in a six-team league with 55 wins and 63 losses for a .466 winning percentage.

22. Ibid. Sept. 18, 1906

23. Ibid. April, 22, 1907

24. Green Bay *Gazette,* April 17 and 22, 1907.

25. The *Gazette* also reported "that Nixon, the Oneida Indian, has been released."

26. Ibid. April 27, 1907

27. Ibid. May 16, 1907

28. Ibid. June, 5, 1907

29. Hancock *Evening Journal*, July 13, 1907. He may have had a sore arm. The paper mentioned that his throws were short hopping to first base.

30. Ibid, August 19, 1907

31. Quoted in Davids, et al p. 1. Ray Nemec found the quote.

32. The Fargo *Forum and Republican*, June 18, 1908.

33. Ibid., July 8, 1908

34. He gave up seven runs on eight hits in three innings. Ibid. June 18, 1908. An earlier edition of the Fargo *Forum noted* "The Fargo infield was dead with Brookins crippled on third, Thompson indifferent and Sturgeon loafing…" June 10, 1908.

35. See the Fargo *Forum and Republican* June 8, 1908.

36. Ibid. June 12, 1908.

37. The Davids, et al. paper suggests that he went home to rest his injury and did not return. However, since his record states that he played 65 games and the shortened season had the Fargo team only playing 79 games this would have been impossible.

38. Ibid.

39. Edmonton *Bulletin* 6/6/10.

40. My guess is that the incident probably took place in a hotel room that the players had gathered prior to the game of May 31; however, the newspaper report is unclear about this merely stating that a meeting took place.

41. Ibid.

42. Edmonton *Journal* 6/6/10

43. The *Albertan* 6/3/10. In what appeared to be a quasisecret meeting between Eckstorm and Medicine Hat officials on May 14 it was decided that Eckstorm would ask Farrell to rule on the matter.

44. Smith had a letter from a school in St. Louis supposedly certifying that Brookins was white. Sharon Huffman, archivist for the St. Louis School Board, suggests that such letters would have been very unusual and thus was probably a forgery. Telephone conversation 9/22/97.

45. Winnipeg *Free Press* 6/10/10

46. Lethbridge *Herald* 5/3/10.

47. *Albertan* 6/3/10

48. Ibid.

49. Ibid.

50. Ibid.

51. Regina *Leader* May 6, 1910

52. Regina *Leader Post*, May 26, 1910

53. cited in Regina *Leader*, May 14, 1910.

54. Lethbridge *Daily Herald, June 3, 1910.* The visiting share of the receipts was suppose to be $40 for each game.

55. Edmonton *Bulletin,* May 30, 1910 The full text of the Cummings letter reads: "I can find no record of the finding of any committee, appointed authoritatively to pass on Brookins' eligibility to play in organized ball, but I wrote to Mr. Robert E. Bruce, secretary of the National Commission, which it seems to me, would have a record of such finding, if made officially. Mr. Bruce sends me this reply 'I wish to say that as far as my recollections goes and an examination of my records the case was never passed upon my commission' (Cummings continues) If the National Commission has never barred Brookins for alleged negro blood, and even though the American Association may have done so as a family affair, the matter will be strictly up to the Western Cnada [sic] League for adjudcation[sic]." The Regina *Leader* also mentioned that Cummings indicated that Brookins' parents lived in an exclusively white area.

56. Phone calls to the American Association Office, August 19, 1997. No correspondence records now exists between the WCL and the A.A.

57. Regina *Leader* June 11, 1910. A headline of an earlier issue (May 19, 1910) gives an indication of white attitudes toward blacks: "Halley's Comet Comes and Goes and Nothing Happens" Subheadlines then stated "NEGROES PANIC STRICKEN" "Colored People in Southern States Frenzied at Comet's Visit."

58. Regina *Leader* June 7, 1910

59. Albertan, Calgary, AB June 10, 1910.

60. Regina *Leader* June 8, 1910

61. Winnipeg *Free Press* June 6, 1910

62. A report in the Regina *Leader* on June 14 compliments umpire Longnecker on umpiring a good game and having to put up with "a lot of chaffing, on account of the raw deals handed out by his confreres" while the names of Brookins and Eckstorm were "frequently heard hurdling either way across the diamond"

63. Eckstorm fined Walters $10 and demanded an apology. The suspension was especially deleterious to the Regina club in that Walters had taken over third base duties with the expulsion of Brookins. It appears that the apology did not occur. However, it seems that Eckstorm was able to extract his due when he reversed a decision made by umpire Wheeler that had awarded a game by forfeit to Regina when a Medicine Hat player refused to leave the field after being tossed from the game.

64. Medicine Hat *Times*, August 31, 1910. The Medicine Hat team franchise had been shifted to Saskatoon five weeks earlier.

65. Davids, ibid.

Jimmie Foxx

Nanci Foxx Canaday as told to John Bennett

To start with, Jimmie Foxx was my stepfather. He married my mother when I was two years old, and he was always a true father to me and my brother John. Much has been written and said about Jimmie, especially in the past few years. I hardly know where to start retelling my memories, but I hope I can add something to your knowledge and image of him.

In my eyes he was the greatest player of them all. He could play all positions and play them well. People tend to think of him as a first baseman, but he started out as a catcher and finished as a pitcher!

I don't think he had anything but pleasant memories of his playing days. Dad loved people. He was a gentle, loving person, and so generous—he'd literally give you the shirt off his back. Once I saw him give one of his game caps to a kid, right off his own head. There'd be times that he would be out to dinner and never get to eat his meal because he was too busy talking to the many people who came over to greet him. That's the kind of Dad I was lucky enough to have.

Dad had a way of making everyone feel comfortable around him, even if they weren't baseball fans. He could always find something to talk to you about. When my husband Jim first met him, he felt awkward because he didn't know very much about Jimmie or even about baseball itself. Dad made him feel comfortable right away, and soon they were having a long conversation. Dad had a very humble and down-to-earth side. I remember he used to surprise my dates by answering the door in a T-shirt and boxer shorts!

Dad always had a lot of fans, and they were extremely important to him. He would get all sorts of fan mail, sometimes simply addressed "Jimmie Foxx-USA." He tried to sign as many autographs as he could up until his death in 1967. I was touched to receive a letter back from one fan a few weeks after his funeral. It contained a baseball card that Jimmie had autographed and mailed out the day before he died.

I had a good childhood with loving parents. Dad loved to spend time with us, going to the drive-in, hitting golf balls, or simply wrestling around on the rug. We lived in a well-disciplined home, to be sure. My brother Jimmie and I decided to bury Dad's strap in the backyard in Miami, because I felt that at fourteen I was too "old" for a spanking! I never told Dad about it until about eight years later. He pretended to be surprised, then admitted that he "kinda knew" all along. It's probably still buried there in the backyard on 47th Street.

The year he coached the Fort Wayne Daisies was terrific. We stayed in a big house on the lake. Dad made me the bat girl for the team and I got to go on some road trips as well. The ladies on the team treated me wonderfully, and I know Dad thought highly of their playing abilities. It was a great summer for the whole family. I also remember that the best corn on the cob seemed to grow around there too.

Speaking of food, Dad sure had a tremendous appetite. Simply put, he liked to eat, and he was also a fine cook. Dad loved that old farm-style cooking. Whenever he went home to Maryland, he would bring back a big side of ham (his favorite dish) and cook us a big feast. No meal for Dad was complete without ice cream.

Nanci Foxx Canaday *operates a farm with her husband Jim in Sumterville, Florida.* **John Bennett** *teaches social studies in Bennington, Vermont.*

Many was the time when he would grab a spoon and polish off a half gallon tub of either vanilla or peach ice cream, complete with a whole canteloupe.

Dad held a variety of jobs after his playing days ended. He lost all the money he made in baseball, mainly through bad investments and his habit of picking up the tab for everyone. He lost a fortune on a golf course venture that was cancelled because of restrictions during World War II. I can remember him driving a coal delivery truck for a dollar an hour. Dad just missed qualifying for the big league pension, although he finally started receiving some Social Security disability funds in his later years. He never had to live off anyone, and he paid all his bills—I still have his checkbook to prove it.

All of us are human and have our faults. It is very true that Dad had a drinking problem. I think this had a lot to do with how much he missed the game after he retired. Going from farm life to the glamour and publicity of the big leagues in just a few years brought many changes to his life. Adjusting back to "normalcy" when he retired was extremely difficult. I think he felt terribly empty during his retirement years, because he missed the game he loved so much and the many friends he made in it.

My mom and dad had a long and happy relationship. When she died in 1966, it really broke his heart. His own health was poor in his later years. He had two heart attacks and was badly injured in a fall. He spent many of his last days reminiscing with his brother Sam, who was with him when he passed away on July 21, 1967. Sadly and tragically, both he and my mother died from choking.

It's been over thirty years now and I still miss him. Happily, I have so many wonderful memories of him that he never seems very far away. I know that many of

The gentle Beast: Jimmie Foxx

Transcendental Graphics

you know about the great things he did on the field. I hope that by sharing some of my memories of Dad you will know that he was just as great off the field too. They called him the "Beast," but he was just a gentle giant, still the greatest ever for me.

Snuffy

Lyle Spatz

While few baseball fans would include George Stirnweiss on a list of distinguished Yankee second basemen, neither Tony Lazzeri, Joe Gordon, Willie Randolph, nor any other Yankee second-sacker ever had a more spectacular offensive season than Stirnweiss did in 1945. Among his accomplishments that year was a batting championship—the only one ever won by a Yankee second baseman.

Stirnweiss was more than just a "wartime player," but his finest years, by far, were 1944, when he was arguably the best player in the American League, and 1945, when he was the best. True, there was a war on. And, unquestionably, he was the best only because men like Joe DiMaggio, Ted Williams, Cecil Travis, Hank Greenberg, et al., were serving in the military. Nevertheless, there remained in the league many excellent players who, for a variety of reasons, were not in the service. Among those active in one or both seasons were Cleveland's Lou Boudreau, St. Louis's Vern Stephens, Boston's Bobby Doerr, Washington's Stan Spence, and Detroit's Rudy York. Stirnweiss was 4-F because of ulcers.

He was the son of a New York policeman; he got the name Snuffy either from comic book character Snuffy Smith or the vaudeville character, Snuffy the Cabman. He grew up in the Bronx, becoming a football star first at Fordham Prep and then at the University of North Carolina. Arthur Daley of the New York *Times* said, "He was a triple-threat back who could do everything

phenomenally well." The Chicago Cardinals of the National Football League drafted him when he graduated in 1940, offering him a starting salary of $4,000. Stirnweiss declined and signed with the Yankees instead. The Yanks sent him to Norfolk of the Piedmont League, where in eighty-six games he hit twelve home runs and batted .307. Stirnweiss played the next two years with the Newark Bears of the International League. While at Newark, in 1942, he stole seventy-three bases.

The Yanks brought him to the big leagues in 1943, where he batted .219 in eighty-three games for the World Champions. He was the team's shortstop from midseason on, replacing Frank Crosetti. But in 1944, after Gordon went into the Army, manager Joe McCarthy moved him to second base. Besides Gordon, the Yanks that year also lost catcher Bill Dickey, pitcher Marius Russo, and third baseman Billy Johnson to the military. They joined DiMaggio, Tommy Henrich, Phil Rizzuto, and Red Ruffing, who had answered the call in 1943. Like all big league teams during the war, the Yanks played with a patchwork lineup of oldtimers, kids, 4-Fs, and an occasional player of major league caliber.

The Yankees slipped to third place in 1944, despite the best efforts of Stirnweiss, first baseman Nick Etten, and outfielder Johnny Lindell, the only bona fide major leaguers in their lineup. Etten led the league in home runs with twenty-two, and walks with ninety-seven, while Lindell led in total bases with 297 and tied for the lead in triples with sixteen. Still, it was Stirnweiss who was the team's best player.

Playing in all 154 games, he batted .319, fourth-best

Lyle Spatz *is the chairman of SABR's Baseball Records Committee and the author of* New York Yankee Openers *(McFarland, 1997). His history of Yankee trades will be published by McFarland in 2000.*

George "Snuffy" Stirnweiss

Transcendental Graphics

in the league, but only .008 behind the leader, Boudreau. His sixteen triples tied Lindell for the league high, and his 296 total bases were just one behind league-leader Lindell. Stirnweiss led the league in hits with 205, and was the only major leaguer to have more than 200. (Stan Musial and Phil Cavaretta tied for the National League lead with 197.) He also led the majors in three other categories with 125 runs scored, 146 singles, and fifty-five stolen bases. He was caught stealing only eleven times. By winning the stolen-base crown, Stirnweiss broke the five-year reign of Washington's George Case, who was second with forty-nine. In the voting for the Most Valuable Player Award, Stirnweiss finished a strong fourth behind Hal Newhouser, Dizzy Trout, and Stephens. But the best was yet to come.

The big year—In 1945, Stirnweiss, again playing in each of the Yankees' 152 games, led the American League in seven major offensive departments: batting average (.309), slugging average (.476), total bases (301), runs (107), hits (195), triples (twenty-two) and stolen bases (thirty-three). The twenty-two triples were the most in the American League in eighteen years, and since then only one major leaguer, Dale Mitchell, with twenty-three for Cleveland in 1949, has hit more. Stirnweiss also led the league in total at-bats, with 632, and his thirty-two doubles tied him for second place behind Chicago's Wally Moses, who had thirty-five. Defensively, Stirnweiss led all American League second basemen in errors with twenty-nine, but also finished first in putouts (432), double plays (119), and chances per game (6.3).

Newhouser, who led the league with twenty-five wins and a 1.81 earned run average, deservedly won his second consecutive Most Valuable Player Award. His teammate on the pennant-winning Tigers, second baseman Eddie Mayo, finished second. Mayo got 164 points in the voting, three more than Stirnweiss, who finished third. I still question that vote. Mayo hit a respectable .285, but with little extra-base power. Some sportswriters cited his fielding, claiming that it was a major contributor to Detroit's championship. That may have been true. Mayo fielded .980 to Stirnweiss's .970. However, he had 106 fewer putouts, ninety-nine fewer assists, and participated in twenty-eight fewer double plays, *Newsweek* columnist John Lardner wrote that "in fact it is possible to imagine putting Stirnweiss on an all-star team in any year, so skillful and valuable has this young reformed football player become." And no less an authority than Babe Ruth claimed, "That sawed-off runt playing second base is the only ballplayer who could've gotten a uniform when the Yankees really had a ball club."

On September 30, the final day of the 1945 season, Stirnweiss trailed Chicago's Tony Cuccinello in the batting race, .308 to .306. The Yanks were at the Stadium, against Boston, while Chicago was at home for a scheduled doubleheader with Cleveland. However, rain canceled the games in Chicago, giving Stirnweiss the chance to win it on his own. He did, going three-for-five as Joe Page downed the Red Sox, 12-2. After doubling in the first, and getting an infield single in the third, Stirnweiss was still trailing Cuccinello, .30846 to .30745, as he batted for the last time in the eighth, against Otis Clark. He came through with a single to

right to raise his average to .30854. Rounded to .309, it enabled him finally to overtake Cuccinello, who had led for most of the season. Had the White Sox not been rained out, and had Cuccinello played in one, or both games, he might have retained his lead. But then Cuccinello had just 402 official at-bats in 1945 compared to Stirnweiss's league-leading 632. For the thirty-seven-year-old Cuccinello, 1945 would be his final big league season. He was released in January 1946. "I'm the most surprised guy in baseball," he complained. "When the season ended, [manager] Jimmy Dykes definitely assured me I'd be back with the White Sox."

After the game, manager McCarthy argued that "Stirnweiss deserved his victory over Cuccinello. Snuffy, for the good part of the war period was the best all-around player in the majors, and certainly in our league." McCarthy noted that "it's a distinction when a leadoff batter makes off with the hitting crown." Stirnweiss is the only major leaguer to win a batting title without ever having led previously at any time during the season, although his .309 average was the lowest to lead the American League since Cleveland's Elmer Flick's .306º won the title in 1905. (In the pitcher's year of 1968, Carl Yastrzemski of the Red Sox hit just .301 to establish the all-time major league low.) Stirnweiss once said that whenever his batting championship comes up in conversation, "somebody is always sure to mention the fact that I hit .309 that year. But it was enough to win."

Gordon returned to the Yankees in 1946, and Stirnweiss split the year between second and third. After the season, the Yanks traded Gordon to Cleveland, and for the next two years Stirnweiss was the team's everyday second baseman. In 1949, a year after setting a major league record for the position (subsequently broken) with a .993 fielding average, he lost his job to Jerry Coleman. In 1950 the Yanks traded Stirnweiss to the St. Louis Browns as part of an eight-player deal. He moved on to Cleveland in 1951 and for one game in 1952, then managed at Binghamton and Schenectady in the Yankee farm system before leaving baseball. Phil Rizzuto would later say that "Stirnweiss wasn't as spectacular as Joe Gordon or Jerry Coleman and didn't have the fire of Billy Martin, but of all of them he was the easiest to work with."

Stirnweiss was working in financial management when he died in a New York commuter-train accident on September 15, 1958. He was thirty-nine years old and left a wife and six children. At the time of his death he had been the director of the New York *Journal-American* Sandlot Baseball program. *Journal-American* sports editor Max Kase said that he "was matchless when it came to handling youngsters."

The Santurce Crabbers

Thomas E. Van Hyning

Pedro (Pete) "Pedrín" Zorrilla a.k.a. "Mr. Baseball" and "El Cangrejo Mayor," was the architect and first owner of the Santurce Crabbers baseball club. Zorrilla, with the help of close friends and associates, did everything from signing ballplayers to securing uniforms for eighteen players prior to the team's October 1, 1939 opener at Aguadilla to face Leon Day and the Sharks. Another Santurce uniform was made for Josh Gibson—one of Pedrín's favorite Santurce players—several weeks later when Josh flew to Puerto Rico to begin his Santurce career.

Zorrilla was an executive with the Shell Oil Company who loved baseball. He played second base on several amateur ballclubs in Santurce—a section of San Juan, Puerto Rico's capital city. Santurce was called "Cangrejos" (crabs) by Spanish planters in the sixteenth and seventeenth centuries because of its crab-shaped land and lagoon topography. Parts of Santurce were still called "Cangrejo Arriba" (Upper Cangrejo) and "Cangrejo Abajo" (Lower Cangrejo). And hence, the team nickname "Cangrejeros" (Crabbers) was created and stuck.

The early years—Pedrín befriended Josh Gibson, Satchel Paige, Leon Day, Dick Seay, and many other Negro Leaguers who barnstormed in Puerto Rico during the mid-1930s. These ballplayers loved Pedrín and

became an informal network that put in good words with other players for the Santurce franchise during the 1940s and early 1950s. Gibson, Willard Brown, and Bob Thurman would emerge as the franchise's top imports through the early '50s, when the league first allowed three, then five non-Puerto Rican players per team.

Gibson twice led the Puerto Rico League in homers—1939-40 and 1941-42—and won MVP laurels that second season based on his thirteen homers and a .480 batting mark. His Santurce debut came in an October 22, 1939, twin bill against the archrival San Juan Senators at Sixto Escobar Stadium, the ballpark shared by these two teams.

Ballclubs played only Sunday doubleheaders during the league's early years, so players had plenty of time during the week to enjoy Puerto Rico's hospitality. Enriqueta Marcano Zorrilla, a niece of Pedrín, recalled that Josh Gibson came to Manatí—Pedrín's hometown—where he met and had a good time with the Zorrilla family. Enriqueta remembers the time a car got stuck in a ditch and how everyone marveled at Gibson's strength when he single-handedly lifted it out.

Gibson's Puerto Rico nickname was "Trucutú," based on a muscular popular cartoon hero of the time. Other Santurce players of the 1940s and early 1950s were also given sobriquets by the Santurce faithful. Thurman was called "El Múcaro" (the owl) because of his ability to pitch and catch outfield flies during night contests.

Brown was "Ese Hombre" (that man) for his home runs. Pitcher Jim Lamarque became "Libertad Lamarque," after a famous Argentine singer by that

Thomas E. Van Hyning *attended school in Santurce between 1960 and 1973, and lived in a Santurce neighborhood from 1960-66. Most of his playmates—including Rubén Gómez's son, Rafael—were avid Santurce fans. He became a true Santurce fan following the 1964 World Series. His book on the sixty-year history of the Santurce franchise will be published by McFarland this summer.*

name. John Ford Smith became "El Teniente" since he had served as a lieutenant in the armed forces during World War II.

A dynamic duo—Brown and Thurman led Santurce to its first league championship in 1950-51, and to its first two Caribbean Series titles in 1951 and 1953.

Brown was a two-time Triple Crown winner in 1947-48 and 1949-50, who still holds the Puerto Rico League records of twenty-seven homers (in the sixty-game 1947-48 season) and ninety-seven RBIs (in the eighty game season of 1949-50).

Bob Thurman's eleven Santurce seasons featured 117 career homers, a franchise record. He hit 120 homers in Puerto Rico—the most in league history—after slugging three more for the Ponce Lions in 1959-60 at age forty-two. The Brown-Thurman duo put Santurce on the Caribbean baseball map, and were as identified with the team as Babe Ruth and Lou Gehrig were with the New York Yankees.

Pedrín's Big League Contacts—Pedrín scouted for the Brooklyn Dodgers and then for the New York-San Francisco Giants in the 1950s. This helped his club secure the services of second baseman Junior Gilliam for three seasons beginning with 1950-51. Gilliam paid dividends as a member of Santurce's first two title winners.

The signing of Roberto Clemente by the Dodgers in February, 1954, was a direct result of Pedrín's coordinating a workout at Sixto Escobar Stadium under the supervision of Al Campanis. Pedrín had signed the eighteen-year old Clemente to his first professional baseball contract (for $40 per week) in October, 1952. Clemente saw limited playing time with the Crabbers in 1952-53, but became a regular in 1953-54.

Rubén Gómez's signing with the New York Giants before the 1953 big league season helped set up a Santurce-Giants working agreement. Gómez pitched well in the big leagues. Pedrín and Giants owner Horace Stoneham hit it off, and Pedrín also became a close friend of Giants coach Herman Franks, who would manage Santurce in 1954-55 and 1955-56. These contacts would bring Willie Mays to the Crabbers in 1954-55.

The Crabbers that season featured an outfield of Clemente in left, Mays in center, and Thurman in right. Harry Chiti and Valmy Thomas shared the catching duties. George Crowe and Buster Clarkson manned the corners at first and third, while Ronnie Samford and Don Zimmer emerged as the keystone duo after Santurce had tried other players at those positions. Zimmer told me in March, 1992, that this was the "greatest winter league ballclub ever assembled."

Franks called this a "special group that with a little more pitching depth could have won it all in the big

Willie Mays at bat for Santurce in 1955.

leagues." Gómez, Sam Jones, and Bill Greason were the team's front line pitchers. Pete Burnside and several Dominican and Puerto Rican hurlers were spot starters. The Crabbers easily won the 1955 Caribbean Series in Caracas, Venezuela.

New Ownership—Ramón Cuevas and his son, Hiram, purchased the Santurce ballclub from Pedrín in late December, 1956. The Cuevas family were businessmen, more concerned with the bottom line than with the well-being of ballplayers. One of their terms for purchasing the ballclub was that $30,000 be handed over to erase the team debt. The result was the sale of Roberto Clemente, Juan "Terín" Pizarro, and Samford to the Caguas Criollos shortly after Christmas, 1956.

Pedrín was brought back as the team's GM for 1958-59, when Santurce won its fourth league title of the decade. Orlando Cepeda was the team's star. Pedrín had signed him to a New York Giants contract in 1955. But the Cuevas family kept players' salaries low. Jackie Brandt made about $800 a month in 1958-59, plus $200 for living expenses. Pedrín, by contrast, had paid Billy Hunter $1,200 a month in 1952-53.

Hiram Cuevas became the team's sole owner in 1961-62, and signed Vern Benson, a coach with the St. Louis Cardinals, to manage the Crabbers. This resulted in Bob Gibson and Craig Anderson forming half of Santurce's starting rotation along with Pizarro and Al Schroll. These Crabbers won the league playoffs and a special InterAmerican Series held at Sixto Escobar in February, 1962. It would be the last time professional baseball was played at Escobar. The action moved to Hiram Bithorn Municipal Stadium in a different part of San Juan after the new park was inaugurated in October, 1962.

Cuevas secured corporate sponsorships in the 1960s and 1970s, but found that winning was the formula that brought fans to the ballpark. Santurce won five league titles in the Hiram Cuevas era—1961-62, 1964-65, 1966-67, 1970-71, and 1972-73.

Some more titles—Cepeda suffered a knee injury playing for Santurce in November, 1964, but that was the only thing that went wrong for the Crabbers. Tony "Tany" Pérez had a superb rookie season with Santurce. Lou Johnson played well in center and won the batting crown. Marv Staehle—one of my favorite Santurce players—was the team MVP with his clutch hitting and defense. And a rotation of Pizarro, Fred Talbot, George Brunet, Manley Johnston, and Gómez was supplemented by Jim Dickson's bullpen work.

"There was a great chemistry on that ballclub," said Dickson. "Jesse Gonder was good at calling pitches...there was a good mix of big leaguers and younger players...a fun season."

Hiram Cuevas developed a close friendship in 1966 with Harry Dalton, director of player development for the Baltimore Orioles, resulting in a seven-year Baltimore-Santurce axis. Earl Weaver, called "Mickey Rooney" by Santurce's fans, managed the Crabbers in 1966-67 and 1967-68. Weaver compared the enthusiasm of Santurce fans to the New York Yankee and Met fans. Paul Blair, Dave May, Larry Haney, Dave Johnson, and Jim Hardin were young Orioles who played for Weaver in Puerto Rico. Sparky Anderson, San Juan's manager in 1968-69, later told me that "Santurce was loaded with Jim Palmer, Ellie Hendricks, George Scott, Joe Foy, Paul Blair, Leo Cárdenas, Wally Bunker, Rubén Gómez, Pizarro."

Frank Robinson began his Santurce managing career in 1968-69 and experienced success with titles in 1970-71 and 1972-73. His first Santurce club won more games (49-20) than the fabled 1954-55 Crabbers who went 47-25. But San Juan upset the Crabbers in the 1968-69 semifinal series when Jim Palmer was knocked out of the box in Game 7.

Reggie Jackson hit twenty homers for Santurce in 1970-71, plus one more, which I saw, in February, 1971, against Venezuela's La Guaira Sharks in the Caribbean Series at Bithorn. The Licey Tigers from the Dominican Republic won that series with a 6-0 mark.

Reinaldo "Poto" Paniagua takes charge—The Santurce Crabbers were purchased in 1976 by well-known Island attorney Reinaldo "Poto" Paniagua. Paniagua, a loyal Santurce and New York Yankee fan since his childhood, was named Puerto Rico's Secretary of State soon after the November, 1976, elections and did the honorable thing by putting the Crabbers in a trust. One of Paniagua's first operational moves after returning to his private law practice in 1979 was to hire Pedrín Zorrilla as Santurce's executive vice-president.

"I sought Pedrín because I knew him well from my childhood as a friend of my father and we had a deep respect for Pedrín," said Paniagua. "Everyone in the baseball world loved Pedrín."

Pedrín worked with Santurce for two seasons before he died on April 9, 1981. The 1979-80 Crabbers won the regular season title under Robinson, but lost in the finals to the Bayamón Cowboys, formerly the San Juan club. Santurce's 1980-81 edition featured closer Lee Smith, among other talented players. But Santurce did not qualify for the playoffs, finishing fifth under manager Cookie Rojas.

The Crabbers had good teams throughout the 1980s, but did not win a league title. Luis Tiant and Pérez played their final winter seasons for the 1982-83 Crabbers. Sandy Alomar, Jr. and Rubén Sierra began their Winter League careers with Santurce in 1984-85.

Paniagua established an informal working agreement with the Los Angeles Dodgers in the summer of 1986. Kevin Kennedy took over as the skipper for three seasons, and Dave Wallace became the pitching coach. Chris Gwynn, Mike Devereaux, and John Wetteland were a trio of Dodgers prospects who plied their trade with Santurce between 1986-87 and 1988-89. Santurce made it to the finals in 1987-88 with a cast including Jay Bell, José "Chico" Lind, and Sierra, but lost to Mayagüez.

Santurce's dry spell ended after the 1990-91 season when they bested Mayagüez in the finals. The club captured some of its international glory upon winning the 1993 Caribbean Series in Mazatlán, Mexico, thanks to a two-run homer by Dickie Thon in a tie-breaker contest against the Aguilas Cibaeñas of the Dominican Republic. Thon recalled that the Dominicans were stronger on paper with Moisés Alou, Andujar Cedeño, Tony Peña, Alex Arias, Henry Rodríguez, José Lima, and others.

Juan "Igor" González put on Santurce flannels during the final month of 1992-93, and duplicated two of Josh Gibson's 1941-42 feats by becoming the league MVP and winning the home run title. González did not play in the 1993 Caribbean Series. He did play one more regular season for Santurce in 1993-94.

Santurce's fortunes since the mid-1990s have hinged on prospects from the Houston Astros. The connection began in 1995-96 when Astros coach José Cruz, Sr., managed Santurce. That Santurce club featured the slugging of Darryl Strawberry, Héctor Villanueva, and José Cruz, Jr. Matt Galante, the Astros bench coach, managed the Crabbers in 1996-97. Houston has sent pitchers Scott Elarton, Chris Holt, Trever Miller, and Billy Wagner to Santurce in recent years, along with their pitching coach, Vern Ruhle.

Frankie Thon, brother of Dickie and a Houston scout, served as Santurce's GM, and for the past two seasons as manager. He told me that the Puerto Rico League salary limit for big leaguers was $5,000 a month in the late 1990s. League rookies were paid $900 a month, while second-year native players could earn about $1,250, based on a three-year agreement.

The future—There are changes on the horizon. Santurce will have a new GM and manager for 1999-2000. Former archrivals, the San Juan Senators, will be the Carolina Giants beginning with that season. Carolina's home games are slated for the new 16,000-seat Roberto Clemente Stadium, east of San Juan, while Santurce has the 20,000-seat Hiram Bithorn Municipal Stadium to themselves.

The Crabbers have been "wired"—http://www.santurcebaseballclub.com—since November, 1998. Santurce's home page, Crabber's Home or the "Hogar Cangrejero," has enabled users to hear radio broadcasts, keep track of individual and team statistics, and enjoy the soundtrack of "Take Me Out to the Ballgame."

Twenty-first-century internet users and fans at Puerto Rico's stadiums may get a glimpse of Santurce superstars. But can this franchise come up with Hall of Fame caliber players such as Orlando Cepeda and Roberto Clemente in the next generation of multi-million-dollar ballplayers?

A Browns watershed

The 1997 death of Al (Boots) Hollingsworth in brought to mind the fourth game of the 1944 World Series in which Hollingsworth pitched well in relief of Sig Jakucki in a 5-1 Browns loss. The World Series Record Book *states that the Cardinals "rapped Jakucki hard" in the early innings and coasted to an easy victory. Not exactly. Jakucki had good stuff, striking out four and walking none, allowing only two solid hits in the three innings he pitched. In the first, a Stan Musial homer followed a scratch hit. In the third, two more infield scratches and a Don Gutteridge error sandwiched around a legitimate single by Walker Cooper produced two rather tainted Cardinal runs.*

The Browns didn't lay down and die offensively, as they put thirteen men on base against Harry Brecheen—nine on base hits. But the crafty "Cat" was tough in the clutch and allowed only the one runner to score.

This game was the turning point of the Series. The Cards won the next two by a cumulative scored of 5-1 to take the Fall Classic four games to two. Actually, this Game 4 was a watershed event in Browns history. It was all downhill from there. They only finished in the first division of the AL one more time (third, in 1945) before departing St. Louis to become the Baltimore Orioles after the 1953 season.

—Hilton Rahn

Born in the U.S.A.— NOT!

Jamie Selko

I fully realize that on a cosmic scale, the issue to be addressed herein is outweighed many times by a feather's dream of a feather, and that there are not hordes of unavenged dead crying out for justice regarding this subject matter. Yet, like many SABRites, I am troubled by seeing a jot where a tittle should be— or vice versa. We are a society of seekers which prides itself on getting every little thing correct, down to the fourth or fifth decimal place. It is this search for accuracy, this spirit of exactitude, which was the genesis for that which follows.

There are not that many demographic facts in the Big Mac or TB that can claim to be unique. Every day of the year is the birthday (or day of demise) for many a ballplayer. There are players of every height (Eddie Gaedel aside) from 5-foot-four to 6-foot-10—and none stands alone. True, there is but one lightest ever and one heaviest ever, but all the weights in between are multipopulated. Every state has had natives grace the major league ball yards of our past and present, including Hawaii. But there is one player from Hawaii who is, indeed, unique.

John Brodie Williams was born, not in the state of Hawaii, not even in the territory of Hawaii. John Williams was born in the independent kingdom of Hawaii, a geopolitical entity which, barring a major shift in the historical trends of the last century, will never again grace the maps of our atlii. Yes, Hawaii *did* have a life before American sugar trusts first engineered the re-

moval of the monarchy and then did away with the republic with which it replaced it (1893 and 1898, for those of you keeping score). Born as he was in 1889, the birth entry for Honolulu Johnny should correctly read: Kingdom of Hawaii.

And that's not all.

Those of you who were paying attention in school may remember a little tiff called "the Civil War." Like it or not, during the period 1861-65, the Confederate States of America considered itself an independent nation. It had its own stamps, printed its own money, had consulates in other lands, had its own army and navy, and for a time controlled its own territory. I think, therefore, Abe Lincoln to the contrary notwithstanding, that the birth data for the following players should be amended with the notation C.S.A. after their natal town, city or state: Beach, "Stonewall" Jackson (1862, Virginia); Caruthers, Robert Lee (1864, Tennessee); Ferguson, Charlie "Parisian Bob" (Virginia, 1863); Ford, E. L. (Virginia, 1862), and Sanders, Ben (Virginia, 1865).

But wait, there's still more. If you were listening really closely in class, you will recall that, during the aforementioned late unpleasantness between the states, the western counties of Virginia chose to stay in the Union, giving us the state of West Virginia. Anyone listed as being born in West Virginia before this time was, in point of fact, born in Virginia, and his birth data should be changed to list Virginia as the state of birth with the following parenthetical notation: (present-day West Virginia). I have found only four players thus affected: Pat Friel, Jack "The Scab" Glasscock, and the Moffett brothers, Joe and Sam.

Jamie Selko *claims to be a bipedal, bilaterally symmetrical non-isodactyl ectomorph. He also claims to be the author of* Human Sushi: The Tragic Fate of the Japanese Trans-Appalachian Expedition of 1959. *He reminds folks that it's* always *fiddler crab season.*

On to Canada—Our northern neighbor was not always the monolithic giant we have come to know and take for granted. Until 1867, Canada, governmentally and politically speaking (if not in the minds of its beholders) meant the provinces of Ontario, Quebec, Manitoba, Saskatchewan, and Alberta. New Brunswick and Nova Scotia did not join the Confederation until 1867, British Columbia until 1871, Prince Edward Island until 1873, and Newfoundland until 1948 (!). Thus, in point of fact, any players born in those provinces prior to their joining the confederation were not, strictly speaking, Canadian. Accordingly, the following players' place of birth information should *end* with the respective province in which they were born and not go on to include "Canada" as part of the information—at least not without the parenthetical (currently part of Canada) notation:

New Brunswickers—Mullen, Henry J.; Phillips, William B.

Nova Scotians—Doyle, John Aloysius; Lake, Frederick Lovett; Scanlon, Patrick; Smith, Charles Marvin "Pop".

Prince Edward Islander—Oxley, Henry Havelock.

(It should here be noted that James McKeever, the sole Newfoundlander to play in the majors may not have been a Newfie at all, and probably should not be included in this list.)

Europe next beckons, so let us away thither—Ah, Europe, thou continent of borders ever changing. To be historically correct is to be politically incorrect, but given the choice, I will go for historical correctness every time. Anyway, here goes—Emil Geiss, listed as born in Germany, should read: Born in Villmar, Duchy of Hessen-Nassau, Kingdom of Prussia (present-day German). William Kühne, listed as born in Germany, should read: Born in Leipzig, Kingdom of Saxony (present-day Germany). John Michaelson, listed as born in Finland, should read: born in Tivalkoski,

Grand Duchy of Finland, Russia (present-day Finland). Henry "Pep" Peploski, listed as born in Poland, should read: Born in Garlin, Duchy of Pomerania, Kingdom of Prussia (present-day Germany). John Reder, listed as born in Poland, should read: Born in Lublin, Congress Poland, Russia (present-day Poland). Gus Shallix, listed as born in Germany should read: Born in Paderborn, Westphalia, Kingdom of Prussia (present-day Germany).

Four other players born in Europe should also have their data adjusted, even though exact birth places are not known. Joseph Miller, and Frank Siffell were born before the founding of the modern German state and should have "Exact birth locale unknown—somewhere in present-day Germany," rather than just Germany. George Meister, likewise, was born in Dorzbach "in present-day Germany." John "Nap" Kloza, born before the restitution of Poland to statehood in 1918 likewise should reflect the uncertainty of the exact locale and say "…in present-day Poland".

Next we come to the original Aussie, Joe Quinn. Saying he was born in Sydney, Australia, is like saying Sandy Koufax was born in Brooklyn, North America. Australia did not become a unified country until 1913. Before that it, like Canada, was a group of politically separate British colonies which may have shared a continent but did not share a ruler—other than the reigning British monarch in faraway England. To be historically correct, his line should read: Sydney, New South Wales (part of present-day Australia).

Well, I suppose we could go on and amend the data for Tom Sullivan (Territory of Alaska) or Jim Scott (Territory of South Dakota) or all of the other "Territory Boys"—I know I would—but some would say in doing so that we would have gone too far in our search for the truth, that we have begun to strain at the proverbial gnat. I am willing, in the interests of social amity to grant that. But, dad-burn it, it's the *Kingdom* of Hawaii for Honolulu Johnny—accept no substitutes.

Big Boy

Clarence (Big Boy) Kraft quit at the top. The popular Forth Worth (Texas League) first baseman smashed fifty-five home runs to establish a minor league record in 1924, then promptly retired. Big Boy became a car dealer and operated his agency successfully for eighteen years. In wartime 1942 cars became scarce and Kraft entered the political arena. He served six years as Tarrant County Judge.

Kraft joined Fort Worth in 1918. At retirement, he held league career records for home runs, most years leading in runs batted in, runs scored, and most years making 200 or more hits. His Texas League homer mark stood until Ken Guettler hit fifty-six in 1956 for Shreveport.

Kraft's major league career consisted of three games with the 1914 "miracle" Boston Braves. He got a single in three at bats. Born on June 9, 1887 in Evansville, Indiana, Kraft died in Forth Worth on March 26, 1958.

—Howard Green

Nate Moreland:
A Mystery to Historians

John McReynolds

"Sorry John, I don't have the information you need on Nate Moreland. He is a mystery to many historians."
—Larry Lester, co-editor, *The Negro Leagues Book*

Of the first twenty black players signed by Organized Baseball between October, 1945, and August, 1947, nineteen went to the major leagues—the Dodgers, Indians and Browns—or to minor league teams in Canada or New England—Montreal; Nashua, New Hampshire; Three Rivers or Sherbrooke, Quebec; Stamford, Connecticut, and Gloversville, New York.

The only player signed in this period by a team located south or west of Gloversville, near Schenectady in upstate New York, was Nate Moreland. He was signed by the El Centro, California, Imperials of the Class C Sunset League on May 18, 1947, barely a month after Jackie Robinson appeared in Brooklyn.

"Why El Centro?" and "Who's Moreland?" were the questions that propelled this inquiry. The Imperials were not an affiliate of the Dodgers, Indians, or Browns. Nor was Moreland a local lad. He was thirty years old in 1947. He spent his formative years in Pasadena, more than two-hundred miles north. El Centro itself, a farm town of 6,000, eight miles from the Mexican border, was known by many as the redneck capital of the league. Its public schools were racially segregated as late as 1954. So why there?

John McReynolds *won the 1998 SABR Macmillan Award for this article, which originally appeared in* The Grandstand Baseball Annual. *He writes sports and the occasional feature for the Santa Maria (California)* Times.

The investigation of this question led to three other stories. One centers on Moreland's association with Jackie Robinson. The highlight was a purported "tryout" by the two with the Chicago White Sox in 1942, which has been included in many Robinson biographies. Another story alleges that Moreland had been promised, then refused, a tryout for the Los Angeles Angels by club president Clarence "Pants" Rowland. Finally, Larry Lester's "mystery" comment was repeated by several sources and merited investigation. What it turned up shows…well, no mystery gives away its climax this early.

Moreland: on the record—Nathaniel Edmond Moreland, Jr., was born April 22, 1917, in England, Arkansas, one of four children of Nathaniel Moreland Sr. and Elizabeth Moreland. The family moved to Pasadena in about 1930. The elder Moreland was a teacher and Baptist minister.

Nate played baseball at Muir Tech High School in Pasadena. The school yearbook, "The Sequoian," published his portrait in 1935 among the graduating seniors and noted his participation on the baseball and track teams. It listed his hobby as baseball and, prophetically, listed his aspiration as "professional baseball."

After graduation Moreland remìned at home and attended Pasadena Junior College. There he continued to play ball. A catcher, he batted .349 in 1936. Also that year he won the Golden Gloves boxing title at PJC. At six-foot-two and 200 pounds he was a heavyweight. In 1937, despite his success the previous year Moreland eschewed baseball and opted for the track team. He threw the javelin and put the shot. That team, called the "strongest JC track team I've ever seen" by USC coach Dean Cromwell, included Jackie Robinson's older brother, Mack, whose last competition had been the 1936 Berlin Olympics.

Moreland continued his education, entering Baptist-affiliated Redlands University in the fall of 1938 majoring in Physical Education and Sociology. He was an all-conference wide receiver on the Bulldog football team as well as a shot putter for the track team. Also, he returned to baseball, but now as a right handed pitcher. "A college Don Newcombe," one observer called him years later. He threw a fastball and occasional slider.

A string of 1940 victories and a conference title, albeit over the small-school opposition offered by such as LaVerne, Occidental, and Whittier, attracted attention. "Moreland is pitching some flossy ball" noted one Los Angeles *Times* sports columnist in the lingo of the time.

"He was as good as we had," said UR teammate Herb Morrelli. "He could throw hard. We didn't have speed guns then, but he probably threw in the nineties."

In June, 1940, Moreland travelled East seeking his high-school dream. He caught on with the Baltimore Elite Giants of the Negro National League. By his own count he won fourteen games and lost five. The catcher for the Elites was eighteen-year-old Roy Campanella.

In 1941, Moreland finished his courses at Redlands, then celebrated his honeymoon by taking his bride, Delma, to Mexico as he pitched for the Tampico Alijadores (Longshoremen). He later claimed that he won thirteen straight games. He threw 223 innings and finished 16-12 with a 3.67 ERA. His sixteen wins led the team.

Delma returned from Mexico before the season ended because she was pregnant with Amelia, named for the Morelands' landlady in Tampico. Delma's health began to deteriorate. Ultimately she was diagnosed with tuberculosis and was interned in the Los Angeles County TB sanitarium for the next four years. Responsible by himself for the baby and Delma's older daughter, Lynne, Moreland remained in southern California during 1942, playing semipro ball for the Los Angeles Colored Giants and the Los Angeles Colored Athletics.

From a historical perspective, the most noteworthy event of Moreland's life took place in March, 1942—the conversation he and Robinson held with Jimmy Dykes of the White Sox. At the time it was only another discouraging footnote.

The highlight of Moreland's year came after the big leaguers came home. On October 11 and 18, 1942, the "Philadelphia Royal Colored Giants" took the field in two doubleheaders at Los Angeles' Wrigley Field against Joe Pirrone's major league and Pacific Coast League "All Stars." The first twin bill drew 6,000 fans, the second 4,000.

Pirrones' lineup included major leaguers Peanuts Lowrey, Babe Dahlgren, Babe Herman, Lou (the Mad Russian) Novikoff, and Gerry Priddy. The Giants included veteran Negro Leagues catcher Biz Mackey, infielder Howard "Slug" Easterling of the Homestead Grays, and Kenny Washington, the former UCLA football star. Moreland took the mound in the first game of both doubleheaders. He was opposed each time by Larry French, 15-4 with the Brooklyn Dodgers that season. The Royal Giants sent Chet Brewer of the Cleveland Buckeyes to the mound in both second games against Jess Flores, recently purchased by the Philadelphia Athletics.

The big leaguers won all four games, beating Moreland 6-1 and 4-1, but they could not drive him from the hill. Moreland gave up ten hits in nine innings each game. In the first game he relinquished four runs on five hits in the first inning, then settled down to hold the All Stars to two tallies on five hits over the final eight. In the second game he gave up only three earned runs. Four of the ten hits he relinquished came off the bat of Novikoff.

In a fit of hyperbole, the California *Eagle*, a black Los Angeles weekly, called Moreland's pitching "consistently brilliant." If not brilliant, he showed he was competitive with the best in the game.

Moreland and Washington played together much of the winter of 1942-43 for the team sponsored by Moreland's employer, the Los Angeles Police Department. In the spring, when the big leaguers of the Pirrone All Stars headed back east, Moreland again remained in Los Angeles. By June he had joined the North American Aviation Mustangs for whom he pitched the remainder of the year and into 1944, often as part of a tandem with Chet Brewer.

Moreland returned to professional baseball in Tampico for the summer of 1944. He pitched 234 innings, but went 8-16 and led the league in bases on balls with 152. His ERA of 3.50 was second best on the Alijadores' four-man rotation.

In winter, 1944-45, he played both for Brewer's "Kansas City Royals" [so-named, according to Brewer's explanation years later, because the players were Kansas City Monarchs in the summer] as well as occasionally for the Los Angeles Police Department.

On Saturday, March 10, 1945, in one of the few semi-pro games given newspaper coverage beyond a line score, Moreland and veteran coast leaguer Tillie Schaeffer combined on a one-hit shutout as LAPD shelled the UCLA Bruins, 16-0, in a practice game. Soon after, he was inducted into the U.S. Army, an eventuality delayed for years because of Delma's continuing hospitalization.

Even in the military Moreland was able to find the mound. He pitched for the Camp Ellis (Illinois) team and managed to pitch a few games with the Kansas City Monarchs while on leave. In 1946 he returned to Mexico with the Monterrey Sultans. In fifteen games he went 2-6, 2.97.

In three years in the Mexican League Moreland was 26-34. He gave up 516 hits in 524 innings. His bases on balls totaled 293, or five per nine innings. His walks doubled his strikeouts (293 to 147). He posted an ERA of 3.50.

Among his more noted teammates at Tampico and Monterrey were Cuban stars Santos Amaro and Claro Duany, Jesus "Cochihuila" Valenzuela (a Mexican Hall of Fame pitcher reputed nowadays to have been an antecedent of Fernando) and Negro Leagues stars Buster Clarkson, Larry Brown, Art Pennington and Verdell Mathis.

Just as Delma's health played a pivotal role in Moreland's career in 1942, her daughter Lynne's did the same in 1946. With her mother still in the TB hospital, and Moreland playing ball in Mexico, eight-year-old Lynne was hospitalized with appendicitis. Driven by worry and suspicions regarding her daughters' child-care providers, Delma Moreland "escaped" from the sanitarium, snatched up Lynne from her hospital, and spirited her off to relatives in Riverside.

"Mama was afraid to come back into Los Angeles County for twenty years," Lynne laughs today. "She thought they were going to pick her up."

Moreland family members say it was the fall of 1946 when the family moved from Riverside south to El Centro, Nate hoping to use his college education to land a teaching job.

During the winter of 1946-47 Moreland, commuting into Los Angeles to play, made occasional appearances for the A.J. Laverenz and Los Angeles Eagles semipro teams.

Having reached age thirty still with no opportunity in Organized Ball, Moreland appears to have resigned himself to his fate. Or perhaps he hoped to sign with the new El Centro Imperiels professional team at their inception. He made no move to Mexico or the Negro Leagues in the spring of 1947.

As late as Sunday, May 11, he *caught* for the Los Angeles Eagles in a 14-13 defeat at the hands of the Paramount Dodgers at Sawtelle Playground in Los Angeles.

After signing with El Centro, Moreland made history with his first appearance on Wednesday, May 21, 1947. The Imperials drew over 1,000 for his debut. He soon became a workhorse and regional hero. He won twenty games for the woeful Imps despite missing the first month .

Moreland was a pitching cornerstone in El Centro in

1948 and 1949 as well. Sold to Mexicali in 1950 he went 13-3. In 1953 with Mexicali he won twenty games. In 1954 he led the Arizona-Texas League with twenty-two wins. In his last season, 1956, at age thirty-nine he was 17-8 for Cananea. In ten years with El Centro, Mexicali, and Cananea, he averaged more than 200 innings a year. This despite pitching fulltime only after school was out in June, due to his El Centro teaching position.

Moreland won 152 games and lost 104 with an ERA of 4.22 over this stretch. His control improved dramatically over his Mexican League seasons. Strikeouts now surpassed bases on balls. His ten-year total in Organized Baseball was 707 free passes and 1,161 strikeouts (5.1 per nine innings).

In 1958 Moreland served as manager of the Mexicali club during spring training, but after receiving an offer from league president Chuck Hollinger he followed Emmett Ashford as the second African-American umpire in the Arizona-Texas League. For a time it appeared that Moreland could finally be on track to the majors, albeit wearing blue.

In a 1958 interview with the Tucson *Daily Star* Moreland minimized racism and discrimination. "There's no trouble at all now," he told *Star* sports editor Abe Chanin. "Everyone's been wonderful to me. I don't have any difficulty finding places to stay. All I want to do is improve and go up to higher classification baseball as an umpire."

Months later came an event which changed all that, the basis of the Moreland "mystery."

Moreland and Jackie Robinson—Moreland's baseball career and that of Jackie Robinson intertwined throughout their Pasadena years, but after Robinson arrived in Brooklyn the public record of their relationship almost completely disappears.

Their most famous moment together took place in the so-called "tryout" with the Chicago White Sox.

It took place on Wednesday morning, March 18, 1942, in the dugout at Brookside Park in Pasadena, the Sox spring training base. Moreland, Robinson, and Herman Hill, the West Coast correspondent for the Pittsburgh *Courier*, then the nation's largest Negro weekly newspaper, approached Jimmy Dykes, manager of the Sox.

In at least three biographies of Robinson the day's events are termed a "tryout." If a "tryout" involves running, throwing, and hitting, this one more resembled a conversation. SOX REJECT RACE PLAYERS screamed the *Courier* of Saturday, March 21, above its story, which was soon picked up by the *Daily Worker*. "Jackie Robinson, Nate Moreland Barred at Camp."

"Personally I would welcome Negro players on the White Sox," said Dykes. "The matter is out of the hands of us managers. We are powerless to act and it's strictly up to the club owners and Judge Landis to start the ball-a-rolling. Go after them!"

The caption below the *Courier* photo of Moreland and Robinson, the latter in his UCLA letterman's jacket, reads: "The pair are pictured at Pasadena's Brookside Park, the Chicago White Sox's training camp, just after they unsuccessfully applied last week for a tryout with the Sox. "

Dykes' famous comments about Robinson being worth $50,000 and "stealing everything but my infielders' gloves" came not that day but "upon a former occasion," wrote Hill.

That occasion was probably in 1938. Shav Glick of the Los Angeles *Times* was a classmate of Moreland at Pasadena Junior College, and editor of the student newspaper. He reports that the quotes were made after a game between the White Sox and the Pasadena Sox, a local amateur team, in March, 1938.

The *Courier* account of the Dykes conversation quotes not Robinson, more well-known even then due to his UCLA football exploits, but Moreland. "I can play in the Mexican National League, but I must fight to defend this country where I can't play," he said.

Moreland and Robinson, two years younger, grew up as neighbors. The Morelands' backyard abutted that of the Robinsons' Pepper Street home.

Moreland and Robinson did not play together on the same Muir Tech baseball team. Due to the enrollment policy of the time in the Pasadena Unified School District when Moreland was a senior at Muir and Robinson was in tenth grade, Robinson was still at Washington Junior High They missed each other again at Pasadena Junior College. Moreland graduated three months before Robinson entered in the fall of 1937, but they played together in the Pasadena recreation department's summer softball league

Approximately forty teams played a version of softball unique to Pasadena that featured overhand pitching. Moreland and Robinson played together on one predominately black team. Moreland pitched, and, as he pitched, whistled, according to Vernie Leif, a PJC pitcher. "I'd never seen that before or since," Lief marvelled.

During the summer of 1939 Moreland and Robinson played together on the Pasadena Sox baseball team which won the California semipro championship. Moreland pitched while Robinson played shortstop. The team was financed by the gate receipts from that annual spring training game with the Chicago White Sox.

In personality, Moreland could not have been more different from the fiery Robinson. "He had an absolutely different personality from Jackie Robinson," says Toni Stewart, Moreland's sister. Moreland has been described to the author as good-natured, quiet, soft-spoken, diplomatic, one of the boys, unassuming, even "sweetheart."

Several sources said Moreland transcended the color line. "He wasn't black or white. He was American," said Leif. "He was above color."

"Nate Moreland was a nice man," remembers Ray E. Viers, a batboy for the Imperials. "It didn't dawn on me that he was black."

Moreland would offer a quiet word to children. His vocabulary advertised his college background. And his dignified personal presence set him apart from the average ballplayer. "Moreland wasn't the kind of guy you ran into every day," said Ed Maljan, owner of the El Centro Imperials for most of their history.

"Nate was just one of the guys as far as I was concerned," said minor league home run king Forrest "Frosty" Kennedy. "Being a college-educated guy probably made him stand out more than the fact he was black."

The Moreland family today emphasizes their closeness to Robinson and the assistance Nate gave to him. " My brother's whole life was devoted to helping others," says Toni Stewart. "His motto was 'we lift as we climb.' And there was no one Nate helped more than Jackie Robinson. When Jackie was younger he ran with a very wild crowd, the Pepper Street Gang they were called. He didn't have a father at home and his mother worked. But Jackie knew he could always come to our house and my mama would give him a meal. So Nate really became a father figure for Jackie, and convinced him to get involved with baseball."

In 1958 Moreland told of playing this guiding role with Robinson as late as 1945. "I was pitching for the Kansas City Monarchs and Jackie was playing shortstop. Jackie came to me during the game and said some fellow by the name of Clyde Sukeforth had told him he was scouting him for Mr. Branch Rickey.

"Jackie said he wasn't sure Sukeforth was a scout. I had to convince him that this was his big chance.

"I remember that Sukeforth tried every trick on Jackie to test his character. He tried to get Jackie to break curfew; Jackie wouldn't. Then he tried to get Jackie to take a drink and to smoke; Jackie turned him down both times. Jackie was bewildered but Sukeforth reported to Rickey that the boy was okay." (Arizona *Daily Star*, July 6, 1958.)

Yet in the detailed account of Robinson's large wedding published in the California *Eagle* early in 1946, there is no mention of Moreland or any of his family. Nor is there any mention of Moreland in any of the Robinson biographies, other than in connection with the White Sox "tryout."

Moreland and Robinson briefly played together one last time after Robinson signed with the Dodgers. In the fall of 1946, after Robinson had torn up the International League with Montreal, he organized the Jackie Robinson All Stars to barnstorm the country.

According to the September 18, 1946, issue of *The*

Sporting News, players he invited to join him included Campanella, Newcombe, John Wright, Roy Partlow, Larry Doby, Monte Irvin and [white] Montreal teammates Marvin Rackley and Al Campanis. Moreland was invited too, but *The Sporting News* didn't mention him as a member of the tour until its article the following May announcing Moreland's signing in El Centro.

One of the Robinson tour stops was little El Centro on October 24. The Robinson stars played the Bob Feller All Stars, filling in for Satchel Paige's touring team after Satch had a falling out with Feller. El Centro was the home of Boston Brave slugger Bob Elliott, a member of the Feller troupe. The Fellers won the weekday afternoon contest and, more important, drew a throng of 1,800. This in a town with a population of 6,000.

The last publicly documented contact between Robinson and Moreland came during the 1947 season, when Robinson sent a telegram of con- gratulations to Moreland in El Centro on "Nate Moreland Night."

The Angels' "Announcement"—The second appearance by Moreland on a national stage took place in 1943. It lends credence to the contention that Moreland was blackballed from organized baseball for speaking out about race.

In 1970, Robert Peterson wrote in *Only the Ball was White* that "Clarence "Pants" Rowland, president of the Pacific Coast League Angels, said trials would be given to three Negro players, Chet Brewer, Howard Easterling, and Nate Moreland. Two weeks later he reneged, apparently under pressure from other league operators, but his retreat brought a flurry of protests. The Los Angeles County Board of Supervisors… went on record opposing discrimination in the Pacific Coast League. The Angels' park was picketed on opening day," wrote Peterson.

Other versions of this story substitute Biz Mackey and Kenny Washington for Brewer and Easterling, but the basics of the story are similar. Interestingly, all five players mentioned participated for the Philadelphia Royal Giants in their doubleheaders with Pirrone's All-Stars at Wrigley Field in Los Angeles in October, 1942. And all versions of the story mention Moreland.

Closer examination of the Los Angeles *Times*, the Los Angeles *Examiner*, the California *Eagle* , the New York *Daily Worker* and the Pittsburgh *Courier* from late 1942 and early 1943 brings into question some details of the Peterson account but confirms a thread of a story connecting the Moreland-Robinson-Hill meeting with Jimmy Dykes in March, 1942, to the "protests" of 1943.

In August, 1942, the New York *Daily Worker* picked up a story from the Los Angeles *Tribune*, a black weekly, that Nate Moreland and Herman Hill had met "recently" with Victor F. Collins, president of the Hol-lywood Stars, in his office. Collins refused to grant Moreland a tryout, wrote Saul Halpert in a special report to the *Worker*. "Collins said that hiring of Negro players would be a change in policy which would require the approval of the stockholders of the club."

If Moreland and Hill approached Collins as they had Dykes, it is likely they sought a meeting with Rowland as well.

On March 24, 1943, the California *Eagle* printed sports editor J. Cullen Fentress' comments that "several months ago, all of the local weeklies carried stories stating that…Rowland had made…commitments regarding tryouts for Negro ballplayers this Spring.

"However, the other day…Mister Rowland reneged. It seems that the war had the smaller loops in its throes, leaving the Angel club with more than the usual share of pre-campaign hopefuls. This, of course, left the Negro ballplayers, who were nominated last winter for tryouts, out in the cold…."

The Pittsburgh *Courier* on April 10 explained that three Negro players—no names, no dates—had asked to be permitted to try out for the Angels, and that they were assured—by an uspecified person—that they would be permitted to do so. "At the start of spring training the three were informed that they would not be considered," the article explained. The only player mentioned by name in the *Courier* and the *Eagle* accounts was Nate Moreland.

His father, identified in the *Courier* as "Professor Moreland," was part of a seven-man delegation that Hallie Harding, former Negro Leagues player and now a representative of the Los Angeles *Tribune*, led before the Los Angeles County Board of Supervisors to discuss this issue. Herman Hill of the *Courier*, and pitcher Chet Brewer were also present. This meeting took place on March 23, before the wartime year's spring training began.

The Board of Supervisors and the City Council adopted watered-down resolutions decrying discrimination in hiring "in organized baseball" with no specific target, minor or major. No speakers from organized baseball appeared.

In April, Harding, Brewer, and Olan "Lou" Dials, a Negro Leagues outfielder, visited Oakland manager Johnny Vergez at Wrigley Field in Los Angeles after Oaks owner Vic Devincenzi had told Hill of the *Courier* he "would gladly give Negro players a trial with the Oaks." The visit drew headlines in the San Francisco Bay Area when Devincenzi instructed Vergez to go ahead and offer the tryout.

Vergez, flabbergasted, refused. "I'll be damned if I'll do it, " he stammered.

In response Harding, Hill, Brewer, and Dials formed the "Committee for Equal Participation in Organized Baseball." The twelve-member steering committee included the Rev. N.E. Moreland.

On Sunday May 24, the California *Eagle* headlined, PICKETS MARCH AT BALL PARK. CARRYING PLACARDS LABELED 'LET'S ALL BE AMERICANS–STOP DISCRIMINATION.' The article noted that "some thirty pickets paraded before the Los Angeles Angels ball park, Wrigley Field Sunday afternoon."

The *Eagle* added some context: "A crowd of over 19,000, one of the largest in the history of the park, was on hand to see the doubleheader featuring the league-leading Angels and the Hollywood Stars."

The mainstream (white) Los Angeles press covered the game and the attendance, but ignored the pickets.

Pants Rowland never held an open press conference to make any formal comment. If he made a private deal with Harding, Hill, or Moreland he never acknowledged it.

Perhaps Rowland's verbal comments were more limited than his visitors wished to hear. Perhaps he was pressured by his Pacific Coast League associates. Or perhaps when lower level minor leagues suspended operation due to the wartime manpower shortage, more white players became available to the Angels and Rowland's interest waned. For whatever reason Rowland made no move toward tryouts in the spring.

One point is undeniable. Victor Collins, Pants Rowland, and other Pacific Coast League brass were familiar with the name Nate Moreland. One can only speculate whether the adjective "troublemaker" accompanied it.

Toni Stewart remembers seeing a letter to her brother from one team regretfully informing Moreland of a club policy against hiring "communists."

Ray Viers—Then how did Moreland come to be signed by El Centro in May, 1947?

The answer is Ray Viers.

Moreland was signed just two days after Raymond Oliver Viers, a fiery second baseman who had played for the Los Angeles Angels in 1945, was hired as the new Imp manager.

Viers, at age twenty-seven, had ten years of minor league experience. Signed out of Hamilton High in Los Angeles, Viers bounced through the low minors (Bisbee, Pine Bluff, Panama City, Pensacola, Clarksdale, Montgomery) for six years before a trial by the manpower-starved wartime Yankees prior to the 1943 season.

In spring training Viers filled in for Joe Gordon at second base during his holdout, but was sent to Newark of the International League before opening day.

At Newark a flying bat changed the trajectory of his career. It hit him in the left thigh and hospitalized him for several weeks. It cost him much of the season. Worse, the injury left "big knots on both legs that still cause considerable pain at times," he told the Imperial Valley *Post Press* four years later.

Traded from Newark to the Atlanta Crackers, Viers, bad leg or no, burned up the Southern Association in 1944. He drove in seventy runs, despite batting seventh most of the season, was named to the league's All Star team, finished second to one-armed Pete Gray in the MVP voting, and led the Crackers to the pennant. For three weeks while manager Kiki Cuyler was ill, Viers, then twenty-four, filled in at the Cracker helm.

Picked up by the Chicago Cubs, Viers received another spring training chance at the majors in 1945, but was sent down again, this time to the Los Angeles Angels where he batted a disappointing .244.

Riding the bench for the Angels in 1946 as war veterans flooded back to baseball, Viers asked for his release. He signed with Memphis where he finished the year batting .218.

With his career on the decline, Viers was referred to El Centro owner George Jackson by Boston Braves scout Johnny Moore after manager Bob Boken suddenly resigned. Viers knew Moore from the Los Angeles winter leagues. Viers knew Moreland from the same place. In fact, they had been teammates.

In January, 1944, Viers and Moreland played together with the North American Aviation Mustangs as they upset the Rosabell Plumbers for the Los Angeles semipro title. In the championship game Viers scored the winning run in the thirteenth inning. Moreland was the Mustangs' starting pitcher.

In January, 1945, Viers and Moreland played again in the Los Angeles title game, this time in opposing uniforms, Viers now with the Plumbers, Moreland with Chet Brewer's "Kansas City Royals." The Plumbers won and reestablished their dominance of the Los Angeles semipro circuits.

At Viers' funeral in January, 1996, the eulogy included a story about Viers and his disregard of racial barriers. It was set in one of the southern cities he played in. The story ran that Viers was one of the few white players to sign autographs for fans of all colors. He was so known for this that after one game from which he was ejected and fined $50, his fine was paid by a collection taken up by black fans.

"Dad had no prejudices," says Viers' son, Ray E., "Little Ray," who became a batboy for the Imperials (along with ticket manager Harold Harvey's boy Doug, who went on to become a National League umpire). "In our home we never heard those words—nigger, kike, dago."

When Viers arrived in El Centro it was easy to see that the Imperials needed pitching. The team was 7-21 and had no pitcher with an ERA under 5.00. Viers took one look at the sad-sack mound staff and knew he could use a hurler like Moreland.

According to the Moreland family, Nate had moved from Riverside to El Centro in September, 1946, in search of a teaching job. A Pasadena teammate, Ellery Prince, had a cousin, Arthur Prince, who was head teacher at still-segregated Washington Elementary School in El Centro.

Whether it was Moreland or Viers who made the first move to seek out the other may never be known.

But Viers faced an argument when he went to club owner George Jackson to talk about signing Moreland. Jackson demurred because of color.

"What the hell difference does that make!" Viers exploded.

"Dad argued…till he got his way," writes Ray E. Viers from the story recounted to him by his mother.

"It sounds like my Dad…when he spotted a winner, nothing else mattered."

Jackson, a thirty-nine-year-old Riverside roofing contractor, may not have been unduly difficult to persuade. Calling him a "baseball Barnum" the Riverside *Enterprise* wrote on June 16 that Jackson's publicity and promotion campaign in El Centro was the envy of other Sunset League operators.

"You've got to have showmanship in this league," Jackson told the paper. "You've got to have an act."

Jackson announced Moreland's acquisition on Sunday night May 18, shortly after Viers made his first appearance in uniform watching the Imps lose a doubleheader to Ontario. The defeats pushed El Centro further into the league basement, now by four games.

IMPERIALS SIGN MORELAND IN UNPRECEDENTED MOVE headlined the Imperial Valley *Post-Press* sports page on Monday.

"President George Jackson pulled an unprecedented move by signing the first Negro player in the Sunset league when he announced that Nate Moreland had been obtained for 1947 Imperial duty Sunday night," wrote *Post-Press* sports editor Dwain Esper.

"Moreland, whose career strangely parallels that of the famous Jackie Robinson, performed for Muir Tech high school and Pasadena Junior College before he finally went into organized ball.

"He is a graduate of Redlands University and was one of the ace moundsmen of the outstanding Negro team in the nation during his term with the Kansas City Royals [*sic*]. Nate also played on Monterey of the Mexican circuit last year, and new El Centro Manager Ray Viers believes that he will be a definite asset to the club."

Years later Viers told Karl Knickrehm of SABR that there was no overt hostility to Moreland. Many others say the same. Tom Lloyd of Rosabell and the Reno Silver Sox was present for Moreland's first game. He remembers it a little differently, at least at the beginning.

Moreland "was a good friend of mine. I had known him (because) we played the colored all-stars all the time [in the LA winter leagues]. I sat down with him up in Reno and told him it's gonna be tough. Fans are close to the field. They're going to call you 'shine boy' and names like that.

"They gave him pretty good hell for a while there, but he showed 'em he could play. None of the players ever said anything, just some fans.

"Later he thanked me. He said he lost his temper a few times."

The first season—Moreland's debut was rocky. In his first appearance on May 21 in front of the first home crowd of more than 1,000 since opening day, he pitched a complete game, struck out three and walked one, but gave up eleven hits and two home runs to lose, 6-1, to Lloyd's Reno club.

His second outing, in Las Vegas, was worse. Wrangler Field's dimensions were 320 along the left field line, 360 to dead center, only 290 down the right field line, and only 304 up the alley to right center. With ten-foot fences, the park was a shooting gallery for lefthanded pull hitters and late-swinging righties. Against a power thrower like Moreland, Wrangler hitters could lift easy chip shots for home runs. On May 25, the big veteran lasted only four innings while giving up fourteen hits but avoided taking the loss as the Imps came from behind to win, 14-13.

Monday night, in a pattern of pitching on consecutive days that would become routine, Moreland drew three innings of relief duty as Las Vegas won again, 9-6.

May 30, after talking with Tom Lloyd, Moreland began to round into form. He took his second loss, but gave up only six runs, several unearned as the Imps committed four errors.

The next day, on its return trip to El Centro, the Imperials' team bus broke down near Bishop. Jackson sprang into action and chartered a plane to rescue the team and deliver them to El Centro in time for game time at 8 PM. By the fifth inning Moreland was back on the mound. Entering a tie game against Las Vegas he allowed only one hit the rest of the way in what the *Post-Press* termed a "magnificent" effort. It gained him his first victory.

On June 1, Viers, with a Sunday doubleheader to supervise, brought Moreland in for the third time in three days late in the second game. It wasn't enough as the Imps lost both contests to the Wranglers.

Wednesday, June 4, marked the turnaround. MORELAND, FUENTE TEAM TO BEAT DONS AGAIN BY 11-2, read the headine in the *Post-Press*. Moreland stopped Riverside on two runs on eight hits while striking out thirteen.

"Aside from the two scoring frames, Riverside was handcuffed in every instance by the fireball slants of Moreland who copped his first victory in a starting role this season," wrote Esper.

Again the next night, with the Imperials on the cusp of blowing an 8-3 lead, Viers summoned Moreland. Despite having thrown nine frames the night before, the big man nailed down the final out of the game, a strikeout, to give El Centro an 8-6 win and a sweep—the Imps' first of the season and only their second series victory.

Sunday, June 8, in Ontario, Moreland gave up two runs in the first, then no more to ace the Orioles, 3-2, on five hits. He struck out three and walked none in nine innings to up his record to 3-2.

Dwain Esper was impressed. "Nate Moreland, off to a poor start, seems to be on his way now as proved by his recent work in the Riverside series when he struck out 13 batters in one game to win easily, 11-2, and came in to quench a rally for Pete Castro the next night," he wrote.

On two days' rest Moreland was back starting on the mound at league-leading Anaheim on June 11. The *Post-Press* headline read, MORELAND COPS FOURTH IN ROW WITH VAL VICTORY 6-3. Moreland shut out the Valencias for eight innings before weakening in the ninth. Still, he pitched a six-hitter.

The Anaheim team drove out to El Centro for the next series and won it, two games to one, losing, 4-2, to Moreland in a seven-inning Sunday night game on June 15. "Anaheim took the series, but Ol' Nate Moreland kept right on rolling along. The dusky right hand fireball artist…lowered the boom…to record his fifth straight victory…," wrote Esper. By the seventeenth of June, Esper was calling Moreland "the most dependable pitcher on the Imperial pitching staff."

MORELAND CHALKS UP SIXTH CONSECUTIVE VICTORY, 4-3, headlined the *Post-Press* after the June 19 night game in Riverside. Moreland gave up two runs in the first, then shut out the Dons the rest of the way.

But on Monday, June 23, it was back to the "pint-sized park" in Las Vegas. Bombed there in May, he was destroyed in June. Moreland gave up nine hits in 2-2/3 innings as the Wranglers sent him to the showers en route to a 25-4 annihilation.

Viers gave him another chance the next night and he responded, holding the Silver Sox to one run on eight hits to pick up his seventh win. He fanned seven and walked three.

"Nate showed tremendous stamina in his performance since he went almost three innings against the Wranglers Monday night, but was not effective," wrote Esper. "The Reno victory was his seventh as against three defeats, and he now challenges the leading percentage hurlers in the loop." By the end of the week Esper was promoting Moreland for the first Sunset League All Star Game.

On June 28 Moreland stopped the Orioles in Ontario, 8-7, in another complete game for his eighth win. He

led, 8-4, going into the ninth. He came back Sunday afternoon in relief and received credit for victory number nine in a 10-9 El Centro win that lifted the Imperials out of the Sunset League cellar for the first time in two months.

The Sunset League All Star team was announced on July 1. From El Centro it included Viers, batting .373; outfielder Gale Bishop, a former Washington State basketball star (.363), and Nate Moreland, 9-3. From Reno it included catcher/manager Tom Lloyd, hitting .348.

On July 2, Moreland won his tenth game, 11-7, over the visiting Anaheim Valencias. Typically, he struck out only two, walked two, gave up eleven hits, and induced eleven ground-ball outs.

In a Sunday doubleheader on July 6, the still-visiting Valencias handed Moreland his fourth loss, 11-10. On Monday night the righthander pitched on consecutive days for the seventh time as he relieved in Anaheim at the first Sunset League All-Star game. A crowd of 4,200 watched comedian Joe E. Brown and singer Peggy Lee, then saw the Anaheim Valencias down the All Stars, 6-2, at La Palma Park.

Moreland was 12-4 by July 13, and his popularity was assured. El Centro management scheduled "Nate Moreland Night" for Wednesday, July 30.

MORELAND NIGHT WILL SET PRECEDENT headlined the *Post-Press*. FIRST PROGRAM IN ORGANIZED BASEBALL TO HONOR NEGRO PLAYER PLANNED FOR EL CENTRO.

Billed as the first such night in America dedicated to a black player, it drew 1,049 in a town of 6,000. The night featured an array of small gifts—electric razor, sports shirts, handkerchiefs, belt buckle, underwear, socks, traveling kit, shaving set, golf balls, writing paper—and telegrams of congratulations from Jackie Robinson and league president Bill Schroeder. New *Post-Press* sports editor Edgar Wilson reported that Moreland's teammates cheered and applauded as he opened his gifts in the clubhouse.

"The fans sure have been nice to me," Moreland told Wilson. "My first year in organized ball has sure been a happy one. I hope things are always as nice."

The Imperials drew more than 1,000 fans for only four of seventy Sunset League home games in 1947. They had Nate Moreland to thank for the two on week nights. One was for his first appearance on Wednesday, May 21, when 1,003 showed up. The other was "Nate Moreland Night."

Despite arriving a month late, Moreland won twenty games in 1947. The rest of the Imperial pitchers combined to win thirty-three. Sportswriters named him to the league all-star team. He finished third in the voting by El Centro fans for most popular player. He and Viers had made the last-place Imperials respectable. The bonus of $150 he earned when he won his fifteenth game seemed a wise investment.

Late in the season Moreland reiterated his enjoyment of the season and compared the Mexican League to the Sunset League in a conversation with Edgar Wilson. "A fellow couldn't help but win with the hits our boys have gotten behind me," he said. "I sure have enjoyed this year. We've got a nice bunch of fellows on this squad. And I hope my future seasons are all as happy as this.

"There is some pretty fast ball in the Mexican League. The players put their heart and soul into the game and give that old school boy try.

"However the league is not as well organized as the U.S. leagues…I liked playing down there but I like it up here much better."

Wilson gave Moreland credit: "It has been his steady work which has kept the shaky Imperial pitching staff from falling completely apart."

Despite his relative stardom, coverage of Moreland's history-making role by Sunset League newspapers was curiously low key. Five papers referred routinely to Moreland in understated fashion as "the first Negro in the Sunset League." Only one, the Nevada *Daily Journal* in Reno, saw a bigger picture—"the only Negro in western Organized Ball."

In comparison to the insult, injury, and potential player strike that Jackie Robinson faced in 1947, reaction to Moreland was restrained.

There are several reasons Moreland's debut was quieter than Robinson's. The managers and older players of the Sunset League were almost all veterans of the Los Angeles winter leagues where the race barrier had been crossed decades before. Virtually all the players were from the West, where racism was less virulent than in the deep South. Moreland was older than most everyone else—three years older than his own manager. He was a diplomat, as his sister described him. Finally, he was a pitcher. He could defend himself with a well-placed fastball.

Moreland threw hard and "let 'em know he was pitching," remembers Lloyd.

Questions remain about Moreland's ten years in organized baseball. One is why he received no offer to play at a higher classification. Another is whether he was allowed to lodge with the team while on the road. Tom Alston, who played for Porterville in the Sunset League in 1952 and later became the St. Louis Cardinals' first black player, said later that the Las Vegas hotels were still segregated when he played there.

Ed Maljan, who bought the Imperials from Jackson in July, 1947, didn't remember where Moreland roomed, but he had a joking explanation. "He had a girl in every port, you know."

The Sunset League did have more than its share of postgame entertainment. One source, pleading anonymity, recalled a particularly accessible establishment in Porterville, a town that entered the league in 1949. Known as Rosie's, it was located behind the first base stands of the Porterville ballpark. The girls would watch the games and socialize with players from both sides afterward. Rosie's was not to be confused with Roxie's, four miles south of Las Vegas. Tijuana, also new to the league in 1949; Mexicali, to which the Ontario Orioles moved in 1948, and Reno had similarly rousing night life.

Unlike Maljan, however, Viers and others described Moreland as quiet and keeping to himself.

In September and October, 1947, Moreland organized, and promoted fifteen exhibition games in El Centro between Sunset League All Stars, Mexicali's winter league club, Pacific Coast League All Stars, Negro Leagues stars, and a return visit by the barnstorming Bob Feller All Stars. Feller's visit, with no Jackie Robinson to help the draw, attracted fewer than 500.

All accounts agree that by then Moreland was teaching sixth grade at segregated Washington School in El Centro. He was a community leader highly regarded by both the black and white communities.

"In my mind's eye I can still see a silhouette of the man," says Sedalia White Sanders, the first African-American woman to serve as mayor of El Centro.

"He was my sixth-grade teacher. He was able to reach young people and transform his athletic abilities into the motivation of young people in their academic pursuits. He often visited in the homes of his students. Since he had a role in both the athletic world and the academic world, he made us think 'Why not me too?'" When she was interviewed in October, 1996, Mrs. Sanders was just leaving office as president of the League of California Cities.

The mystery around Moreland—Research into Moreland kept running into people who would eventually stop talking about him and say, "You know, he got in trouble later." This reticence came in marked contrast to friends and relatives of Ray Viers.

It turns out that Moreland was arrested on February 15, 1959, at the El Centro Greyhound station for selling twenty pounds of marijuana to an undercover agent. It was only thirteen days after the death of his father.

The shock was immense. Imperial Valley *Post-Press* front page account of Moreland's arrest began, "Say it ain't so, Nate. Say it ain't so," recalling the anguish of fans at the fall of Chicago White Sox idol Shoeless Joe Jackson. It also included Moreland's statement of occupation given to the arresting officers. "'It used to be teacher,' he said with a rueful smile," wrote the paper.

The arrest and trial received banner headlines in the *Post-Press* from February through April. To counter character testimony from a dozen witnesses, including the Imperial County Superintendent of Schools and an off-duty Superior Court judge, the prosecution contended that Moreland had a residence in Mexicali and was living a "double life." The defense argued entrapment. His wife and his mother appeared in the courtroom daily.

After four hours deliberation the jury returned a verdict of guilty on all three counts of narcotics sales. Moreland was sentenced to five years to life in state prison.

Maintaining his innocence, Moreland taught classes in prison at San Quentin. He used books his daughter Amelia secured from the Los Angeles school book depository. But first he instructed her firmly to scratch out all the grade-level numbers. He didn't want his students to know they were reading from elementary school texts.

Moreland was paroled in 1964, but he never again lived in Southern California. Delma divorced him. He married Virginia Vasquez, an acquaintance from Mexicali, in 1967, and did youth work and coaching before he died of bone cancer on November 27, 1973 in Alameda, California at age fifty-six.

At his death his family was showered with condolence cards, including many from former inmates who wanted to express thanks for the contribution Moreland made to their education. Some were signed only with an 'X'.

Old timers in El Centro still remember him, many fondly. But many, fifty years after "Nate Moreland Night," and thirty years after the parole, are still reluctant to talk about him.

Like foul territory at Stark Field in El Centro there are corners of this story invisible to the press box. The image of Nate Moreland remains shrouded in the shadows of minor league lights.

"My brother said one team was very interested in signing him. This may have been the White Sox or one of the PCL teams. I'm not sure. But this team wanted him to 'pass' as an Indian. My mother's mother was Cherokee and my father also has Indian blood, so Nate probably had more Indian blood than Negro blood. But Nate didn't want any part of 'passing.' That would be like getting into baseball by the back door. He always walked tall. It wasn't about race, it was about accepting him as he was."
—Toni Stewart

Sources:

Newspapers:

Arizona *Daily Star*, California *Eagle*, Imperial Valley *Post-Press*, Los Angeles *Examiner*, Los Angeles *Times*, Nevada *Daily Journal*, Pittsburgh *Courier*, Redlands *Daily Facts*, Riverside *Enterprise*, San Bernardino County *Sun*, San Gabriel Valley Newspaper Group, *The Sporting News*.

Books:

Cisneros, Pedro Treto *Enciclopedia Del Beisbol Mexicano* 1996.

Clark, Dick and Lester, Larry *TheNegro Leagues Book* 1994.

Falkner, David *Great Time Coming* 1995.

Holway, John B. *Voices from the Great Black Baseball Leagues (Revised Edition)* 1992.

_____ *Black Diamonds* 1989.

Johnson, Lloyd and Wolff, Miles *The Encyclopedia of Minor League Baseball* 1993.

Peterson, Robert *Only the Ball Was White* 1970.

Rust, Art Jr. *Get That Nigger off the Field* 1992.

Tygiel, Jules *Baseball's Great Experiment* 1983.

Winegardner, Mark *The Veracruz Blues* 1996.

Articles:

"Tom Alston" *Sports Collectors Digest* October 30, 1992.

"Forgotten Pioneer" by Jim McConnell San Gabriel Valley Newspaper Group, August 9, 1998.

"Get After Landis" *Daily Worker* March 23, 1942.

"Hollywood Club 'Too Busy for Negro Stars'" *Daily Worker* August 8. 1942.

"Moreland: Mystery Man" by Obrey Brown, *Redlands Daily Facts,* August 9, 1998.

"Robinson a Baseball Star?" by Shav Glick *Los Angeles Times* March 31, 1997.

"Statue of Limitations" by Shav Glick *Los Angeles Times* December 10, 1996.

"The Umpire Who Learned the Hard Way" by Abe Chanin *Arizona Daily Star* July 6, 1958.

"U of R Alumnus a Sports Pioneer" by Gregg Patton *San Bernardino County Sun,* August 9, 1998.

daily coverage *Imperial Valley Post-Press* 1947.

Interviews

Bob Andrews, Ray Bartlett, Lynn Bogdan (Imperial Valley Historical Society), Obrey Brown, John Dormann, Shav Glick, Stan Gray, Karl Knickrehm, Vernon Leif, Larry Lester, Amelia Moreland Lett, Tom Lloyd, Jim McConnell, Ed Maljan, Dianna Osborne Newton, Gregg Patton, Fred Peltz, Lester Rodney, Sedalia White Sanders, Toni Moreland Stewart, Gil Stratton, Jules Tygiel, Ray E. Viers, Lynne Moreland Walters, Bill Weiss

A Man For All Seasons

Kit Crissey

Minor league pitcher, major league pitcher, assistant farm director, pitching coach, scout, and currently scouting consultant: "Broadway" Charlie Wagner has filled all of these roles in his remarkable run of sixty-four years with the Boston Red Sox. At age eighty-six he is still physically fit and ever the sharp dresser that his nickname implies. Furthermore, he is unfailingly polite, has a wonderful wit, is a good listener, and acts as a quiet sage when the situation warrants. As one who has experienced both triumph and tragedy in his life, he dispenses good advice when asked, particularly in times of discouragement and depression: "Be thankful that you can get out of bed in the morning. Many people cannot."

Charlie grew up in Reading, Pennsylvania, and still lives there. He played amateur ball for the local Ajax team before beginning his pro career at age twenty-two with Charlotte of the Piedmont League in 1935. A 7-15 won-lost record that year provided scant evidence of better things to come, but Charlie was learning. He blossomed into a twenty-game winner with Rocky Mount in the same league the following year. It was Rocky Mount manager George "Specs" Toporcer who responded to Charlie's question about an appropriate "baseball age" by suggesting he lop off four years, hence a birth year of 1916 instead of 1912 in guides of the time.

Promoted all the way to Double-A in 1937 (the equivalent of modern Triple-A), Charlie again won

twenty games, this time with Minneapolis of the American Association under manager Donie Bush. He started the next season with the parent Red Sox, but was sent back to Minneapolis, where he played for the first time with Ted Williams. For the rest of Charlie's days in the American League, he would be Williams' roommate. What a smart move it was on the part of the Boston management to match steady Charlie with tempestuous Ted! Thus was formed a strong friendship that exists to this day.

In 1939, Charlie divided his time between Boston and the Bosox's new Double-A farm, Louisville of the American Association. The following year he had the parent club made after spring training, but Boston owner Thomas Yawkey asked him to go back down to Louisville to help get that franchise off to a good start. Rather than complain, Charlie willingly accepted the demotion and performed brilliantly, posting a 9-1 record and a 1.84 ERA before being recalled. It has been said that this cooperative behavior earned him Yawkey's lifelong respect.

Charlie came into his own during the 1941 and 1942 campaigns, going 12-8 with a 3.07 ERA for the Sox in '41, and 14-11 with a 3.29 ERA in '42. Never an overpowering pitcher, Charlie got by on his brains, even throwing an infrequent spitter in a pinch. He was the beneficiary of excellent teaching by two very wise old heads who are revered today because they are among the greatest minor league pitchers of all time: Bill Burwell of the American Association and Frank Shellenback of the Pacific Coast League.

Kit Crissey *teaches English as a second language to foreign adults for English Language Services on the campus of Saint Joseph's University in Philadelphia.*

Heading for "Broadway"—Another important influence on Charlie during that period was the legendary catcher Moe Berg. Charlie had first seen Berg as a child in Reading when Moe, recently graduated from Princeton and at that time a shortstop, teamed with Heinie Scheer to give the home town club a Jewish double play combination. Over a decade later, they were teammates on the Red Sox. Berg took a liking to Charlie and one spring specifically asked to catch him. Charlie was fighting to make the club and was slated to pitch an exhibition game as the club made its way north after breaking camp. With Berg calling the pitches, Charlie performed magnificently and stayed with the club.

The intellectual backstop had a much more lasting impact on the hurler, however. It was he who gave the relatively young high school graduate the polish and sophistication to live life fully on the big league circuit, including a good background in history and the arts. Charlie had the great good sense to tag along with Berg to museums, theaters, historical sites, and classy restaurants on the road, and he got an education in the process. He deplores the tendency of modern players to go from the airport to the hotel to the ballpark and back to the hotel bar or a nearby watering hole after the game. They're the beneficiaries of free travel but are missing out on so much! To talk with Charlie is to occasionally be transported back to a bygone world in which a foursome of Berg, Wagner, erudite sportswriter John Kieran, and pianist Oscar Levant, famous for his Gershwin interpretations, occupy a table at Toots Shor's or Sardi's after a game in New York, with the chain-smoking Levant firing questions at Berg and Wagner as to why the Sox can't catch the Yankees.

To war and back—Like several other ballplayers who were getting into high gear in the early forties, Charlie's playing career was derailed by World War II. He joined the Navy after the 1942 season ended and married Elynor Becker, his wife of fifty-seven years. He also had to cope with the death of his father. In 1943, he was the prime hurler on the Norfolk Naval Station squad managed by Gary Bodie. This team of professionals went 68-22-1 on the year, often playing other top-notch service teams and major league clubs. Charlie himself won seventeen games and lost only five. After the season ended, he was shipped to Brisbane, Australia, where he performed athletic specialist duties but played no serious baseball. Then it was on to the Philippines, where misfortune struck in the form of dysentery.

Released from the Navy, he returned to the States weak and underweight. This condition persisted through the 1946 campaign, but the gaunt Charlie remained on the Red Sox roster for their first American League championship year since 1918. He was doubt-less the beneficiary of the rule that allowed major league clubs to carry thirty rather than twenty-five players that summer; and the excellent relations he had with both management and teammates must have had a bearing on his retention. His contribution on the field was minimal, however. He appeared in only eight games, winning one and losing none with an ERA of 5.87. His one win was against the lowly St. Louis Browns, 13-6, in a night game in Sportsman's Park on July 27, when Rudy York tied a major league record with two grand slam home runs and drove in ten runs, one shy of the AL record. But Charlie kept his hand in as a clubhouse cheerleader as Boston surged to an early lead in the standings, was never headed, and eventually coasted to a 104-50 won-lost mark. He was not destined to pitch in the World Series.

From field to office—By the end of 1946 he had recovered from the effects of the dysentery but decided to pack it in at the age of thirty-four and accept a front office job as assistant farm director. From then until now he has been involved in the scouting and development of talent, including one season on the field (1970) when he served as Boston's pitching coach. He has been very positive about young pitching talent, encouraging managers to give young hurlers a chance, let them make their mistakes and learn from their experiences, just as he did long ago.

If one were to pick the best game Charlie ever pitched, which would it be? The 1-0 win over Bob Feller and the Indians on a July night in Cleveland in 1941? His whitewashing of the powerful Yankees in his final appearance before entering the service? The 12-11 game he won in relief in Philadelphia on the final day of the '41 season, when he dumped a two-run single into right field to secure the victory in the first game of a doubleheader, then joined the intermission celebration of his roommate's .400 average?

My choice is the $2,125,375 war bond game in Washington, D.C., on May 24, 1943. In a highly touted contest attended by British General Sir Archibald Wavell, singer Kate Smith, and many notables in the government, Norfolk Naval Station faced the Washington Senators at Griffith Stadium. Charlie, who had beaten the Nats the previous season as a major leaguer, was opposing them again as a sailor. With the help of former Bosox center fielder Dom DiMaggio, who threw two runners out at home plate, Charlie stymied Washington until the ninth inning when he weakened, but Norfolk held on for a 4-3 victory. "Broadway" Charlie had done it again. It was the last great game he would throw at major league opposition. That night he was not only the toast of the town but in a larger sense, given the goals and ideals of the war effort, the toast of the nation as well.

Monumental Failure

A.D. Suehsdorf

In the spring of 1884, Baltimore had three professional baseball teams. The American Association's Orioles were embarking on their third season. After two years in the cellar they would ascend to sixth place. The Union Association was about to launch a Baltimore entry which would finish a respectable fourth. And Dr. George W. Massamore, a dentist, was single-handedly creating an Eastern League franchise of uncertain pedigree and unpredictable future.

Appropriately, the team would be called the Monumentals. Baltimore is pleased to be known as "the Monument City." Even today more than a few downtown businesses incorporate the adjective in their names. It derives from the city's Washington and Battle Monuments, which date from 1815, when their cornerstones were laid—Washington's for the nation's earliest commemoration of its first president, Battle for the Battle of North Point, where Fort McHenry's bombardment by the British in 1814 inspired a Baltimore lawyer to compose the poem that, set to music, became our national anthem.

Dr. Massamore left few footprints in the sands of time. He graduated in 1867 from the Baltimore College of Dental Surgery (now part of Johns Hopkins). He evidently was a coin collector, though not a notable one. (A modern dealer who belongs to five numismatic societies has never heard of him.) He lived at 94 Eutaw Street, and his middle name was William. But one thing is certain: he was a baseball enthusiast and an optimist.

Sporting Life first calls our attention to him in its issue of January 2, 1884. A letter from Dr. Massamore says that he has a five-year lease on "suitable grounds" for his club and has paid the first year's rent. The site is at Madison and Boundary Avenues, at the eastern outskirts of the city, a "much sought-after" area served by five street-car lines. "Monumental Park," as it will be called, can be reached from the heart of the city in twenty minutes.

In February, *SL* notes that the Doctor's ground rent is $2,000 a year, a big hit for a minor league club. Dr. M. must be a man of means. In the March 5 issue, we learn that his park is 456 feet by 400 and will have a covered grandstand shaped like "half a hexagon" with private boxes to seat 1,800 spectators comfortably. The home-to-second axis will face northeast, thus assuring "perfect shade" throughout the grandstand. Open stands extending beyond each wing will seat another 3,000. They will be partially shaded by 'the foliage of surrounding trees." An outfield area will permit carriages to park while observing the game.

By April, *Sporting Life* is downright enthusiastic. "A visit to Monumental Park...found the wood butchers chewing up material very fast. The grand stand, which is a very fine one, is nearly completed and is so arranged as to give a good view from every seat in it, of the highest fly or the lowest daisy-cutter. Everything has a thrifty appearance and indicates the contemplation of a long stay. The virgin sod has a rich appearance and no doubt will have a pleasant effect on the eye in hot weather."

At the league level two accommodations have been agreed to. The Eastern League, organized as the Union

A.D. Suehsdorf *invites Baltimore-area SABR members to see what more can be discovered about the elusive Dr. Massamore.*

League, changed its name to avoid conflict with the new Union Association. And the American Association, which prohibits recognition of, or games with, any new team in a city where it is already established, will make an exception of the Monumentals so they can be a party to the National Agreement..

The Eastern will have eight clubs (Active [Reading], Allentown, and Harrisburg in Pennsylvania; Domestic [Newark] and Trenton in New Jersey; Virginia [Richmond];Wilmington, Delaware, and the Monumentals), playing a 98-game schedule from May 1 to October 1. The pitching distance will be 50 feet, shoulder-high delivery is permitted, and although the National League now permits a base on six balls, the Eastern will require seven.

The Monumentals' meager roster of a dozen players is managed and captained by its twenty-six-year-old third baseman, Harrison L. "Harry" Spence. An article on the team's progress in *Sporting Life* rates him highly. Mr. Spence, it says, "gives one the impression of being able to handle his men with good judgment and of making the most of the material at his disposal…He believes his team will make a good showing." The players are "said to be…of modest demeanor and superior intelligence, and incapable of causing shame to their adopted city by lax discipline or ungentlemanly behavior."

The season begins on May 1, after some exhibition losses to Princeton University and the crosstown Orioles. It is immediately clear that modest demeanor and superior intelligence will not be enough. Three straight losses at Wilmington—26-6, 11-1, and 15-8—are followed by a split of two at Harrisburg. Returning home to Monumental Park, they lose two of three to Virginia, and another three to powerful Wilmington, one of them a 21-9 shellacking.

The club is applauded for its treatment of the press. "At Oriole and Union [Association] Parks, those who keep the record of the game for the public are placed where there are the least facilities for observing—i.e., perched up high on the roof—while at Monumental Park they are placed immediately behind the catcher on the lowest floor of the grand stand and protected by a screen of fine wire."

But things are not going well for Dr. Massamore. On May 20, as umpire Wesley Curry calls, "Play," at four o'clock there is confusion on the field. The Harrisburg nine, in uniform and ready to go, take their positions, but the Monumentals are milling about in street clothes, explaining that they have no intention of playing until they are paid their salaries, which in some instances are two weeks in arrears. For about five minutes Harrisburg's pitcher throws "various curves" to his catcher. (Now and again he is cautioned by the crowd to "keep his arm down"—to avoid illegal overhand throws.) Umpire Curry, having called nine of them strikes, now declares the game forfeited to Harrisburg, 9-0.

The Monumentals gather up their bats "and other appliances" and depart. The club, in effect, is disbanded, the season ended with a record of three wins and ten losses, including the forfeit.

Dr. Massamore is distraught. He admits that some salaries have not been paid, but some players have received advances, "so that if equally divided the sum total would have been sufficient to meet all that was due." Well, maybe. He also says that if "certain unnamed persons" had kept their promises to help him, he would have been able to bridge this temporary difficulty. He hopes to reorganize in a few days and complete the season.

The *Sun* is less sanguine. Aside from the high rental and expensive grandstand, the "other expenses of the club were also heavy and, after exhausting the funds on hand, the management went into debt, expecting to realize profit enough from the gate receipts…to liquidate all claims against the club." But their games were poorly patronized. Not one took in even enough to pay the League guarantee of $65 to the visiting club. *Sporting Life* estimated debts at $1,000 for player salaries, $1,000 owing to lumber suppliers and contractors, $300 to hotels where the players boarded, and $130 to the Eastern League, which assessed each club $100 monthly for umpires and "incidental expenses." In short, a lot more than Dr. Massamore's amalgam fillings and nitrous oxide—"laughing gas"—extractions can pay for. The collapse, *Sporting Life* comments bluntly, "demonstrates the fact that Baltimore will not support three clubs."

Manager Spence is optimistic. Good players are in demand. He is sure they can join other clubs at better salaries than they had with the Monumentals. Actually, they do not fare well. Three of the "good men…bemoaning their sad fate on the stoop of the Howard House hotel" join Harrisburg at salaries "almost doubling" what they got as Monumentals. By mid-July, however, this franchise will also collapse. Pitcher Jim McElroy and catcher Joe Kappel will have brief, unsatisfactory stints with the Philadelphia Nationals. Two others will catch on with American Association teams. Infielder Gil Hatfield will have a modest career—317 games over eight seasons with National League, Players' League, and American Association teams. Harry Spence will manage the National League's Indianapolis entry to a seventh-place finish in 1888. Of rash Dr. Massamore nothing more is known.

Walt Dropo Goes 12-For-12

Bob Mayer

It was a golden summer. Like being in heaven." That's how Walt Dropo remembered his Rookie-of-the-Year season in 1950.

Dropo was the big Red Sox first baseman whose first-year stats inspired him to ask owner Tom Yawkey for $50,000...ten times more than the $5,000 major league minimum salary he was paid as a rookie.

"I told Yawkey I had a better year than Williams," he recalled. "I said I should be in Ted's salary category."

Needless to say, Walt wore a sheepish grin when he recounted his meeting with the Boston owner and how he readily settled for less. Forty-nine years later, Dropo speaks eloquently and with perspective of his days in the sun, reciting a litany of names from the era. When he mentions the uniform numbers he wore, for example, he invokes the names of his predecessors.

"I wore number three with the Sox," he recalled. "That was Jimmie Foxx's number. When I went to Detroit, they gave me number eleven, which was Dizzy Trout's old number."

Dropo established career highs during his rookie season, although twelve more big league years were to follow. He led the league in RBIs with 144, drilled thirty-four home runs, batted .322, and scored 101 runs.

"They couldn't get me out the whole year," he said. "I was prepared mentally, physically, emotionally, every way. Nothing could bother me. They weren't going to get me out. I had Williams in front of me and [Vern] Stephens and [Bobby] Doerr in the middle of the order, so they couldn't really afford to pitch to me as though I was alone. The pitchers thought they had the

book on me, but they were wrong." Trying to pump fastballs by him didn't work.

A ballplayer's maiden home run is always a memorable event, as it was for Dropo on May 3, 1950. "I remember the day vividly," he recalled. "I hit it off Bob Feller at Fenway Park. It went into the nets above the left field wall...and while rounding the bases I said to myself, 'if I can hit Feller's fast ball, who do I have to worry about?' I *knew* I was a major leaguer."

Boston's ballpark was his favorite. "Fenway was cozy," he said. "You felt like you were in a real ballpark, not a concrete mausoleum like all those other stadiums. And you were close to the fans."

The righthanded-hitting Dropo was a mountain of a man. At sox-foot-five and 220 pounds, he was nicknamed "Moose," partly because of his size and partly because of his hometown of Moosup, Connecticut.

On June 8 he homered twice and knocked in seven runs against the St. Louis Browns. "We had a field day," he recalled. "We scored twenty-nine runs, a major league record."

A month later he started at first base for the American League in the All Star Game. "It was at Comiskey Park," said Dropo. "We lost, 3-2. What I remember most was Ted running into the wall on [Ralph] Kiner's drive. He fractured his elbow, but stayed in the game. His next time up he got a base hit. I'll never forget it." Nor will he forget the triple he laced to right center field off Don Newcombe in his first at bat.

Dropo topped off the year with therookie award. His thirty-four homers remain the ninth most ever hit by a rookie, while his 144 RBI are second only to Williams' rookie record of 145 in 1939.

Bob Mayer *lives in Westwood, New Jersey.*

Walt Dropo in 1953.

year later he was gone—traded to the Detroit Tigers on June 3, 1952, in one of those renowned multiplayer, "blockbuster" deals.

For Dropo it was the first of four trades. His take on all the deals is upbeat and philosophical. "You know, I always took it as a compliment. To me, it meant that these different ball clubs wanted me in their lineup." To Walt, baseball was a way of life. "No matter where they sent me I took it in stride. All I cared about was…'just let me play ball'."

On July 14 and 15, 1952, just six weeks after his arrival in Detroit, Dropo batted his way into the record book with an unparalleled display of hitting consistency. It began in a getaway game against the Yankees in New York when Walt went five-for-five.

"I don't think I had an extra-base hit," he recalled. "They were all singles. I remember I saw the ball well and stayed away from trying to pull and from going for the long ball. It was my first five-hit game and I was elated. And to come at Yankee Stadium made it extra special.

"The next day," he continued, "we had to play two at Griffith Stadium in Washington. I was hoping my stroke would hold up."

In the first game, facing Walter Masterson of the Senators, Dropo went four-for-four. "I had three singles and a double," he said. "But they beat us."

Heading into Game 2 of the doubleheader, he was nine-for-nine. "Now I'm in a zone," he remembers. "There's nothing else in the world but the ball; when they throw it up there, you know you're going to hit it. Nobody understands what the zone is unless they're in

"I was elated to put up those numbers," he says, "but I was realistic enough to know that I couldn't burn up the league like that every year. If Ted Williams and Joe DiMaggio couldn't do it…who am I?"

Indeed, his productivity took a dramatic turn in '51. He managed only eleven home runs and batted .239. A it. You're unencumbered by any other outside influence. That's the zone. A great place to be.

"When they told me I was approaching the record," he said, "I decided I'd just keep whaling away because I was still in the zone. They weren't going to stop me."

Dropo hit safely his first three times up in the second game. He was now an incredible twelve-for-twelve, tying the record established in 1938 by Pinky Higgins of the Red Sox, whose streak of hits was interrupted twice by bases on balls.

Walt remembers waiting for a "perfect pitch" against reliever Lou Sleater, a lefthander. "He threw me a fast ball, but I waited on the ball too long and I popped it up. The catcher, Mickey Grasso, caught it. The streak was over, but I got two more hits after that. They told me I had the record…fourteen hits in three games."

For Dropo, 1952 was a bounce-back year. He stroked twenty-nine homers and had ninety-seven RBIs, a dramatic return to form. But Walt was unable to sustain a consistent stroke and played out the string with the White Sox, Reds, and Orioles before the ax fell in 1961. "I started fouling off pitches I used to kill," he said.

Dropo's last hurrah involved his fists and a rush of moral indignation, rather than his bat or glove. He was a major player in what was known simply as "the Melee," which erupted in Chicago on June 13, 1957. He was with the White Sox, in the on-deck circle. The Yankees were in town.

Dropo vividly recalls the incident. "Larry Doby was at the plate," he said. "Art Ditmar was pitching and, with two strikes, he walked toward Doby and called him a really ugly racial name. Larry swung at him and landed a haymaker, then they both went to the ground. I was closest to the action and tried to break them

apart, which I did with the help of some others. But Billy Martin, when he returned to second base, turned back to Doby and promised, 'We're not through with you' and used some more racial stuff. He wouldn't let it go and kept at it until Doby challenged him."

Both dugouts emptied. "The first guy I saw was Enos Slaughter and I said to myself, 'With him involved there'll be no more peacemaking.' So I grabbed him and hit him a shot in the head and I tore his uniform off. Hearing all those remarks about race brought me to the boiling point and I decided to make a stand and end it once and for all."

Slaughter's disheveled appearance was recorded in newspapers all over the country and made the centerfold of *Look* magazine. It would be one of baseball's classic pictures—one of its toughest competitors, the rough-and-tumble prototype, in shredded uniform, hat worn backwards, his bare chest exposed like a casualty of war.

"It was all about a principle that I was trying to prove," said Walt.

At age seventy-six, Dropo fittingly lives in a tall building overlooking Boston Harbor. Healthy and robust, he plays golf, dabbles in real estate, and keeps tabs on his son Jeff, who operates the family's interest in a fireworks business in Alabama.

He reflects on being a big leaguer. "It was my dream come true…to play in the majors with Ted Williams, who was my idol when I was growing up, and was the icon of hitting baseballs…and to be a teammate of his gave me a great thrill, obviously. I'll never forget what Ted once said to me one day during batting practice. 'Moose, not even Jesus Christ could get a fastball by me'."

So there!

Long before the days of the Bronx Zoo in Yankee Stadium, there was the Colts' corral in Chicago, starring manager Cap Anson and his .350-hitting shortstop, Bill Dahlen. While researching Connie Mack's time in Philadelphia, I came across the following evidence to support my thesis that there is nothing new in baseball:

From the Pittsburgh Press, *September 29, 1896.*

Cincinnati, O.—It remained for the last trip of the Chicago ball club to develop the worst quarrel that has been seen in a team for years. Dahlen and Anson had a falling out and one of the $10,000 beauties for the Chicago club was hustled out of his berth and put off a train in the wilds of Indiana last night, and left to make his way to a place of shelter as best he could.

The quarrel was over the most trivial affair imaginable, a sleeping car ticket. Dahlen had gone to bed without getting his berth ticket from Anson, having retired some time in advance of the other members of the team. When the conductor asked Dahlen for his ticket, the shortstop referred him to Anson.

"If he wants his ticket, let him come and get it," said Anson.

The man in blue clothes and silver buttons returned to Dahlen and told what Anson had said. Dahlen's reply was not couched in parliamentary language. But the import of it was that Mr. Dahlen had no present intention of getting up and asking for the little red cardboard.

—Norman Macht

The Queen of Diamonds

Bob Fulton

Back when John Kovalchick managed a semipro baseball team every bit as invincible as that era's New York Yankees, he hoped that one of his players would ultimately make the Hall of Fame.

One has, in a manner of speaking. But in a delicious twist of irony, the player whose name is now part of a special display at Cooperstown, New York, was not one of the standouts Kovalchick groomed for a major league career.

No, this player wore braids and a skirt during games and was hailed as "the prettiest first baseman in baseball." She was his daughter, Dorothy.

Dorothy Kovalchick was the most acclaimed member of a troupe that barnstormed through Pennsylvania during the 1940s, attracting overflow crowds. The team was based in the tiny coal-mining community of Sagamore, located about forty-five miles northeast of Pittsburgh, but its fame reached far beyond the borders of the state.

The "colorful Kovalchicks," as they were billed, drew national—even international—attention because of the only female member of the cast, a spunky teen-aged girl able to hold her own against hard-nosed men who toiled in the mines by day and played no-nonsense baseball in the evening.

"Other teams tried harder to get me out than the men," says Dorothy Kovalchick Roark, a retired real estate agent who now lives in West Monroe, Louisiana. "If a guy gave up a hit to a girl, well, you can imagine the razzing he took. Those teams played harder against

us because they didn't want the stigma of having lost to a team with a girl."

The Kovalchicks, notwithstanding the extra measure of motivation they provided the opposition, were rarely vanquished. John, an astute judge of talent, recruited some of the premier players in the area: Billy Hunter, who would spend twenty-one seasons in the major leagues as a shortstop, coach, and manager; Bud Souchock, an outfielder with three American League clubs during the 1940s and 1950s; and outfielder Alex Kvasnak, who played briefly with the 1942 Washington Senators.

Kovalchick did some of his best recruiting under his own roof. At times, five of the team's nine starters were family members. Besides managing, John would play at shortstop, third base, or behind the plate. He was joined in the lineup by three sons: Nick, a shortstop; Ed, a pitcher, and Johnny, who could catch and pitch. Dorothy was a fixture at first.

Her presence on the field was anything but a gimmick designed to attract crowds. She could play. Roark was such an accomplished first baseman that she signed with the Fort Wayne Daisies of the All-American Girls Professional Baseball League, the focus of Penny Marshall's 1992 movie, *A League of Their Own*.

It was Roark's experience in the AAGPBL that put her name on the wall of the Hall of Fame's museum as part of a Women in Baseball exhibit. She is included on a list of the nearly 600 women who played in the league during its twelve-year existence (1943-54). Roark also has her own file in the archives of the Hall's National Baseball Library, filled with articles and photographs chronicling her career. Heady stuff for someone raised

---

Bob Fulton *practically grew up at Pittsburgh's Forbes Field, where his father worked as an usher. He lives in Indiana, Pennsylvania.*

in a poor mining town where broken dreams darkened the landscape like so much coal dust.

The baseball career that landed Roark in Cooperstown began almost by accident in 1941, when she was fourteen.

"I was the scorekeeper for my dad's team," she recalls. "One day the team was practicing and he asked me to help out by shagging some flies. When he saw me in the outfield he said, 'My gosh, that's my ballplayer.' When I came in he asked me if I wanted to play an inning or two in a game."

Roark debuted as a right fielder, but her enthusiasm for the position quickly ebbed. When she complained about the lack of activity, Kovalchick switched his daughter to first base, even though she stood only five foot two.

By 1943 she was playing regularly. Fans flocked to see the Kovalchicks, especially the pigtailed teen-ager who was adept at handling both a glove and a bat. Soon enough, young Dorothy Kovalchick was attracting notice on a national scale.

A female reporter for the Seattle *Post-Intelligencer* wrote, "She is the prettiest first baseman in baseball and perhaps the only girl, playing for the Sagamore nine. She fields her position with the ease of a Gehrig or a [Rip] Collins. She hoists a regular Louisville Slugger and last year had an average of .240."

The All-American Girls—Photos of Roark appeared in *Life* and *Stars and Stripes*, the latter triggering a veritable avalanche of fan mail (and a handful of marriage proposals) from servicemen overseas. By then she was playing professionally, in the fledgling AAGPBL.

The women's league was founded by chewing gum magnate Philip K. Wrigley in response to manpower shortages caused by World War II. Military call-ups ravaged rosters on the major league level and forced many minor leagues to cease operations entirely. By creating the AAGPBL, Wrigley not only filled a void, he

Dorothy Kovalchick Roark

Dorothy preferred a 34-inch Louisville Slugger, and she wore men's size 2 spikes. She was the best bunter on the family team, and her father once put her in as a pinch hitter with the bases loaded to squeeze the winning run home. "I could bunt a ball anywhere my father signalled me to do so," she remembers.

filled ballparks that would otherwise have lain dormant. The Rockford (Illinois) Peaches, South Bend (Indiana) Blue Sox, Kenosha (Wisconsin) Belles, and Racine (Wisconsin) Comets formed the original lineup.

Fort Wayne entered the league in 1945 under the direction of manager Bill Wambsganss, who recorded the only unassisted triple play in World Series history as Cleveland's second baseman in 1920. One of Roark's teammates that year was outfielder Helen Callaghan St. Aubin, whose son, Kelly Candaele, filmed a documentary about the AAGPBL that served as the inspiration for *A League of Their Own*. Another son, Casey, spent nine seasons in the majors as an infielder.

Players received between $75 and $125 a week in 1945 (as a rookie, Roark earned the minimum), with their teams furnishing room and board. The AAGPBL took steps to ensure that its star attractions projected a ladylike image at all times: Wearing shorts or slacks was prohibited, as was smoking or drinking in public. What's more, attendance was compulsory at a league-sponsored charm school, where the curriculum consisted of lessons on how properly to sit, walk, talk, and apply makeup, which the players were expected to wear during games.

"Oh, that was a must," Roark says. "You had to have lipstick, rouge, and eye pencil on. They wanted us to look feminine."

"The queen of the diamond"—Roark returned to Sagamore before the 1945 season ran its course. She was disenchanted, not with the league's emphasis on glamour, but with its modified rules: a slightly larger ball, shorter distances between the bases and between the mound and home plate, and a ban on overhand pitching, which was not lifted until 1948. Roark preferred regulation baseball, the kind she played back home. Besides, she missed the celebrity that came with playing for her father's team.

"This may sound self-centered, but I was queen of the diamond on the men's team," she recalls. "In the All-American League I kind of got lost in the shuffle. I was just one of the girls."

Roark clearly stood out on the Sagamore team, given her signature pigtails and unorthodox uniforms. Because she was allergic to wool—the material of choice in baseball uniforms of that era—Roark favored peasant blouses and tennis-style skirts. She even donned a satin uniform, with mortifying consequences.

"We were playing a night game and in the fifth inning came a downpour," Roark recalls. "It soaked me right through. Well, once it got wet, that uniform clung to me. You could see right through it. I was so embarrassed. I knocked in the winning run, I think in the tenth inning. But I never wore that uniform again."

Funny thing, that satin ensemble brought Roark good luck on an earlier occasion. She wore it at a Pittsburgh Pirates tryout in 1947 and performed so capably that the team offered her a minor league contract. The Pirates actually proposed a unique package deal involving Roark and her mother—one to play, the other to act as chaperone. But Anna Kovalchick refused to sign.

"She said, 'I saw my daughter play one game and I died a thousand deaths. I will never watch that child in another game.' She was so afraid that I'd get hurt," Roark recalls. "So she didn't sign the contract. I can remember it like it was yesterday. I was crying, saying, 'I want to go, I want to go.' But without my mother, they wouldn't take me."

Roark's career ended a year later when a wild left-hander plunked her with a pitch. She had put in parts of eight seasons with her father's team by then and drawn national attention to the colorful Kovalchicks and a speck on the map called Sagamore.

Today Roark's name is inscribed in an exhibit at Cooperstown, where baseball's greats are immortalized. Back when she was barnstorming with her family, neither Roark nor her father could have envisioned her winding up in the hallowed halls of Cooperstown.

"This is the absolute truth: My greatest pleasure and my greatest joy is not the fact that I'm realizing my dream. It's the fact that I'm realizing my father's dream," Roark says. "He always hoped to send someone to the Hall of Fame. Who knew it was going to be me?"

Dorothy Kovalchick Roark

"The Kovalchicks" before a game at Adrian, Pennsylvania, just after Dorothy returned home from the AAGPBL. She singled and stole second, third, and home. Her father, "Bounce," is at the far left of the front row. Brother Nick is at the far right, next to his sister. Brother Johnny is fifth from the right in the back row, and Brother Ed stands behind Nick.

Bert Shepard

Joe Naiman

Bert Shepard, the only one-legged player ever to appear in a major league game, lost his right leg below the knee after he was shot down during World War II. Shepard was flying a P-38 for the United States Army Air Corps in England, where he was also the manager of a service baseball team. He was planning to pitch in a game after he got back from his mission over Germany.

Flying low, Shepard was hit in the leg by enemy ground fire. He was able to radio that he was wounded, then was hit on the chin and lost consciousness. He woke up in a German hospital with his leg amputated and a plate in his head. He didn't learn many of the details until a few years ago, when an Englishman on a hunting trip in Hungary encountered an Austrian, Dr. Loidl, who had been in the German medical corps. The doctor wanted to know what happened to the American pilot on whom he had operated during World War II. The Englishman managed to find the Bert Shepard who had been shot down while flyng a P-38.

"From then on my whole life has changed," says Shepard, who didn't even know how he ended up in the German hospital until he visited Europe to meet his rescuer. Dr. Loidl told him that he had been called to the wreck, where he found civilian farmers menacing the unconscious pilot with pitchforks. Loidl drew his Luger and chased them away before easing Shepard out of the cockpit. Loidl also arranged for Shepard to be properly treated, pulling strings to force the German hospital to take a P-38 pilot. Loidl then had to explain to the Gestapo why he saved an American. The

doctor responded that being injured and being a human being was enough to merit being saved.

"It was a great reunion to meet the doctor who had saved my life," said Shepard.

Dr. Loidl's wife had made a dress out of Shepard's parachute, which Loidl had taken.

Shepard's trip also involved a visit to the town in which he crashed, a town with one street and about a hundred people. Two ladies who had been teenagers during the war remembered the crash and showed Bert the site.

On the last night of the trip Loidl gave Shepard a hug. To Shepard it was a strange feeling. Those were the same two arms which had taken him out of the cockpit decades before. "To go see the doctor and thank him was the most wonderful thing that could ever happen to me."

Shepard's leg was amputated eleven inches below the knee. He became a prisoner of war, which acquainted him with German interrogator Hans Scharff. Scharff, who later lived in Tehachapi, California, and kept in touch with Shepard, died about two months before Shepard received the letter about Dr. Loidl's inquiry.

Scharff helped a number of American prisoners. Five other P-38 pilots had been shot down that day, and they faced trial for "dirty strafing" which had been committed by another P-38. Scharff determined that the five pilots were not guilty and saved them from a firing squad.

In September, 1944, Shepard was exchanged and admitted to Walter Reed Hospital. During his stay Secretary of War Robert P. Patterson visited the hospital

Joe Naiman *is secretary of the Ted Williams chapter of SABR. He is a freelance writer and lives in Lakeside, California.*

and asked former POWs what they would like to do.

"I said, 'If I can't fly combat in the South Pacific, I'd like to play baseball'," says Shepard.

Patterson called Clark Griffith, who was hard-pressed to turn down a Cabinet member. Griffith told Patterson to have Shepard come out when he was ready.

Baseball—Shepard was fitted with an artificial leg on March 10, 1945. He worked out behind the hospital, practicing his pivots. Four days after Shepard received his artificial leg a Washington sportswriter took him to the Senators' training camp. He pitched batting practice and attracted the attention of one of the other sportswriters.

"From the publicity Clark Griffith had to think: 'This is a pretty good thing. I better hang onto it'," remembers Shepard.

During 1945, each American League team played a National League team in an exhibition game to raise money for the war effort. Shepard started in the game against Brooklyn and shut the Dodgers out for three innings. He allowed two runs in the fourth inning, but left with a 4-2 lead.

Later in the season manager Ossie Bluege put Shepard on the mound against the Red Sox with the bases loaded and two out. George Metkovich took Shepard to a full count before Bert whiffed him. Shepard pitched five more innings, allowing only one run on three hits.

Shepard knew his career was limited. The Senators were in a pennant race. "It's hard for a manager to realize that his best chance of winning today is a guy with a leg off," he says. Shepard and his teammates were ready to board the train to Detroit for a playoff until Hank Greenberg's grand slam gave the Tigers the 1945 AL pennant.

Shepard had the chance to meet Bluege's former teammate, Walter Johnson. He also met Ty Cobb, George Sisler, and Connie Mack. "That's something I will always remember," Shepard said. "I think that's great about baseball. A person gets their heroes and they stay with them the rest of their life."

Shepard's Senators teammates included George Case, Joe Kuhel, Buddy Lewis, and Cecil Travis. Travis had also sacrificed a promising baseball career to the war; he suffered frostbite at the Battle of the Bulge.

Lewis had flown in India. Shepard told a story of Lewis's first game back, in which umpire Bill McGowan called some pitches over the plate as balls so that Lewis would have an enjoyable first at-bat.

Shepard spent the winter on an all-star team which faced a black all-star team. He lost a 1-0 game in Canada but faced the same team two weeks later in North Dakota. Having trouble hitting Shepard, the team tried bunting against him, but Shepard had ten assists.

When the prewar players returned to the Senators, Shepard was dropped from the big league roster. He was a coach until the middle of the season, when he resumed his minor league career at Chattanooga.

At the end of the 1946 season, Shepard barnstormed with an all-star team. When it faced Bob Feller's all-stars Shepard played first and went one-for-two against both Feller and Johnny Sain. In Yakima, Washington, Shepard struck out Bob Lemon three times, giving Lemon cause to think about becoming a pitcher. "Bob gives me credit for making a pitcher out of him," says Shepard. Stan Musial went oh-for-four against him.

Shepard notes that he could compete with two-legged players because his amputation was below the knee (Monty Stratton's was above the knee), and because the right leg of a lefthander isn't the "push-off" leg. "I wouldn't get out on the field if I couldn't do everything the other person could."

He was fired as manager of the St. Augustine, Florida, team in 1947 because he supported his players. The team was tired and Shepard refused to conduct a public practice which the owners had hoped would provide hometown support. "I was never a stooge for the owners."

Shepard also managed in Waterbury, Connecticut, in 1949, playing some first base and the outfield. He had four home runs and five stolen bases. "I have an advantage stealing bases. Nobody expects me to run. I could take a bigger lead and I could leave a little earlier. Take advantage of your weaknesses." Shepard also beat out a couple of bunts that year.

Shepard has great respect for another baseball figure who lost a leg during World War II. "The best owner in baseball was Bill Veeck," said Shepard, basing his opinion on Veeck's accessibility to the fans, including keeping his office open throughout the day. "It's a shame we don't have more like him."

Lester Rodney, the Daily Worker, and the Integration of Baseball

Tom Gallagher

The whole history leading up to Jackie Robinson has usually been that an electric light went on in the head of the noble Branch Rickey one morning and he ended baseball discrimination." As the lean, white-haired Lester Rodney speaks in his living room in Rossmoor, the sprawling retirement community across the bay from San Francisco, these events are now nearly half a century and three thousand miles removed. Important details now seem in danger of being lost forever.

Given the power of the pen Rodney once wielded and its influence on baseball's integration, the former *Daily Worker* sportswriter might well have written the history himself. But everything in life—no matter how long a life it may be—is a matter of priorities, and in recent years Rodney has switched his from writing about sports to playing them. Had he taken the time to write the book, he might not have stayed in such extraordinary shape and might never have become the first top-ranked tennis player in California's eighty-five-and-over bracket. So, for now, an important chapter in the story is known mostly to those who know Rodney—and who happen to ask.

Although he scoffs at the notion that Brooklyn's "Great Mahatma" acted alone, Rodney doesn't mean to minimize the credit due the Dodgers president. Some club owner actually had to put a black ballplayer into a major league uniform and Rickey acted while the others mumbled. It's just that he knows there were a lot of other people generating the electricity that finally turned on that light.

Tom Gallagher *has been a Socialist all of his adult life and a Dodger fan longer than that. He lives in San Francisco.*

"A Communist sportswriter"—Not the least of them was Rodney himself. By the time Robinson took his position at first base in Ebbets Field on April 15, 1947, more than a decade had passed since Rodney first took up the cause of integrating baseball as sports editor of the Communist Party's New York *Daily Worker.*

Today the concept of a "Communist sportswriter" seems a strange proposition. In Rodney's day it was not quite so exotic, but still no one would confuse the *Daily Worker*'s sports department with the "toy department" of any other newspaper. By tradition, the sportswriter's job is merely to interpret the world of sports; the Communist sportswriter's job was to change it.

The first thing Rodney tried to change was what *The Sporting News* in 1923 called baseball's "tacit understanding that a player of Ethiopian descent is ineligible." In one respect, the cause was a natural for a group that considered itself "the Party of Negro and White." After all, the Communists had distinguished themselves in defense of the nine black "Scottsboro Boys" charged with the 1931 rape of two white women in Alabama—a cause few others would touch.

The basics of baseball's integration story are, of course, familiar to baseball fans: Rickey signed Jackie Robinson, whose athletic achievements had already prompted one sportswriter to call him the "Jim Thorpe of his race,"and took him from the Kansas City Monarchs of the Negro American League. He sent him out for a season of minor league ball in Montreal and finally put him in Ebbets Field the following year. But, until the 1995 publication of David Falkner's *Great Time Coming: The Life Of Jackie Robinson From Baseball To Birmingham,* no mainstream publication had ever provided any detail of how in 1936 "the *Daily Worker* began a steady and unremitting campaign for integration… spearheaded by sports writer and editor Lester Rodney," or noted that it was not even until "A year or so after the 'Worker' began its push," that "the Pittsburgh *Courier*, the most widely circulated Negro weekly in the nation, initiated its own campaign."

Digging out the story—Rodney's method was quite simple. He would ask questions other writers wouldn't or couldn't. The first goal was to locate the exact whereabouts of *The Sporting News*'s "tacit understanding." He recalls, "First we'd go to the top officials and they'd say, 'There's nothing written, it's up to the club owners.' We'd go to the owners and they'd say, 'My heart is with you but the players would never stand for it.' Then you go to the players and shoot that down."

A typical July 19, 1939, *Worker* story, "Big Leaguers Rip Jim Crow," quoted members of the Cincinnati Reds. (The franchise often found its fate intertwined with that of Rodney's party. According to one team historian, each "crisis in affairs between the United States and Soviet Russia" brought new demands "that the management change the team's name" despite the fact that "the Reds have been the Reds since 1869, one year before Nicolai Lenin was born and ten years before Stalin's birthday.") Manager Bill McKechnie claimed, "I'd use negroes if I were given permission." Bucky Walters declared them "some of the best players I've ever seen," and Johnny VanderMeer concluded, "I don't see why they're banned." "Sensational stuff in 1939," Rodney remembers.

Two seasons earlier he'd published an interview with Satchel Paige, the most famous Negro League star. Rodney recalls, "At the end of the interview I said to Paige that Dazzy Vance came to the Dodgers at twenty-nine years of age, which was old for a ballplayer, but that when he was thirty-three he won twenty-eight games. Paige, who was then thirty himself, says, 'I don't think they can keep us out three more years.' But he was wrong. He had to wait another eleven years. Very tragic and it bothers me that Paige is always portrayed as an egocentric guy, content to be a big fish in a small pond. It's absolutely false." (Joe DiMaggio once told the *Daily Worker* that Paige, whom he'd played against in postseason exhibitions was, "the best pitcher I ever faced," but Paige ultimately became the first player elected to the Baseball Hall of Fame primarily on the basis of his Negro League career.)

Campaigning—In 1941, Rodney and his confederates stepped up the campaign, sending telegrams to all major league team owners asking them to try out black players. "The only fully positive response we got was from William Benswanger of the Pittsburgh Pirates. The next spring we arranged a tryout for Roy

Campanella—who was about twenty-one then—and two other players. And then Benswanger came under intense pressure—I've never known the exact nature—not to hold the tryouts, and he backed out as gracefully as he could.

"I never slammed him for it, because he was the first honest guy who answered, 'You're right and I'm willing to give it a try.' And then he came under all that pressure. So that was the first tryout that never happened.

"Imagine how baseball history would have been changed if Benswanger had told all the other owners to go f--- themselves and hired Campanella, Satchel Paige, and maybe three other players from the [Negro National League] Homestead Grays who were the best team in baseball and played in Pittsburgh. Pittsburgh was the heart of black baseball then. The Pirates would immediately have won five straight pennants."

Invisible Men, Donn Rogosin's 1983 history of the Negro Leagues, is fairly typical of the short shrift usually accorded the Communists' efforts, dismissing the Benswanger affair as a "nonexistent tryout," and concluding that "the black players and the black press were unimpressed by the Communist campaigns."

The Communists, however, clearly impressed at least one black player: Roy Campanella's 1952 autobiography acknowledges that the *Daily Worker* had "pounded hard and unceasingly against the color line in organized ball." What makes this recognition particularly compelling is the fact that the book's author, New York *Daily News* sportswriter Dick Young, was known neither for left-wing sympathies nor graciousness. The Hall of Fame catcher himself insisted on it.

According to Rodney, "Campanella believed that baseball was the most important reason why the Supreme Court struck down segregation in 1954. When I heard that I said, 'Come on, Roy, what are you talking about?' Campy said, 'All I know is that the ballclubs going down south traveling together, playing together, living together, were the first all the time. They were the first in hotels; they were the first in trains. Don't tell me it wasn't the most important thing.'

At first Campanella's conclusion may seem that of a man overestimating the significance of his own corner of the world. But the record shows that Birmingham, Alabama, actually ended its prohibition of interracial sports a month before the Court ordered its schools desegregated in the landmark Brown versus the Board of Education decision. The reason? To allow Campy, Jackie, and the rest of the Dodgers to play a spring training exhibition game there.

And a letter to the August 20, 1939, *Daily Worker* appears to give the lie to the alleged indifference of black sportswriters. The letter-writer takes the "opportunity to congratulate you and the *Daily Worker* for the way you have joined with us in the current series concerning Negro Players in the major leagues, as well as all your past great efforts in this aspect," and goes on to express the hope of further collaboration. The author was Wendell Smith, sports editor of the Pittsburgh *Courier*, a black newspaper whose nationwide readership would exceed 400,000 in the following decade.

"You know, Jules Tygiel's book [*Baseball's Great Experiment: Jackie Robinson and His Legacy*] was the first to acknowledge our efforts and that wasn't until 1983," Rodney recalls. "In that Ken Burns series [the nine-part 1994 Public Broadcasting System documentary of baseball history] it mentions that [manager] Leo Durocher told a sportswriter he would use some of the great Negroes in a minute on the Dodgers if he were given permission. I'm the sportswriter he told that to. Burns, of course, had a big corporate-funded series and he did manage to push the role of the Negro to the center, as he did with his Civil War series. But even PBS is not so radical on these things," he adds with a grin, "as you can tell by how many radicals you'll see on the McNeil-Lehrer news hour. So you can't fault Burns for not mentioning the *Daily Worker*."

Starting a career—It's probably less accurate to say that Rodney and the integration campaign—eventually including "End Jim Crow in Baseball" petitions with two million signatures gathered by the Young Communist League and labor organizations like the National Maritime Union—were written out of history than that they were just never written into it in the first place, although David Falkner's recent book noted how "remarkable was the passion and the insistence of the campaign which was generally lost on white America—though not on those in government who were always vigilant on the twin menaces of Communist agitation and black unrest."

Foremost among the vigilant was FBI director J. Edgar Hoover, who singled Rodney out for individual mention in *Masters of Deceit*, the central text of anticommunism. "We're sort of considered folk heroes by many young people now, but things like that created problems for our children in high school in the 1950s," Rodney says today.

Rodney himself was no Red Diaper Baby. He recalls his Republican father displaying a window sign in their Brooklyn house mourning the death of President Warren G. Harding in 1923. But then "in 1931 or '32—during the depression—three of us rented a cold water flat on McDougal Street in Greenwich Village—ten dollars a month. We were there for the Bohemian atmosphere, the cellar clubs, poetry readings. We were poor as hell, but we didn't know it.

"I wrote some pulp magazine stuff to pay the rent—cheap romances, love stories, just junk. Then we all did our creative writing and critiqued each other. We sold a few stories; I don't even have them anymore. It all got lost or thrown out when I went into the Army. It was just about life and the torments of youth. It was a very heady New York, Greenwich Villagey atmosphere; the cafeterias were humming with literary discussions and the Communists at that time were impinging on everybody's consciousness."

Bohemianism never dulled Rodney's interest in sports, so one thing that was clear to him about the Communists was that when they addressed sports it was an embarrassment. When he told them so in a letter to the *Worker*, he was invited in to discuss it and he wound up doing the occasional weekly piece—gratis. By 1936, the Communists were eager to shed sinister or foreign identifications in the public mind and entered their "Popular Front" period. "Communism Is Twentieth Century Americanism" replaced "Towards Soviet America" as the party's slogan. The *Daily Worker* wondered whether it should now deal with popular concerns like sports on a more regular basis. When a readers poll came back 6-1 in favor of daily sports coverage, the paper asked Rodney to take it on.

Of course, since this was the Communist party's newspaper, the question would not be settled as simply as that. There were those who thought the paper should cover "people's sports" like soccer, not "corporate sports" like baseball. But once the paper decided that a commitment to "Twentieth Century Americanism" required coverage of the national pastime, that coverage would be activist.

It must be noted that even if Ken Burns did not give Rodney his due, Leo Durocher did. In his 1993 book, *The Era 1947-1957: When the Yankees, the Giants and the Dodgers Ruled the World*, Roger Kahn quotes Durocher telling Rodney, "For a f----- Communist, you know your baseball."

"I was a fan," Rodney reiterates today. "That's crucial. They couldn't have hired just an ideologue to run the campaign. You had to know baseball."

Innovations—The integration campaign was not the limit of the *Worker*'s innovative baseball coverage. By 1938 the Americanization of the party had progressed sufficiently to allow it to engage New York Yankee third baseman Red (hair, not politics) Rolfe to cover the World Series from a player's point of view.

"I'd go up to Yankee Stadium after a World Series game and I'd jump in the locker room," Rodney remembers. "I'm in a hurry. Our deadline is the earliest of any of the papers and so I'd try to speed things up. I'd say, 'Red, that was pretty much a key moment when Crosetti decided to go to third instead of going for the doubleplay' and he'd say, 'No'—you couldn't speed him up—'No, no, no. I wouldn't say that at all.' And he painstakingly would go into his own view of the game. This guy was a Dartmouth College graduate. He had just got married and wanted to show his wife that he was more than just a jock. That's why he agreed to do it for the nominal payment we could afford. He took great pride in these things."

Rodney once introduced heavyweight champion Joe Louis to novelist Richard Wright, author of *Native Son*. "Joe Louis was training at Pompton Lakes, New Jersey. Sportswriters were invited to go to these things as part of the prefight publicity, so I told them I had a guest along, a rather well-known writer. Louis and Wright had about twenty minutes alone. Apparently Louis had once seen a collection of Wright's stories, so he knew about him. Richard told me on the way back that although Joe wasn't formally educated he was no fool, and that they'd had a fascinating discussion."

Since Rodney usually operated as a one-man sports section it might take him a while to get to every sport, but there wasn't much he missed. Given that more than three out of every four current National Basketball Association players are black, it will surprise some to know that there ever could have been an issue about letting blacks play the professional game, but there was. And the *Worker* was in the middle of it.

"Joe Lapchick, who was the center on the original Celtics, coached the Knickerbockers, the first New York professional team, and his son Richard later told me that his father, a devout Catholic, said 'That damned *Daily Worker* has done more good helping me to get Sweetwater Clifton [the team's first black player] on the Knicks.' This came after Jackie Robinson and it just flowed out of it. There was no big fuss about it. We wrote about it, but not in a scolding way as if the Knicks were the only sinners. There was actually more work done on basketball integration in Boston [where the Celtics signed the first black NBA players] than in New York."

Religion and tennis—It's over forty years now since Rodney left the Communist Party following publication of Soviet premier Nikita Khrushchev's speech in 1956 denouncing Joseph Stalin. While Rodney may now think of himself and his comrades as having been "rigid simpletons" back then, he has never renounced the goal of social equality that led him to join. Nor does he have any difficulty finding political relevance in events of half a century ago. He gladly explains his belief that Brooklyn Dodger shortstop Pee Wee Reese articulated the principles behind affirmative action years before anyone had given the theory a name.

"In 1947, when Jackie Robinson had first come up he was taking a lot of punishment because he had promised Rickey not to fight back, no matter what. And the bad guys were taking advantage of him. Enos Slaughter of the Cardinals came down on his heel at first base. Another time some little-known shortstop for the Chicago Cubs pretended that Robinson had done something wrong sliding into second and jumped on top of him and began pummeling him and Robinson lay there until the umpires came and pushed the shortstop off. We sportswriters spent time in the dugout before games and knew some of the white players on the Dodgers were troubled by what was happening. The discussions would go something like this: 'Democracy means that everybody's the same, so you treat everybody the same, so that means we don't do anything special. You treat Jackie the same way as anybody.'

"Pee Wee cut a layer deeper and he scratched his Kentucky head and he said, 'Yeah, democracy means everybody is the same, but things aren't the same for Jackie because he's the only colored guy and he's catching special hell because of that, so maybe there's a way we can make things the same for him.' If that isn't affirmative action! Here's a baseball player saying this. That's the special contribution of Pee Wee Reese."

When Rodney moved to Los Angeles in 1958—coincidentally the same year Walter O'Malley turned Pee Wee and the rest of the Trolley Dodgers into Freeway Dodgers—he continued in journalism, eventually becoming religion editor of the Long Beach *Press Telegram*, a Knight-Ridder paper.

"How did I become religion editor? How does the real world work? The managing editor is unhappy with the religion pages and comes into the press room and says, 'One of you guys has got to be able to do a better job. Rodney—you!' I found it quite interesting; it was the time of the ecumenical movement. I was actually cited by the National Council of Churches for my coverage of churches and the Vietnam War."

But unusual as that particular turn in his life was, his 1975 retirement from the *Press Telegram* gave him the time to do something even more remarkable—to pursue the second career in sports that caused a local newspaper to dub him the "George Burns of tennis." He joined the senior circuit at age sixty-five with mixed results, but reached number seven ranking in Southern California in the seventy-plus bracket. From then on he has outlasted—or maybe outlived—the opposition. At age seventy-nine, Rodney and his wife Clare moved north to be closer to their children, but he still teamed with a southern partner to become the top-ranked doubles combination in Southern California in the eighty-plus category. In singles, he reached as high as number two statewide and number six nationally.

Rodney still keeps his hand in journalism with the occasional article for the weekly Rossmoor *News*. In a 1995 piece he explained the secret of his tennis success: a player's best chance for attaining high ranking in any five-year age bracket comes in the first year when he is still relatively "young," and he predicted that "come 1996 yours truly will magically metamorphose from a tired old eighty-four to a frisky young eighty-five." And sure enough, after winning his first two singles tournaments Rodney finally achieved the number one spot—at age eighty-five.

The Forgotten War

Bob Bailey

War between baseball leagues has broken out on many occasions. Today we might characterize "baseball war" as fierce, all-out competition between rival baseball organizations for the economic upper hand. From the stealth campaign of William Hulbert in 1875-1876 to form the National League at the expense of the National Association to the *sitzkrieg* of the Continental League in the early 1960s, baseball wars have dotted the history of the major leagues.

This is the tale of the battles between the American Association and the National League in 1891 that led to the amalgamation of the two leagues into the twelve-team "Big League" in 1892. It is a story that has gotten lost in the backwash of the more famous 1890 Players' League "Brotherhood War." It is barely mentioned in most baseball histories and was totally ignored in the most recent A. G. Spalding biography. It was a small war, seriously violent only at the end. If the Brotherhood War with the Players' League in 1890 and the battle royal between the American League and the National League in 1901-1903 were the baseball equivalent of the Civil War or World War II, then the AA-NL action of 1891 might be compared to the Spanish-American War in scope and fierceness: smaller scale, relatively quick, and not changing the local landscape radically.

The relationship between the American Association and the National League went back to 1882 when the AA was founded to be a direct competitor of the estab-lished league. Formed primarily by western backers, it offered Sunday games, beer at the park, and pricing below that offered by the National League. The two circuits banged heads for a season, then entered into an alliance. The National Agreement of 1883 called for cooperation in scheduling, respect for each other's contracts, and peaceful resolution of disputes. It was essentially an economic settlement that divided territory, protected clubs' investment in players, and undermined the players' ability to play off one league against the other—your basic robber-baron agreement.

The National Agreement functioned relatively well during the 1880s as the established leagues brushed aside a challenge from the Union Association in 1884, and effectively dealt with players' rising economic discontent through the remainder of the decade. The NL always seemed to hold the upper hand, though. During the 1884 battle with the Unions, the NL induced the AA to expand from eight teams to twelve as the NL stood pat. This added such marginal locations as Toledo and Indianapolis to the AA map. The NL was denying the Unions access to certain territories on the American Association's nickel.

When the Players' League made its serious run at establishing a rival organization, the National League again took control of the battle with veteran executive Al Spalding as commanding general. In the process, the NL grabbed the AA franchises in Brooklyn and Cincinnati and left the Association to fill in with such nineteenth-century baseball backwaters as Rochester and Syracuse. The AA made a loud but brief squawk and focused on the immediate battle with the PL.

Bob Bailey *is a frequent contributor to SABR publications. He writes about baseball because he can't hit one. He is currently researching the history of the Dixie Stars.*

The Brotherhood settlement—After the brutal three-league 1890 season, it was obvious to all sides that none of the leagues could stand another season of ruinous competition. All sides had lost money, and the AA and NL had lost control of a sizable number of star players. The press reported through the final months of 1890 that the Players' League intended to take the field again in 1891. Behind the scenes, though, representatives of all three leagues were privately discussing what could be done to avoid another season of strife. A number of the Players' League backers were looking to cut their losses and get out of the baseball business. Others had designs on NL franchises. In Brooklyn, where three teams—the NL Brooklyn team that moved from the AA after the 1889 season, the Players' League aggregation and a sorry new squad slapped together by the AA—vied for the borough's patrons in 1890, there were talks between the Brooklyn NL owners and the Players' League Brooklyn contingent about merging operations. Al Johnson of the Cleveland Players' League club was angling to recoup his loss from the 1890 season. As a major financial backer of the PL, he was disliked by the NL owners and he knew that he was unlikely to be the beneficiary of any accommodation made to PL interest. Johnson, from a politically potent Ohio family, acquired the AA Cincinnati franchise as leverage in future dealings.

In the end, Spalding outmaneuvered the Players' League backers, and only the NL and AA were left standing in a pool of blood in the form of red ink all over every team's ledgers. The peace agreement was not, however, an unconditional surrender. Several Players' League owners were brought into the older leagues. Franchises were shuffled a bit as the AA received the right to compete with the NL in Chicago and Boston, and the victorious leagues agreed to buy out the weak franchises in Toledo, Columbus, Rochester, and Syracuse. The only real losers in the deal were—surprise!—the players. One of the items agreed to in the new National Agreement was that all players who jumped to the Players' League would revert to the teams they had played for in 1889.

Control of player contracts was at the heart of the baseball war. The return to the *status quo ante* was a natural result. The Chicago *Tribune* reported on January 17, 1891, that the Players' League "agrees to return to their respective clubs all the league players now under contract or held by them." This really meant that with the demise of the rebel league, the players would not be free to sell their services on the open market. The return of players was the key demand of the American Association. It appeared that the peace accord would allow the 1891 season to open in relative harmony.

Maneuvering for position—The kettle that would boil over into the next war began to bubble within a week. It was discovered that the old Athletic club of the American Association had not reserved any players with the Association office. This was natural enough as the franchise had collapsed during the 1890 season and was taken over by the league. This same situation faced the National League's Cincinnati franchise. In this situation of uncertainty, the National League club in Boston signed fleet outfielder Harry Stovey and the Pittsburgh League club signed second baseman Louis Bierbauer, both late of the AA Athletics. National League owners, even after the catostrophic battle with the Players' League, saw no reason not to take advantage of a family problem.

Reading the news reports of the day it appears clear that the intent of the peace agreement was to have all players from the Players' League return to the clubs they played for in 1889. But the actual wording of the National Agreement referred to players under contract or under reservation by the respective clubs. The issue went before the National Board, a three-man body set up to hear contract disputes among the clubs. The members of the Board were American Association president Allen Thurman, a board member of the Association's Columbus club; John Rogers, owner of the National League's Philadelphia operation, and Louis Krauthoff, president of the minor league Western Association's Kansas City club.

The National Board met in New York on February 13, 1891, to begin hearings on disputed player claims. There were several disputes, but the Stovey and Bierbauer cases were clearly the key tests. The Board issued its ruling on February 14, granting Bierbauer to Pittsburgh and Stovey to Boston. The National League had prevailed. The Board's decision stated, "Undoubtedly the Pittsburg club has the legal right to the man [Bierbauer] but morally it has not. It ought to withdraw its claim, but as it does not, we must reluctantly decide in favor of Pittsburg." The same reasoning applied to the Stovey claim. The Board's decision was technically correct, but went counter to the intent of the owner's earlier agreement.

The National Board vote was, as expected, two to one. The composition of the vote shocked Association interests, because Thurman sided with the National League. This set off an explosion. Bill Barnie of Baltimore and Art Irwin of Boston were in full howl. They could not understand how the AA president could vote against their league's interests. The board of Thurman's own Columbus club had similar misgivings. Newspapers in Cincinnati and St. Louis labeled Thurman a "tool of Spalding."

There might be some truth to this accusation. Thurman held a private conference with Spalding in Chicago two days before the National Board hearing. Both men stated that they met to discuss the American

Association placing a team in Chicago, but that had been settled in January. When the press went looking for Spalding's reaction to the abuse that was heaped upon Thurman following the decision, they found him huddled with the Ohioan in Spalding's hotel room. Neither of these incidents prooved any skullduggery on the two gentlemen's part, but it looked suspicious.

War—The American Association met five days after the Bierbauer-Stovey decisions, removed Thurman from the presidency, and formally withdrew from the new, month-old National Agreement. The war was on. The AA gave the Bierbauer-Stovey decision as the reason. The NL countered that the AA always wanted out as a way to bring Cincinnati into the Association. Neither organization was completely truthful.

The Bierbauer-Stovey loss was the proximal cause of the split, but the rift already existed. The NL had agreed to put AA teams in Boston and Chicago prior to the January 14 meeting. The AA agreed to the deal thinking the NL representatives (which included Spalding) were authorized to speak for the NL. When the Boston NL ownership objected, the NL wanted to take the Boston part of the deal off the table and leave the rest in place. St. Louis owner Chris Von der Ahe fumed, "They [the NL] are trying to give us another deal and we won't stand it. The Association has been playing second fiddle to the League long enough, and its high time that we...declared ourselves. We came here expecting to be treated fairly, and now the League men are playing their old game." The New York *Times* baseball reporter had much the same sense as he discussed the agreement to let the AA into Boston and Chicago, "At the time the [National] League was in a bad condition and made all sorts of promises, but today it is on top and shows a tendency to ignore the Association."

The Association chose Louis Kramer as their war president. Kramer, a Cincinnati native and lawyer, had been on the board of the Association's Cincinnati club in the 1880s, and served as the club's attorney for several years. Kramer and the AA placed new teams in Cincinnati, Boston, Philadelphia, and Washington to go head-to-head with the NL. The Cincinnati club landed King Kelly as player-manager, and hopes were high that the Association could continue to challenge the National League. But Kramer wasn't the kind of aggressive leader that the AA's circumstances demanded. He ran a quiet war with the National League. There was competition among the cities that had two teams, there was some player raiding, but by and large the battle was on the playing field.

The first evidence of a break in the war came in Cincinnati. The NL entry was operated by John Brush, a department store magnate from Indianapolis. Brush and the National League had earlier acquired Al

Johnson's AA Cincinnati rights and shut down the potential rival club. Brush would later move on to own and operate the New York Giants, but now he was the new owner of the Cincinnati Reds and was not doing well due to competition from a hastily assembled replacement American Association Cincinnati club. Near the end of July Brush approached his opponents with an offer to buy them out. The offer was refused, but other Association owners were starting to look for ways to cut their losses. Only Von der Ahe of St. Louis and Von der Horst of Baltimore were for holding fast.

For the next few weeks rumors continued to fly that Cincinnati or Louisville would move to Indianapolis. Cincinnati continued to draw poorly. Boston manager Art Irwin, during a visit to the Queen City ballpark, commented, "there are not enough people here to hiss the umpire."

Hardball—In mid-August the Cincinnati franchise died of natural causes: no money. The Association awarded a new franchise to Milwaukee and transferred crowd-pleasing Mike Kelly to his hometown of Boston. The evacuation of Cincinnati removed a point of contention between the National League and the American Association, and sensing that the AA might be in enough trouble to consider some type of accommodation, the NL requested a peace conference. The Association accepted, on the assurance that there would be no player raids during the negotiations. The two factions met in Washington on August 25, and on the evening of the first round of meetings the Boston National League club announced the signing of Mike Kelly away from the AA's Boston team.

Phelps—There was blood on the moon from that moment on. The AA withdrew from the peace talks. President Kramer, who apparently had no stomach for a real fight, resigned. The AA selected Louisville attorney Zach Phelps as the new president. He had served in that position during the 1890 Brotherhood War, was the former president of the Louisville franchise, and was the American Association's lawyer. He was also a savvy, well-connected politician who had no qualms about getting into a high stakes game with the National League.

Two days after the Kelly signing Phelps announced that the Association would place a team in Chicago in 1892 and would actively attempt to sign NL players in the off-season. The NL was in for a more active war than that waged by Kramer. Phelps began looking for ways to attack the older league with the limited resources the Association possessed.

Meanwhile, the NL had an outbreak of internecine warfare. The 1891 pennant race came down to Chicago and Boston. With the addition of Kelly the Bostons edged out Cap Anson's Midwesterners. But Chicago president Jim Hart was having none of it. He questioned a late season series that Boston swept from New York, accusing New York owner John Day of "helping" Boston by holding stars Amos Rusie, Roger Connor, and Danny Richardson out of the games. The fact that Boston owned a small portion of the New York franchise because it had bailed Day out during the 1890 season tended to support Hart's concerns. Except that Chicago also owned a piece of the Giants for the same reason. Besides, Al Spalding's brother was an executive of the New York club.

During the NL dispute, Phelps decided on his strategy. He knew that given the League's resources, he needed either a quick knockout or a merger. He decided to concentrate his attack on one particular franchise. Since August there had been intermittent reports of dissention among New York players, who were grumbling about manager Buck Ewing. Roger Connor and Jack Glasscock requested their releases. There were rumors, too, about Danny Richardson.

At the beginning of November, the AA sprang its offensive. The new AA Chicago franchise signed Amos Rusie. The Philadelphia Athletics snared Connor and Richardson. St. Louis picked up Jack Glasscock and Dick Buckley. In a little over a week the Giants lost three-quarters of their infield, and their top battery. The Philadelphia *Inquirer* reported, "The New York Club's management is hustling for players."

Having won the skirmish, the AA announced that, in addition to competing directly with the League in Chicago, it would also move into New York and was considering Brooklyn. It would also reinstitute the twenty-five-cent admission.

The National League was now faced with potential competition offering bargain prices in five of its eight cities. It countered by trying to induce several Association clubs to jump leagues. But Phelps had seen this one coming and had required each franchise to deposit half of its stock with the league office.

The NL next copied Phelps's tactic and targeted his Louisville club for raids. New York, undoubtedly with the assistance of other NL owners, signed infielders Hughie Jennings and Harry Taylor off the Louisville roster.

The Big League—Battered, the NL proposed another peace conference. Battered, the AA accepted. On December 15, the two leagues met in Indianapolis. The AA proposed one eight-team league with four franchises from each league. The NL countered with a twelve-team proposal: the eight NL teams and four from the American Association. The AA, which had only four solvent franchises, accepted.

The AA teams in Boston and Philadelphia were bought out. Other cities were paid to go away. The NL added St. Louis, Baltimore, Washington, and Phelps's Louisville club to form the "Big League" of twelve teams that would last until 1899. Reinforcing the fact that this was a merger, the new league adopted the name The National League and American Association of Base Ball Clubs. Showing who was really in control, NL president Nick Young was named president of the new organization.

The term "Big League" was fashioned by the newspaper reporters and fans of the era. Only during the Union Association War of 1884 had a league, the AA, grown to this size, and it had been a disaster. The new attempt lasted a bit longer, but was no more successful than the first. In the 1890s, the National League tried split seasons, the Temple Cup post-season series between the top two teams in the league, and any scheduling trick it could think of to raise profits. After the 1899 season, it dropped its four weakest teams. But by that time the term "Big League" and its companion "Big Leaguer," had entered the language to stay.

Unlike its earlier wars, this was not a one-sided victory for the National League. It did eliminate a competitor outside the National Agreement. Dual-team cities were eliminated. The League kept its core owners' group intact. Young retained the presidency. But Phelps's brass-knuckle tactics had salvaged something for the American Association. Unlike other NL opponents, the AA lived on in the four franchises that merged into the new league.

Future NL president Harry Pulliam first joined baseball's executive suite when Phelps appointed him American Association secretary in 1891.

Today's St. Louis Cardinals are the lineal descendants of Chris Von der Ahe's American Association Browns, and the Cincinnati Reds trace back, not to the famous pioneering professional squad of 1869, but to the AA club that jumped to the NL in 1890.

The American Association clearly came out second best in its war with the National League, but it was the only competitor—until the NL met its match in Ban Johnson's American League—that wasn't simply demolished.

Grove's Grandest Groove

Dixie Tourangeau

Christy Mathewson, Walter Johnson, Sandy Koufax, and Greg Maddux make up part of a short list of great pitchers who, at some point during their reigns, enjoyed streaks of omnipotence. Wins, ERA, and strikeouts are just the most readily evident examples of their statistical and competitive dominance. Another charter member of this group is baseball's fiery Golden Age southpaw, who hurled Connie Mack's second dynasty to its greatest heights.

SABR has printed several articles concerning the pitching exploits of Robert Moses Grove, and few players are more deserving of the space. This article focuses on his magnificent string of five seasons from 1928 through 1932 when he was the game's top hurler. But since his wins are well documented, here the losses and oddities are scrutinized.

When Grove entered the American League wars in 1925 he was already twenty-five years old, having been a semi-willing captive of Jack Dunn's International League Baltimore Orioles for five seasons (109 victories). At the start of 1928 Lefty's major league record was a solid but unspectacular 43-38/3.45. On the positive side, he had won the ERA title in 1926 (2.51) and top strikeout honors each of those first three seasons (484) on his way to seven straight. Manager Mack was slowly fine-tuning his rebuilt Athletics, finishing second in 1925, third in '26 and second in '27. Grove's

Richard Dixie Tourangeau *has been a SABR member since 1981 and began to author the* Play Ball! *calendar that same year. He is a U.S. Park Ranger in Boston and lives 1.2 miles from Fenway Park. This Grove piece could not have been produced without the research help provided by Scot Mondore at the National Baseball Library in Cooperstown.*

"grand groove" blankets Philadelphia's three pennants and the bookend campaigns before and after. The simple numbers are in the box on the next page.

For these five campaigns Grove posted twenty-five percent of Philadelphia's wins and lost but thirteen percent of its defeats. During this reign he completed seventy-six percent of his 160 starts and was 13–5, with twenty-nine saves, in fifty-four relief appearances. In his major league high of 1,408 innings thrown, Lefty struck out 925 batters. The second best whiff artist over the same period was Dodger Dazzy Vance with 752, followed by Grove's teammate George Earnshaw, 720; Cub Pat Malone, 695, and Red Sox-Yank Red Ruffing, 680.

Second in wins and innings pitched over the 1928–32 span was Washington's Alvin "General" Crowder (100–60/1,351 innings), who topped the AL with twenty-six wins in 1932 (Grove had twenty-five). Ruffing edged Lefty in strikeouts, 190 to 188 that year. In 1928 Lefty (2.58) finished behind Washington's Garland Braxton (2.51) and Herb Pennock's 2.56 for New York in earned-run average.

Getting in the groove—In 1928 there is an interesting curiosity connecting the career of Grove and that of Henry "Hank" Johnson. In 1925, Florida native Johnson was a twenty-two-year old Yankee rookie who had pitched sixty-seven innings for the Bombers, but only one in '26 and was absent in '27. Back with the Yanks in 1928, he led the AL in walks, hit batsmen, and balks (1), according to research ace Bill Deane, yet managed a 14–9 record. However, his claim to fame is that he beat Lefty Grove four times that season, a feat

The Five Years of Grove's Groove

Year	Record	BA	FA	ERA	Grove	Wins	Ks	ERA	Innings
	Philadelphia's team rank in AL					Grove's rank in AL			
28	98-55	2	2	1	24-8	1	1	3	6
29	104-46	2	1	1	20-6	3	1	1	3
30	102-52	4	1	2	28-5	1	1	1	4
31	107-45	3	2	1	31-4	1	1	1	2
32	94-60	1	1	5	25-10	2	2	1	2
	505-258				128-33				

1928-1932

	Batting	Fielding	Pitching
Philadelphia	.292	.975	3.78
Rest of AL	.280	.968	4.44

no other pitcher *ever* matched. Grove was a poor 1–6 versus New York, and Johnson benefited most from that one-year hex. (Hank's 1982 *Sporting News* obituary said five wins, but the number was only four.) Only five *clubs* ever defeated Grove four or more times in a season—the 1925 Senators, 1926 Indians, 1928 Yankees, and 1935 Indians and Senators). Here is how Lefty's 1928 W–L columns evolved.

On April 11, opening day, Shibe Park hosted the Yankees and their fine lefty Herb Pennock. In cold weather Grove was knocked out in three innings in an eventual 8-3 loss. Pennock's two RBIs and Babe Ruth's three runs paced the Yankee offense. In retaliation, Grove beat New York's Wilcy Moore (relieving George Pipgras) in New York's Stadium opener on April 20, in a 2-1 thriller, for his only win against the champs that season. Ty Cobb (a triple and a run scored) and Tris Speaker (two RBIs) were the A's batting heroes.

After five more wins Lefty faced the Yanks again on May 24 back at Shibe. Down 6-5 in the eighth, he was lifted for a pinch hitter. New York scored three in the ninth for a 9-7 victory for Al Shealy, who spent only one year with the Yanks. Trying again four days later, Grove blew a 4-2 lead to Johnson. The game ended 11-4 Yanks. On June 7 at Sportsman's Park, Browns second baseman Otis Brannon's home run powered Crowder over Grove, 4-1. Two weeks later at Yankee Stadium, Hank "chicagoed" Philly and Grove, 4-0 behind a Tony Lazzeri homer and two doubles by Mark Koenig. Johnson made it three wins over Lefty on June 27 at Shibe. Lazzeri and Koenig again pounced on Grove offerings in Johnson's 7-4 complete game victory. Lefty exited in the eighth.

Through July, August, and early September Grove carved out a fourteen-game win streak, which helped the Athletics stay in the race. Johnson, who became Grove's mound mate in Boston in 1934–35, finished his unlikely skein on September 11, hosting and beating

Grove, 5-3, as both went the distance. Ruth homered with Lou Gehrig aboard, and Earle Combs and Koenig also scored in the deciding eighth-inning rally. This was the third of three straight Yank wins over Philadelphia, and it gave them the AL lead for good. In the ninth inning Cobb pinch hit and popped to Koenig for his final career at bat.

Elam Vangilder pinned the final loss on Lefty on September 21 at Detroit's Navin Field. Harry Rice's grand slam and two of rookie John Stone's (.354) four hits (three runs, three RBIs) beat Grove, 9-4. Rice's blast was one of his three lifetime home runs off Grove. It was Vangilder's final contested career win. He pitched on September 29 and beat a New York B squad, 19-10, allowing seventeen hits the day after New York clinched the flag. The Tigers got twenty-eight safeties.

Grove ended the year with a 24-8 record thanks to a 5-3 win over Chicago's Alphonse Thomas to end the campaign. Lefty gave up six hits and homered as each Athletic in the lineup got exactly one hit. Philly won ninety-eight games to New York's 101.

The second dynasty's first flag—In 1929, Cobb and Speaker were gone, and Eddie Collins played in only nine games. But the team was loaded with terrific players in their primes. Most important, George Earnshaw, 7-7 as a rookie, was to own the AL as a sophomore. Grove took no prisoners, beginning his year by beating New York on April 21 at their Bronx inaugural, 7-4. Revenge was sweet as jinx Johnson was pounded out in the first inning and the game called after five frames due to a drenching rain and gale winds.

By May 25, Grove had rung up a 12-1 mark, losing only to White Soxer Thomas, 4-2, at Comiskey Park on May 7. Thomas knocked in two runs, while three errors by shortstop Dykes encouraged Chicago's offense. On June 29, Yank Pipgras held on to beat Lefty, 7-5, on Ruth's two clouts and three errors by usu-

Lefty Grove holding a silver cup presented to him in 1931 by the Philadelphia Sportswriters Association.

ally sure-handed second baseman Max Bishop. Reeling off six more wins gave Lefty an 18-2 mark before he dropped consecutive games to St. Louis and Chicago, each by a 4-3 score. Grove might have been a little fatigued following his eighteenth win, since it took seventeen innings to beat Indian reliever Willis Hudlin, 5-3. Foxx's home run won it despite Joe Sewell's and Wes Ferrell's combined nine hits.

On August 18, Sam Gray beat Lefty in St. Louis on Gray's own two RBIs, despite Foxx's two solo home runs. The Chicago loss was to ace Ted Lyons. The White Sox won in the ninth inning on clutch swings by Art Shires and Bill Cissell. Workhorse Gray (305 innings, 18-15 in 1929) defeated Grove again on September 18 at Shibe, 6-3, on Red Kress' homer and a dozen other hits in seven innings. Playing the Red Sox

at Braves Field in Boston on September 29, Lefty was pummeled for eight runs in five innings in a 10-0 whipping by Boston's Red Ruffing and Milt Gaston. All they gave up were two singles each to Dykes and Haas. Grove's final record was 20-6, while Earnshaw led the AL with twenty-four wins, allowing the fewest hits per game, and finishing second to Lefty in strikeouts. This Philadelphia edition captured its first flag easily with 104 victories to New York's eighty-eight.

Lefty, can you spare an out?—Depression ball was not kind to those paid to work off the slab. In 1929 the AL batting average was .284. It swelled to .288 in 1930. ERAs jumped from 4.24 to 4.65. Unfazed, Grove started 1930 by beating nemesis New York in the opener at

The Competition

Team	Record	Who beat Grove in the groove, and when
Boston	26-2	Ruffing 1929, Durham 1932
Detroit	22-2*	Vangilder 1928, Hogsett *1930
Cleveland	21-4**	Hudlin 1930, Hudlin *1932, Hildebrand 1932, Brown *1932
Chicago	20-6**	Thomas 1929, Lyons *1929, McKain *1930, McKain, 1931, Lyons (2) 1932
St. Louis	17-6***	Crowder 1928, Gray (2) *1929, Coffman 1930, Coffman *1931, Fischer *1932
Washington	12-3***	Jones *1930, Jones *1931, Crowder *1932.
New York	10-10	Pennock 1928, Shealy 1928, Johnson (4) 1928, Pipgras 1929, Rhodes 1931, Gomez (2) 1932

Each * denotes a one-run loss

Grove was 1–7 versus Washington his first three seasons. For the same period his record was 10-3 against New York, including the 4-hit, 12-K, 4-1 victory over Bob Shawkey in which Lefty achieved his nine-inning strikeout career high.

Tough contemporaries

1928-32

GROVE	128-33
Alvin Crowder	100-60
George Earnshaw	93-48
Wes Ferrell	91-50
Pat Malone	91-58
Guy Bush	83-42
Freddie Fitzsimmons	83-49
Carl Hubbell	77-52
Dazzy Vance	76-62

Tough contemporaries
1933-37

Carl Hubbell	115-50
Dizzy Dean	115–60
Tommy Bridges	95-56
Lon Warneke	94–60
Lefty Gomez	88-58
GROVE	86–49

Shibe. Pipgras was mauled, 6-2, and 1928 wonder boy Johnson was relegated to mopping up after him. Holdout Simmons, who signed his contract two hours before the game, homered, and Lefty fanned nine. He won his next six decisions, beating every AL club except Chicago. The White Sox were the first to mar his record, besting Lefty on June 10 at Comiskey, 7-6. In his relentless relief role Grove shut down a Chicago rally in the tenth, but two walks and Bud Clancy's RBI single cost him the game in the eleventh. The win went to Sox reliever Hal McKain.

In Cleveland the next day, Lefty was hit hard and was down 3-1 after seven. The 6-2 final went to Hudlin behind the bats of Earl Averill and Carl Lind. Grove then posted three fine wins, including an eleven-strikeout, 2-1 victory over White Soxer Red Faber. Bill Cissell's three hits and run scored prevented the shutout. On June 27, Grove hosted the Browns and Dick Coffman. Lefty himself homered off Coffman to tie the score at 1-1 in the third, but Brownie bats whacked Grove around for a 7-1 lead by the fifth. Coffman won, 8-2, on four productive hits by Oscar Melillo and rookie Ted Gullic. It was Coffman's first season as a regular—he went 8-18/5.14—and it would not be his last battle with Ol' Mose.

Nearly a month later (three more wins and decisionless relief stints) in Detroit, Grove suffered a heartbreaking relief loss. He stemmed one Tiger rally off starter Bill Shores in the seventh. Tied at 4-4 in the bottom of the eighth, Grove faced ageless Indian ace and pinch hitter George Uhle (.308 in 1930), who singled home two runners for an eventual 6-5 win for Elon "Chief" Hogsett. Foxx made this outcome more frustrating by failing to get Dale Alexander on a simple grounder in the eighth. The Beast decided to race Alexander to first instead of throwing to Grove, who was covering. Dale won the sprint and the rally ignited. Then at 13-4, Grove won eight in a row, lost once, then came back with seven consecutive victories to finish 28-5. Washington visitors Joe Cronin and Sad Sam Jones destroyed what could have been a sixteen-game win streak for Lefty, 3-2, on August 25. Jones, thirty-eight, held the AL champs to six hits (two by Grove). Cronin's home run and single to score Sam Rice drove in all three tallies. At that time Washington was only two games behind the Athletics. Philadelphia finished with 102 wins to ninety- four for the Senators.

Just about unbeatable—Just when baseball fans thought Grove could not be better, he ascended to a higher level. There are limitless "ifs" during a long season, but Lefty's 1931 effort, with few changes, could have been an undefeated campaign, an incredible accomplishment for a pitcher with more than thirty decisions. Rube Walberg started on opening day in Washington before President and Mrs. Hoover. Grove

relieved in the ninth with the score 2-2. Philadelphia won in the eleventh, 5-3, tagging reliever Crowder. Four days later, old Sam Jones took back a victory at Shibe's opener on Grove's first start of 1931, besting him, 2-1, with help from relief ace Firpo Marberry. Cronin again was the batting culprit, his triple scoring Heinie Manush. Joe then came home on Ossie Bluege's hit. Both Harry Rice and Sam Rice tripled later in the game, but were stranded at third. Mickey Cochrane and Al Simmons both fanned with the sacks full in the seventh against Marberry. Washington took three of four contests.

Grove then won eight for a 9-1 mark before losing another relief debacle. Mack called for Lefty's services on June 5 in the seventh inning at Shibe. Chicago quickly scored to tie the score, 5-5, and the game ground into the twelfth. McKain relieved in the sixth for the Sox and did splendid work while Lefty struggled every inning, but Mack would not sit him down. Lew Fonseca whacked his first pitch of the twelfth into the seats and Chicago scored another for a 7-5 McKain victory. After this painful defeat Grove went on to win sixteen consecutive games. With an Athletics' rally in the Chicago game, he might have had a twenty-four- or twenty-five-game record streak. Instead, he tied the existing record of sixteen straight set by Smoky Joe Wood and Walter Johnson in 1912.

Enter Dick Coffman for a second time. After sweeping through the AL for sixteen wins, including three against St. Louis, Grove faced Coffman at Sportsman's Park on August 23. Dick was enjoying his own modest streak of three wins—about as long as any Brownie hurler could hope for. He had beaten Chicago, 1-0 (allowing only a single to Johnny Kerr), Boston, and Washington, all with only two strikeouts.

It has been written many times that Simmons asked out of this monumental Grove game for medical reasons, which is why AA Newark Bear call-up Jimmy Moore was in left field. In fact, Bucketfoot Al, leading the AL with a .385 average, hadn't played since spraining his left ankle on August 16, a day after Lefty's twenty-fourth win. A skin infection prolonged the healing process, and Al didn't play again until September 6 in Boston, as a reluctant courtesy to fans wanting to see him. A few days later Simmons returned as a regular after missing twenty-four of twenty-five games.

Lefty's record-breaking attempt was Moore's sixth game. The kid was batting cleanup and had homered the previous day in Chicago in a 7-1 win over Lyons. Jimmy, however, was not Jo-Jo or Terry as a fly chaser, and in the third stanza he misjudged Melillo's fly into an RBI double, which drove Fred Schulte with the only score of the game. Coffman gave up only three hits (one of them to Moore), while striking out four to snap Lefty's string. It was the only time all season the Mackmen were blanked. (They had played Washington to a 0-0 standstill on July 6 before the game was called after seven innings due to rain.) Cochrane, playing at half speed, got a hit off Coffman too, but quickly flew back to Philadelphia because he was exhausted from little sleep due to pennant pressures and depression. Rally-starter Mule Haas was also absent because of a fractured right wrist, while third baseman Dykes was just coming off an injury. (In Coffman's first start after shattering Grove's streak, Cleveland shelled him for six runs in the second inning.)

Enraged by the loss and the lack of support, Lefty reportedly tore the clubhouse apart and loudly berated Simmons for being absent. In the second game of the twin bill, his club drubbed the Browns, 10-0, behind Waite Hoyt and seventeen hits.

Nevertheless, Grove chalked up another six straight wins. The first was over New York, 7-4, as Foxx's five RBIs outdid Gehrig's grand slam. Another was a 3-2 payback victory over St. Louis in which Moore's triple was the winning smash. His thirty-first victory, 9-4 over Boston's Wilcy Moore, made him this century's winningest southpaw.

At Yankee Stadium on September 27, Lefty pitched three innings and left trailing, 5-1, in a 13-1 final. Grove scored Philly's sole run off winner Gordon "Dusty" Rhodes, but he also gave up a home run to Gehrig. Walberg and Earnshaw followed Grove in this World Series tune-up. Lefty could have avoided being charged with the loss merely by not being the game's starting pitcher. Even Mack probably would have changed his hurler sequence for the meaningless contest if Lefty had been 34-0 at the time. Losing 2-1, 7-5 in twelve innings, and 1-0, is how close he came to being just that in 1931.

This game also cost Grove the best winning percentage for twenty-five or more decisions, or at least twenty wins in a season (Ron Guidry 25–3/.893), and a sub-2.00 ERA. Philadelphia accumulated 107 victories to New York's ninety-four. Simmons hit .390 for his second batting title.

Total domination starts to fade—The other end of Grove's groove was 1932. The Yanks retook the pennant and Lefty was a mortal 25-10, acceptable for most but not the Maryland firebrand. After beating Washington on April 16, he lost to Lefty Gomez and New York, 8-3, on Ruth's hitting; Eddie "Bull" Durham and Boston, 10-2, after the Sox were hitless for five innings, and Crowder and Washington, 2-1, on hits by Cronin and Moe Berg.

Then, in true Grove style, he won eleven straight, beating each AL club at least once, before twisting his ankle chasing fungoes in St. Louis and missing turns at St. Louis, Chicago, and New York, and home against Boston and Washington. During his eleven wins, he

gave up only nineteen runs over ninety-four innings, twenty-four straight of them scoreless—his personal high. Rusty when he came back from his injury, Lefty lost three in a row, pitching the worst ball of the five-year span (nineteen innings, seventeen runs).

In five July days, he lost to Chicago, 7-0 (Lyons four-hitter), and Cleveland twice, 7-6 (Hudlin), and 7-5 (rookie Oral Hildebrand). The Lyons game was Lefty's first start since June 13, and he was hit hard especially by Bob Fothergill (three hits and three RBIs). In the five-game set with visiting Cleveland, the teams combined for ninety-six runs. Though Hudlin didn't get a hit off Lefty on August 12, all the other Indians did, eighteen in all. The barrage included Eddie Morgan's game-tying home run and Bill Cissell's game-winning RBI double in the ninth. Next day, Cissell's RBI single in the tenth beat Lefty in relief. After this slump dropped him to 12-6, three wins raised him to 15-6 before three losses in four decisions leveled him to 16-9. Yankee southpaw ace Gomez won, 9-3, behind Joe Sewell's five hits. Carl Fischer of St. Louis beat him, 9-8, after Lefty hit a go-ahead homer but then gave up a game-winning double in relief to Rick Ferrell. Lyons beat him, 3-1, on Carey Selph's RBI triple and run scored. In Gomez's victory the Yanks rolled up the most runs Grove personally allowed during the five seasons.

Lefty, however, finished with a flourish, winning nine of ten decisions. Only Cleveland's Clint Brown was able to defeat him, 2 to 1 on September 8, on late-inning clutch hits by Willie Kamm and that menace Cissell again. Grove scored the A's run.

Lefty's fluke injury in St. Louis cost him a legitimate shot at a second thirty-win season. Though Foxx was tremendous (.364/58 HR/169 RBI), New York and Philadelphia switched records from 1931.

Not far from fantasy—On the previous page is the franchise won-lost record for the five-year span in which the AL averaged .282 but hit .242 off Grove. He benefited, of course, from having the AL's top defense behind him, and from not having to pitch to Cochrane (520 runs), Simmons (1,002 hits) and Foxx (171 home runs). Mack's Hall of Fame mashers bailed out Grove nine times for wins when he allowed five or more runs during those five years. Philadelphia averaged 5.93 runs per game. In games against Washington ('31) and New York ('32), home runs by Cochrane, Simmons, Foxx, and "Camera Eye" Max Bishop in each gained victories of 12-7 over Marberry and 10-7 over Hank Johnson. In wins, Grove never gave up more than seven runs. All baseball aspects considered, it is within the realm of possibility that with a key hit or pitching change here and there, Lefty could have been 140-20 during his five-season, magnificent GROoVE.

Randy Gumpert

Victor Debs, Jr.

On a sunny September afternoon following a pleasant two-hour drive along the scenic New Jersey and Pennsylvania Turnpikes, I pull into the driveway of a charming rustic home in Douglassville, a secluded Pennsylvania community located ten miles from Reading. Accompanying me is my wife, Lola, a clothes designer by trade but camerawoman for the day. Alighting the minivan, we are greeted by the sound of cackling from a hen house, then by the slender, six-foot, Randy Gumpert, former major league hurler now eighty years young, alongside his equally-trim spouse, retired schoolteacher Anne Gumpert.

We enter the Gumpert home, for which Randy evinces fondness and pride. "I've lived here practically all my life, and after Anne and I got married, we've been fixing the place up ever since. We have about seven acres, and it's a beautiful place to live." He qualifies the remark with "most of the time," then describes a particularly harrowing experience. "In 1972, we got hit with a flood, and I have a plaque on the wall that shows the high-water mark. We were treading water, that's how bad it was. Afterwards, they built a dam near Reading and that's controlled the flooding ever since."

The principal reason for the visit is Randy's recollections of Yankee teammate Ernie "Tiny" Bonham for a book I'm working on that focuses on players whose careers were ended by death. Bonham was the portly

pitcher for the Yankees and Pirates who succumbed to complications following an appendectomy in 1949. Former Buc Wally Westlake has already provided reminiscences of Bonham, and I am hoping Gumpert can as well. "Ernie was a very likable fellow, kind of a rotund, jolly kind of man," Randy recalls. "He would talk to anybody, and didn't have any hang-ups of any kind."

Well, maybe one. "I remember he used to carry an iron ball the size of a baseball that weighed about three or four pounds. He said that carrying the ball made the baseball feel light. I guess his thinking was the same as batters when they swing a couple of bats in the on-deck circle. Bonham would walk around all the time throwing that iron ball up and down. Maybe it worked. He won about thirty more games than he lost in his career."

The conversation turns to Randy's career. He recalls his pre-professional experience. "When I was a youngster, every little village had a Sunday baseball team. There were no leagues. You just played some other team. I could throw better than the rest of the players, so they made me the pitcher. We didn't have any standard uniforms. If your father played and wore one, that's the one you'd wear."

Major league teenager—In 1934, a letter written in Randy's behalf by his father resulted in a tryout with the Philadelphia A's. Manager Connie Mack was sufficiently impressed to suggest that Randy work as a batting practice pitcher at Shibe Park until finishing high school. In 1936, at the age of eighteen, Gumpert became a big-league pitcher. "I should never have been on a club at that age," Randy admits. "Some guys could

Victor Debs, Jr. *is the author of* Still Standing After All These Years, Missed It By That Much, *and other baseball books, and has interviewed dozens of former big league ballplayers. He is currently working on* Diamond Darkness, *which focuses on players whose careers were ended by death, and is gathering research for a biography of Dodgers and Reds first baseman Jake Daubert.*

do it. Mel Ott was only sixteen, and so was Joe Nuxhall. But I just wasn't mature enough."

Gumpert reflects on his career with cheerful humility. "I was always a hard worker. I'd run all the time. If running could have made a good pitcher out of me, I'd have been a wizard." Again, he jokes. "In my first game in 1936, I beat the White Sox on a two-hitter. But I never won another game until ten years later. That's kind of a long gap isn't it?"

Indeed, but circumstances rather than insufficient talent provide the explanation. Randy followed the 1936 season with a couple of seasons in the minors, which included playing for Baltimore manager Rogers Hornsby whom Gumpert describes as "self-opinionated and a terrible manager," then a three-year stint during World War II.

His prewar big-league career left him some fond memories. One is especially pleasing. On September 13, 1936, eighteen-year-old Gumpert faced Cleveland's seventeen-year-old Bob Feller. The game was close until A's shortstop Russ Peters let loose with an errant toss to first, leading to a pair of unearned runs. Feller won the duel while setting a new American League record for strikeouts.

Feller's erratic control, which resulted in nine walks, contributed to his record-setting effort. Relates Randy, "The thing I remember about Feller that day is that none of the A's batters were taking a toehold. He was a little bit on the wild side. And everyone today talks about Feller's good arm and great fast ball, but he had an outstanding curve ball, too—a great, big looping curve."

Yankee success—Randy's next break resulted from another letter, written by himself to Yankee executive George Weiss following World War II. Gumpert's pitch was his 10-5 record and impressive ERA with the minor league Newark club in 1942, and his maintaining arm strength during the war with appearances on the base team on Sundays and some weekdays. Weiss called, instructing Gumpert to report to the 1946 spring training camp. "At that time, they had all these fellows coming back from the service, so the Yankees had two camps—one in St. Petersburg and another in Bradenton. Luckily, I was placed in the St. Petersburg camp under [manager Joe] McCarthy while the coaches were running things in Bradenton. Evidently, McCarthy took a liking to me.

"I started a game and pitched three scoreless innings. In my next outing, I pitched three more scoreless innings. Then I pitched five and seven scoreless innings. We came up to Brooklyn and played that city series, and I shut them out for seven innings. I pitched twenty-five innings without allowing a run, so they almost had to do something with me.

"So if you asked me what my biggest thrill was, it wasn't on the field. It was in the manager's office at Ebbets Field after that game with Brooklyn when McCarthy called me in and said, 'Here's your contract.' It was the minimum salary—$4,000. They weren't taking any chances."

It was a bargain for the Yankees. Gumpert displayed masterful mechanics throughout the regular season, and finished with an 11-3 record and 2.31 ERA. His 1946 performance is arguably the finest by a starter playing in his first season with the Yankees. By comparison, first-year Yankees Joe Bush, Johnny Allen, Hank Borowy, Whitey Ford, and Joe Cowley have slightly better winning percentages, but their ERAs are inferior. Considering his flawless spring training exhibition, Gumpert's season rates as the best.

While Gumpert was enjoying a fabulous year, a Yankee legend bid a reluctant farewell. "McCarthy was fired in midseason," Randy says of the pinstripe skipper of sixteen years. "I didn't get to know him too well, but I couldn't help liking him and feeling sorry when he was fired. But McCarthy had a drinking problem. It was uncontrollable. It got so bad they would have to take his wife on road trips to keep him sober. So I guess the Yankees had to get rid of him."

Injury—In 1947, Gumpert's fortunes changed. Continual use of his favorite pitch, a hard-breaking slider, resulted in a sore elbow. "They didn't do anything like they do now," Randy recalls in a matter-of-fact tone. "Ed Foley, the trainer, just put hot packs on my elbow. That didn't amount to anything. So I pitched with a bad arm for the next five seasons." He laughs. "It used to take me twenty minutes into the game before my arm was warmed up and my elbow wasn't clicking. It used to click all the time."

Despite the injury, Gumpert derived satisfaction from the 1947 season. He entered eighteen games in relief, and won three of four decisions as a starter. The Yankees set a still-standing club record of seventeen consecutive victories, with Gumpert winning one by defeating his former team, the A's, 8-2. The victory string arouses a sour memory for Randy. "I lost the game that broke the streak," he notes. "Freddy Hutchinson beat us on a two-hitter. Of course, I wasn't too happy about it afterwards, being the goat, more or less."

Ultimate gratification came from the Yankees winning the pennant, then beating Brooklyn in a World Series that fans recall more for the heroics of the losers than that of the champions. With two out in the ninth inning of Game 4, Brooklyn pinch hitter Cookie Lavagetto ruined a no-hit bid by Bill Bevens with a double that brought home the tying and winning runs. Two days later in Game 6, left fielder Al Gionfriddo made a running, over-the-shoulder snare of Joe DiMaggio's long drive with two aboard in the sixth frame. Randy reiterates what many have said regarding Joltin' Joe's reaction to the catch. "It was the only time I saw DiMaggio show any emotion of any kind, kicking the dirt the way he did."

Gumpert received a world championship ring, along with a Series share that exceeded his salary. "It was around $5,200 per player. That was quite a bit of money then. Today, I don't know why they bother to pay for playing in the Series with all the money the players make."

On to Chicago—The Pennsylvanian won his only decision with the Yankees in 1948 before being sold to the White Sox in midseason. In his two-and-a-half years with New York, Gumpert's record was 16-4. He did not enjoy the same success with Chicago. While resuming the role of starter, Randy accumulated a 29-42 record and 4.00 ERA in three-and-a-half seasons.

One performance in the Windy City was memorable. "The game in my career that stands out was a twelve-inning game at Comiskey Park," says Randy. "Hal Newhouser was the opposing pitcher. There was no score in the twelfth, and Hoot Evers hit a drive off me to right field. Dave Philley thought the ball was going to hit the wall so he moved away from the wall to play the carom. Well, the ball hit the base of the wall and stopped. Evers got a triple, and came in to score on a single. I lost 1-0." Randy ends the anecdote by kidding, "We were both in the groove that day. And Newhouser went into the Hall of Fame. For some reason, I never got there."

Gumpert doesn't attend modern ball games often, but does watch them on television. "Today's pitchers fall behind on the count too often because they're trying to be too perfect. I was always told to get ahead of the hitter, then make him hit your pitch. And I think this idea of pitch counts is ridiculous. If

Randy Gumpert holds framed photo of himself as a member of the 1947 Yankee ball club.

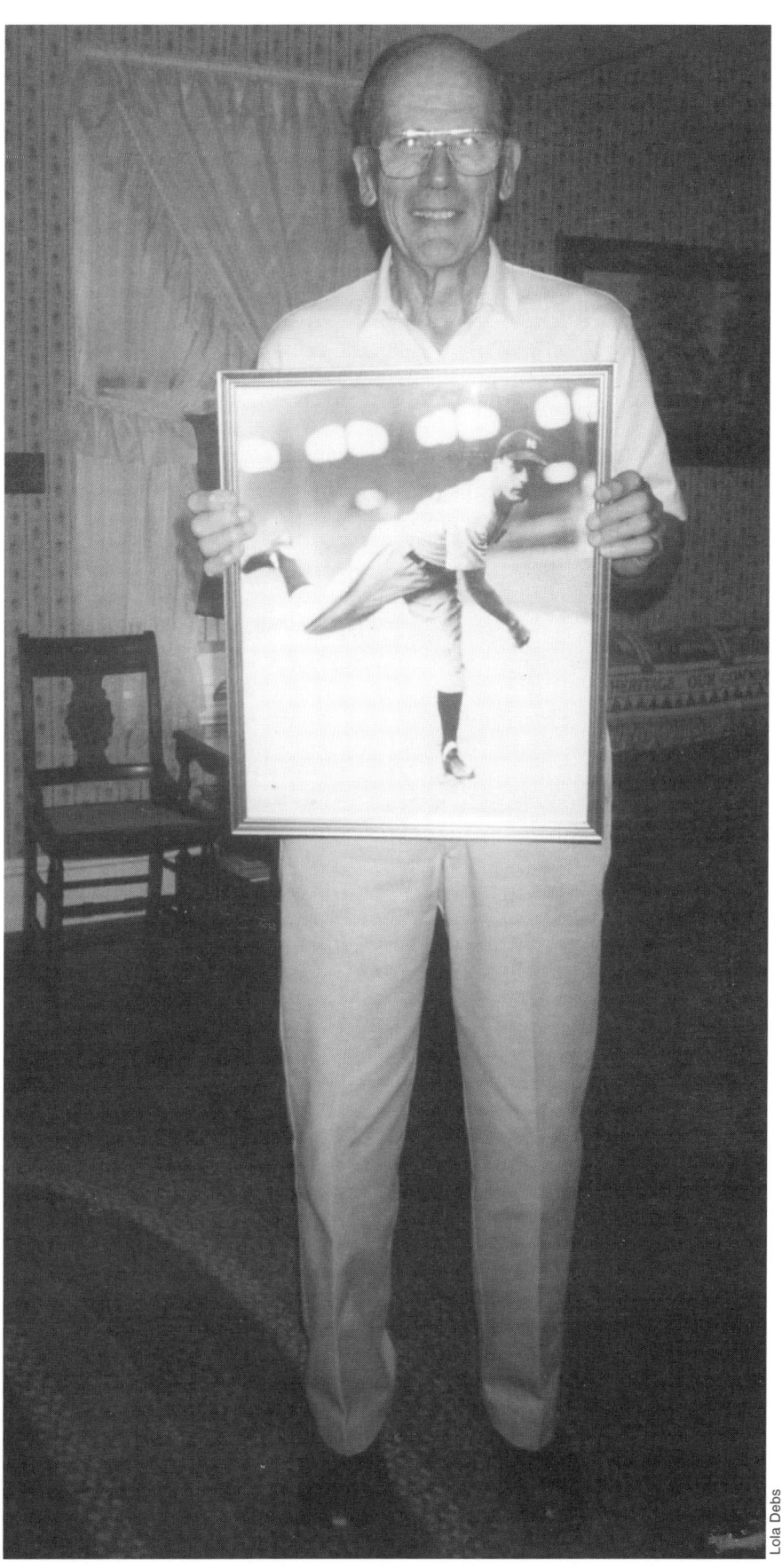

Lola Debs

a starter has thrown a hundred and twenty pitches, his arm isn't bothering him, and he's winning, why take him out?"

Gumpert is critical of current umpires. "It seems different umpires have different strike zones for different pitchers. For example, that pitcher for Atlanta, Tom Glavine. When he throws the ball it's three inches outside, but they call it a strike. Another pitcher might not get that pitch. I can't understand it.

"But I don't agree that today's umpires take less guff from players. I think they have always been a little thin-skinned. Some are just tougher than others. I remember you couldn't question any of Bill McGowan's pitches. But everybody in the league knew that's the way he was, so they wouldn't argue with him."

The Mick's first victim—The interview ends, and Lola and I are offered snacks. I politely decline, giving as a reason my latest in seemingly endless attempts at dieting, but the pair of homemade muffins placed before me nonetheless disappear during a twenty-minute conversation which includes another baseball anecdote. When Anne mentions her surprise that Mickey Mantle's first major league home run, surrendered by Gumpert, has not been discussed, the tape recorder is hastily restarted. "That's right. I gave up Mantle's first homer. Five, one, fifty-one [the date]. I was with the White Sox and pitching at Comiskey Park. I threw Mantle a screwball. Evidently, it didn't screw very well and he hit it into the bullpen in center field.

"Many years later when he was no longer playing, Mantle went to spring training camp to help out. I was down there as one of the instructors. We were sitting in the clubhouse at Miller Huggins Field in St. Petersburg and he said, 'Remember that home run I hit off you at Comiskey Park. That was the first homer I ever hit.' I told him I wasn't aware of that fact, but that I remember he hit it well."

Gumpert's major league career can be described as average, but considering his contributions to Yankee history—his outstanding 1946 record, his attaining a victory in the record seventeen-game winning streak, his 4-1 record on the world championship club of 1947, even his yielding Mantle's first 400-footer—the fact that one of the oldest living Yankees has never been asked to attend Old Timers' Day at Yankee Stadium is puzzling. "I wasn't even there when they honored the 1947 club last year," Randy admits. "It's a mystery to me why I haven't been invited."

Anne wraps a few muffins for the road, then asks us to stay a while longer. She leaves the kitchen and returns with Randy's old uniforms, which are in superb condition. Lola gets to work as Randy and Anne pose. Before leaving, we thank the Gumperts for their hospitality. They insist we visit again.

About an hour later, while driving on the Pennsylvania Turnpike, I ask Lola for another muffin.

Source:

Interview with Randy Gumpert at his home in Douglassville, Pennsylvania, September 2, 1998.

News from Leavenworth I

"A remarkable feat was accomplished by Harding [probably five-foot-nine-and-a-half, 213-pound Lou "Jumbo" Harding] and Smith [probably Sam "Skyrocket" Smith], the catcher and first baseman of the St. Joseph, Mo., club," said the Toronto Globe *in 1886. "They retired the entire Leavenworth team in a recent game. The former had eleven putouts and the latter sixteen." The reporter then jumped to the highly unlikely conclusion that "the other players therefore had nothing to do in the field."*

News from Leavenworth II

James, the Leavenworth pitcher, is a curiosity," reported the Globe *in 1887. "He is deaf and dumb, but can utter one word, 'rats.' He constantly cries 'Rats' at the umpires."*

Fanatical Fans

In 1887, according to the Binghampton (New York) Democrat, *a Connecticut man was declared insane because all he talked about was baseball. Said the* Democrat, *there are "about 10,000,000 such lunatics in the country."*

—David McDonald

Bob Crues

Bob Rives

Not many minor league baseball players, or professional players at any level, accomplished more than Bob Crues.

Playing in the minors' headiest days, immediately after World War II, Crues in 1948 set an organized baseball record for runs batted in that probably will last forever: 254 of them in just 140 games. (Hack Wilson's major league mark of 190 has stood since 1930.)

But good as he was, Crues might have done even more. When he played, no one had ever hit seventy homers in a single season. In 1948 he almost did. Did he fail because of an umpire's bad call? Or did he fall short because his conscience wouldn't let him take an inside-the-park home run when the opposing team gave him the chance in his final time at bat during the season? At least some evidence says "yes" to both questions. Let's take a look.

In 1948 Royce "Rooster" Mills, pitched in hitters' heaven, the Class C West Texas-New Mexico League, where pitchers earned their money more for ducking than for throwing. In both 1947 and 1948, six of eight clubs in the league had team batting averages greater than .300. And pitchers' ERAs looked like numbers that today would be produced at the Jenny Craig Center weigh-in.

Mills was no exception. He won sixteen games while losing only three in 1948 for the Lubbock, Texas, Hubbers. That gave him a league-leading won-lost per-

centage of .842. But his earned run average was 5.14. Only six pitchers in the league had an ERA under 5.00.

In 1954, Mills talked with sports columnist Ed Boykin of the Artesia (New Mexico) *Advocate* about the final day of "Round Trip's" chase.

"Round Trip" was Robert Fulton "Bob" Crues, an outfielder for the Amarillo Gold Sox when his number came up on the wheel of baseball fortune. When it did, he rocked a league already storied for its hitting. In the seemingly magic season of 1948, he batted .404, recorded sixty-nine home runs, thirty-eight doubles, and two triples, and batted in an all-time professional record 254 runs, all in a 140-game season.

His home run record tied the all-time mark for organized baseball, a standard that lasted six more years until it was broken by Joe Bauman, once Crues' teammate, who hit seventy-two in 1954 for the record that still stands. Until Mark McGwire in 1998, he was the only batsman with seventy or more homers in a single year. Crues' sixty-nine still is good for a two-way third-place tie.

But Crues' solar-system-leading record for runs batted in seems coated with eternal Teflon, unlikely ever to be broken. Bauman, the contemporary runner-up to the Crues mark, had "only" 224 runs batted in. Tony Lazzeri hit sixty home runs in 1925 for Salt Lake City, the first player to hit that many in a year. In that 200-game season, he had "just" 222 runs batted in.

Crues hit home runs sixty-eight and sixty-nine off Pampa's George Payte in Amarillo on September 5, the last Sunday of the 1948 regular season. Crues drove a curve over the 360-foot center field fence to tie the record of sixty-nine set in 1933 by Joe Hauser with

Bob Rives *is fascinated with power hitters of the minor leagues. He lives in Wichita, Kansas, where he is retired from business.*

Minneapolis of the American Association.

September 6, 1948, was Labor Day, last day of the regular season for Crues and the Gold Sox and thus Bob's last chance to reach seventy. Amarillo was at home against Lubbock. Both teams already had qualified for the playoffs which would begin two days later. But half a game separated their claims for second place. If Lubbock won both games of the doubleheader, it would move ahead of the Sox into a better seed for the championship series. Amarillo needed to win only one.

The offer of a little help from some friends—Mills told Boykin that the Hubbers were willing to help "Round Trip" Bob become history's first seventy home run hitter and unlock his day-old tie with Hauser, especially after Amarillo won the first game of the twinbill, 4-3, to lock up second place and make the final game meaningless in the standings.

Helping a hitter set a home run record was not new, according to Harry Gilstrap, sports editor of the Amarillo *Globe*. In a late August story, he quoted Harry Brown, a member of the 1925 Sacramento Solons, who said Tony Lazzeri's sixtieth home run in 1925 had been a gift. Though this story has come up nowhere else, Gilstrap and Brown had it that a gift made Lazzeri the first player in history to record sixty homers in a season. According to Gilstrap's account of Brown's story, the final game of the 1925 PCL season had arrived when Lazzeri still had fifty-nine homers.

"You see, we all liked Tony," Brown was quoted as saying.

"Salt Lake let him lead off so he could come to bat more often…But Tony didn't get a home run in the morning game at Stockton nor did he get one in the first three times at bat in the afternoon game at Sacramento.

"The fourth time he punched a hard grounder on the left side of second base. Ray French could have made the play, but he deliberately ran the other way. Bill Cunningham was in center, and he let the ball roll by him on its way to the fence. So Lazzeri got his sixtieth home run…inside the park."

Buck "Leaky" Fausett, who made a cameo appearance with the 1944 Cincinnati Reds, was co-owner of the Amarillo franchise and manager of the Gold Sox. Just as Lazzeri's manager had done twenty-three years earlier, Buck moved Crues into the leadoff spot for the final doubleheader.

Crues' possible record was popular with fans. An Amarillo record crowd of 4,851 forced itself into the park, filling the stadium, the space between the fence and foul lines, and in front of the outfield fence. So far had Crues fever spread that the crowd included not only fans but national media and promoters as well.

"Wheaties were there," Billie Crues, Bob's widow,

recalls. "If he'd hit that home run we'd have been eating Wheaties the rest of our lives."

Look had a photographer among the cameramen at a time when the magazine was one of the nation's most widely circulated news outlets. Billie remembers the crush of the crowd, the flash of cameras, and the interest of the city as building pressure that affected her husband that night.

"He wanted the homer bad, real bad," she would say later. Bob agreed. He called hitting homer number sixty-nine his greatest thrill in a long sports career. Failing to get number seventy was his biggest disappointment. Yet Mills said Crues did not take the record-setting hit when it was offered to him in the way Lazzeri was said to have garnered his number sixty more than two decades earlier.

Crues almost gave the crowd what it came to see in his first time at bat. Bob Clodfelter, 11-9 and 5.40, was pitching for Lubbock. Crues slammed the ball against the left field fence, just inches from the top. Bob himself and the newspaper writer covering the game both said it was an ill wind that kept the ball inside the park.

In Amarillo and most other cities in the league, home plate was in the southwest corner of the diamond. Prevailing winds blew fly balls toward left field. It was a rare inbound north wind that early September day that forced the fly ball down and in, keeping it in the park and turning it into a long single.

It was Game 2 before the Hubbers' help became evident. Since Lubbock's loss in the first game made the second meaningless in the standings, the team could afford to be generous.

After Crues' long first-inning single, he hadn't come close. And by the sixth inning of the scheduled seven-inning nightcap, with Amarillo down, 3-1, it was evident that Crues would not bat in the last inning without help.

"The Hubs wanted to see him get that last chance," Gilstrap wrote. "And when they went into the lower half of the sixth with a 3-1 lead, it was apparent that at least four Gold Sox must go to the plate in order to insure Crues coming up again in the seventh.

"With two out, therefore, Red Ramsey walked Earl Harriman, plainly by intent. He walked Jack Shumacher also, not intentionally, before he got the side out." Mills' story as reported by Boykin agrees.

With the stage set, Lubbock brought Don Moore in to pitch. Although Moore pitched some, he was normally an outfielder. And Gilstrap reported he had trouble getting a pitch over the plate for Bob to hit—until Crues ripped a ball into left that appeared to be destined to become a single.

Chick Fowler was the Lubbock left fielder. According to Mills, he must have read the account of Sacramento's attempt to help Lazzeri get a homer. Fowler "fell" going after the ball, then picked himself up slowly while "picking stickers" from his shirt. The path from first to home was wide open to Crues.

But Crues refused, Mills said. He stayed at first. His first sixty-nine home runs had no air of taint about them. If the record was to be broken, the last one would be equally clean.

Some question whether the Boykin-Mills account is correct. There is no question that the Hubbers tried to give Crues the chance to be all-time champ. But neither Amarillo sports accounts, Bob's own statements, or Billie's memories support the idea that Bob stayed at first when a clear chance loomed to break the record.

In fact, Bob later felt slow pitches being fed him by Lubbock pitchers may have hurt rather than helped. "They lobbed the ball to me all day," he would say. And those slow throws forced him to supply all the power—like a batter in slow pitch softball.

Bad call—Some later argued that he deserved to take number seventy when offered because he had been cheated of a home run earlier in the summer.

On June 30, Amarillo played the Abilene, TX, Blue Sox in Abilene. Crues smashed a towering hit toward the scoreboard, which was behind the fence. The ball bounced back onto the field.

Umpire Frank Secory, who only three years earlier had two World Series hits in five tries for the Cubs and later went on to a big league officiating career, squelched the homer. He ruled the ball had hit the top of the fence, and held Crues at third base.

After the game, Abilene outfielders, the youngster who operated the scoreboard, and the official scorer all said the ball had not hit the fence but the scoreboard itself. It should have been a home run. Ironically, it was Secory, regarded as one of the league's better umpires, who worked behind the plate in Amarillo on September 5 when Bob hit his record-tying homer.

Bill Chick, Abilene's official scorer on June 30 and the league statistician, worried prophetically about the call. In a letter he said:

"Won't it be awful if he fails to get it [number seventy] when I'll always believe he should have had that one here in our park...and Frank Secory ruled that it hit the fence, when several Blue Sox players and fans who should have been able to see the ball said it hit the scoreboard? I, too, thought it hit the scoreboard and should have been an automatic homer. I've been afraid ever since that home run might play a big part in breaking or not breaking that record."

Bad ball—With or without a record, Crues had one of the best years a batter ever experienced in baseball. What made it so special?

Obviously, he had great ability and was big enough

to generate home run power. His body would be called "rangy" at six foot two and 185 pounds. In 1948 he started fast and maintained the pace, hitting thirty-four homers in the first half of the season and thirty-five in the last.

Billie believes personal contentment had something to do with it. They were well-settled that season, their third in Amarillo, a city they liked. Bobby Layne, who went on to a major league sports career but as a football star, not on the diamond, also offered an answer.

Fresh from the University of Texas backfield he shared with another immortal, Doak Walker, Layne in 1948 was pitching for hometown Lubbock, where he also owned a sporting goods store. He was one of the few pitchers in the league to escape the year without giving up a home run to Crues.

Layne believed Crues was the best bad-ball hitter in the league. The Amarillo star could hit a ball outside the strike zone better than one thrown down the middle, Layne concluded. And in a league where pitchers who could regularly throw strikes were rare, the ability to hit bad pitches gave Crues more opportunities than other hitters might receive.

Before and after—While an umpire's bad call and Crues' possible refusal to accept a tainted homer may have kept Bob's name off the record as the first to hit seventy, it took an unlikely web of coincidences even to put him in a position to enter the books.

Bob comes from a family tree that is almost impossible to trace. As children, his father and uncle were the first two boys admitted to the Buckner Orphan Home in Dallas. There his dad was given the name "Crues," and his uncle was labelled "Cruse." Thus two branches of the family had differently spelled last names and neither was their birth name.

Bob was born the last day of 1918 at Frisco, Texas, north of Dallas. The family soon moved to the Texas Panhandle where he spent much of his life. When he was just three, Crues climbed a windmill, stuck the index finger of his right hand into it and lost it to the pumping mechanism.

Possibly in part because of the way his oddly shaped right hand forced him to hold a ball, he became a promising pitcher. Late in the 1939 season he was signed by Lamesa, Texas, of the West Texas-New Mexico League, then a Class D circuit. He played in only two games and went hitless in two times at bat. In 1940 he started the season with Lamesa, then joined the Borger, Texas, Gassers, in the same league. He went 20-5 as part of what Gasser manager Gordon Nell called the best pitching staff he ever saw in the league.

Based on Bob's Borger success, his contract was purchased by the Boston Red Sox, who posted him to the Class A Eastern League at Scranton, Pennsylvania, a remarkable one-season leap for a youngster. It was in the spring of 1941 with Scranton that fate again wiggled its finger.

After pitching five innings of an exhibition game in Greenville, South Carolina, Crues was in the dugout when an extraordinary stray pitch struck him in the soft part of his shoulder. The injury refused to heal and although he kept trying, Crues could never pitch effectively again.

With war clouds darkening, Crues went to work in the Pantex Ordnance Works at Amarillo, helping make ammunition for the growing conflict. Here he met and married coworker Billie. That union lasted the rest of his life and produced four sons.

Before the 1943 season, Crues went into the Army. Even then fate continued to play a role in his assignments. He became ill as he entered the service and was hospitalized before seeing a day of real duty. After he recovered he was sent to Texas posts to play ball. He remained stateside, playing the outfield, a position he had sampled briefly in 1941 and '42 with Borger.

War's end brought him back to civilian life and what he hoped would be continuing work in baseball. In Lamesa he tried out with his old team, the Lobos, but they released him. A later Amarillo *Globe* story noted that Crues always hit well in Lamesa—except when he tried to play there.

Cut by the ball club, he went to work in a poultry processing plant.

It was "Suitcase Bob" Seeds who rescued him from the feathery life of poultry plucking. Seeds was everything in Amarillo baseball. Like Crues a native Texan, he started his career in 1926 and later spent nine seasons as an outfielder-first baseman for the Indians, White Sox, Red Sox, and Giants, batting a combined .277.

By 1946 he had a hardware and sporting goods store in Amarillo and had taken over the Gold Sox. When Seeds found Crues out of work, he signed him for the Gold Sox. The march toward Crues' home run and runs batted in records was underway. Seeds had made one of his best investments.

The 1946 season was good for Bob. He batted .341, hit a respectable twenty-nine home runs and batted in 120. He was labelled a "flashy outfielder" in sports page reports. His 1947 numbers were even better. He hit fifty-two home runs, batted in 178, and compiled a .380 average. Based on that, his career again headed upward. He was sold to Little Rock of the Class AA Southern Association for 1948, where the newspaper reported he was hitting well in spring exhibition games.

Then, suddenly, he was wearing gold stockings again. Amarillo embraced him when he came back. He explained that he was homesick and that "a homesick ball player is no good to anyone." That was a fair analysis. Billie credits herself for his sickness. She was tiring of the demands being placed on minor league players' wives, including frequent moves with small children. If Bob was to play in front of his family, it would be in Amarillo, not Arkansas, she told him.

Actually, the backward move was also financially sound. Pay in AA leagues was not impressively higher than in Class C. And WT-NM fans in 1948 were famous for generosity. A league habit was to push money through the backstop to players after every home run and Bob would wear out their charity.

Billie cannot recall how much Crues made in 1948 in cold cash. "But we lived off it," she said. Joe Bauman had hit only forty-eight home runs at Amarillo in 1946, but bought a Buick with the proceeds. And with forty-one homers in front of Amarillo crowds, Bob could easily have taken in twice as much through the screen as he got in his paycheck.

One fan, a successful car dealer, once tore a $100 bill in half, giving Crues $50 worth of it one night with the rest to come when he hit another one out of the park. Even road crowds gave him money as he neared the record. He also received $200 from a firm which each year honored the player fans voted to be most popular.

Fans honored him with a Bob Crues Night in late August. There he earned $125 from the newspaper which had offered $100 for a home run, $75 per triple, $50 for a double, and $25 per single on his special eve. He responded with five total bases and resisted stretching a single into a double for "the good of the club" when it appeared it might be close at second.

The crowd liberally brought gifts for the second Crues son, who was born during the game. Bob sped from ball park to bedside to be with Billie and their new baby boy afterward. "When I came home the entire living room was lined with packages that had been brought to the park for us that night," she recalls.

That was Bob's last record-setting year. He was drafted following the season by the Jackson, Mississippi, Senators of the Class B Southeastern League, who offered him $250 a month. A Cuban team wrote, asking him to play with several major leaguers over the winter. But he said no to that offer.

Bob was slow to respond to Jackson's requests to sign a contract. Instead, he went to Elk City, Oklahoma, to play on a semipro team being built to contend for the National Baseball Congress title decided each year in Wichita.

But Bob and Elk City's management had a contract dispute, Crues feeling his verbal agreement was not being honored. Instead, he got a release from Jackson and went to Roswell, New Mexico, in the Longhorn League to manage and play first base and the outfield. Manager's pay was exempt from team salary caps and often averaged $500 per month or more, better than double players' salaries.

That 1949 season would be his last big one. He batted .365, hit twenty-eight homers, and batted in 129 runs. Into 1951 he continued play at San Angelo in the Longhorn League, then at Lubbock, Amarillo, and Borger in the WT-NM. But his batting tailed off. In 1953, he retired at age thirty-four only eleven games into the season.

Still, he was a competitor. He played on a company softball team and a small-town sandlot baseball club. An athlete of many skills, he amassed bowling trophies while working in a series of jobs for oil companies, his final one as day manager of a neighborhood service station. He was inducted into the Panhandle Sports Hall of Fame and honored as one of the region's finest baseball players.

Bob's final years were difficult. By 1965 he suffered the first in a series of disabling strokes. Therapy restored his ability to speak but it still was hard for him to articulate his thoughts and difficult for many to understand him. When he walked it was with a cane. Much of his time was spent in a Veterans' Hospital or with Billie in front of a television set, watching sports he once dominated, now locked in the prison of a failing body.

On the day after Christmas in 1980, he died a week short of his sixty-second birthday. He took with him not only the league's home run record but the all-time RBI mark. More important, he took with him the integrity that precedes true greatness.

Walk-A-Game Club Initiates McGwire

In 1998, Mark McGwire chased not only Roger Maris, but also Babe Ruth—for the season walks record (170 in 1923).

McGwire's 162 free passes fell short of Ruth's record, but the redhead did become the ninth player in major league history to draw more than 100 walks and average more than one per game. McGwire is the first player since Jack Clark in 1987 to maintain that pace. The two Cardinals are the only National League players this century to achieve that milestone.

McGwire did break the NL mark of 148 walks in a season by Eddie Stanky (1945) and Jim Wynn (1969). Neither Stanky nor Wynn averaged a walk per game.

Ruth had two of the fourteen walk-a-game seasons in major league history. Both came before Lou Gehrig arrived in New York. After Gehrig's arrival, pitchers no longer could work around The Bambino. Ted Williams never had a lot of protection in the Red Sox lineup. That fact and an excellent batting eye brought him five of the fourteen seasons with at least a walk a game. Williams (thirty-five in 1954) was the only player older than McGwire, who played the '98 season at age thirty-four, to average a walk a game.

The Walk-A-Game Club

Name	Year	Games	Walks	Team, League	Age
Yank Robinson	1890	98	101	Pittsburgh, PL	30
Jack Crooks	1892	128	136	St. Louis, NL	25
John McGraw	1899	117	124	Baltimore, NL	26
Babe Ruth	1920	142	148	New York, AL	25
Babe Ruth	1923	152	170	New York, AL	28
Ted Williams	1941	143	145	Boston, AL	22
Ted Williams	1946	150	156	Boston, AL	27
Ted Williams	1947	156	162	Boston, AL	28
Eddie Joost	1949	144	149	Philadelphia, AL	33
Ted Williams	1949	155	162	Boston, AL	30
Ted Williams	1954	117	136	Boston, AL	35
Mickey Mantle	1957	144	146	New York, AL	25
Jack Clark	1987	131	136	St. Louis, NL	31
Mark McGwire	1998	155	162	St. Louis, NL	34

—Larry Bump

From Dreams To Suicide

Al Figone, Ph.D.

Most current baseball fans know little about Bruce Gardner, one of University of Southern California's all-time winningest pitchers. Even for those who have followed Trojan baseball, he is just a name in the media guide, ranked above Hall of Famer Tom Seaver, and major leaguers Bill Lee, Jim Barr, Brent Strom, Peter Redfern, Steve Busby, and Tom House in career wins. This is true despite the bizarre circumstances surrounding his suicide on June 7, 1971.

Two university groundskeepers discovered Gardner's body that morning lying face down a short distance from the pitcher's mound at Bovard Field, which USC had used for years before moving to its modern Dedeaux Field. In his left hand he held the Smith & Wesson .38 caliber revolver with which he had shot himself in the left temple.[1]

In his right hand he held a laminated plaque of his bachelor's degree from the university. Next to his body investigators found another plaque, this one proclaiming him the 1960 All-American College Baseball Player of the Year, in essence, the best collegiate player in the country. Taped to a board a few feet away was his unaddressed and unsigned suicide note.

Gardner's suicide made more headlines than had his minor league career in the Dodger farm system. After leaving baseball in 1964, Gardner fell back on his other great love, music, and attempted to make it as a ballad singer. For a time he was a successful securities dealer, and finally he was a teacher and coach at Dorsey High School in South Central Los Angeles where he was working when he took his life.

Al Figone, Ph.D. *is a professor of Health and Physical Education at Humbolt State University in Arcata, California.*

After signing with the Dodgers in 1960, Gardner was assigned to Montreal, where he compiled an unimpressive 0-1 record. The next year, he was assigned to Reno in the Class C California League. He went 20-4 with an ERA of 2.82—the last time he would enjoy real success in baseball.[2]

In those days of the draft, Gardner found himself in the Army after the season in Reno. In the service, he fell off a truck and injured his arm. His career declined rapidly from there. After completing his military duty, he was assigned to Spokane in August, 1962, and went 1-5. Thoughts of suicide entered his mind for the first time. The suicide of Marilyn Monroe that summer, according to Gardner, "cemented itself" in his thinking.[3] Reassigned in 1963 to Great Falls, Montana, after a demotion from Salem, Oregon, he went 10-4, but with an ERA above four. On September 30, 1964, the Dodgers gave him his unconditional release.

A month later, he bought a pistol and told a friend, "I went home to shoot myself but the phone rang and got my mind off it."[4] When the friend asked if he was serious, Gardner replied, "Yeah. Everything's so low. The baseball's over and there's nothing left for me."[5]

Gardners classmates in the class of 1956 at Fairfax High School in Los Angeles believed life had tapped him on the shoulder for a special destiny. A campus hero, teenage heartthrob, and athlete, his talents attracted a $50,000 offer from the Chicago White Sox after his senior year. Gardner wanted to sign, but his mother would not consent. He would later recount that his high school coach, Frank Shaefer, and USC coach Raoul "Rod" Dedeaux strongly influenced her. A year later, after a perfect 10-0 record on the freshman team and being named USC's Freshman Athlete of the Year, he was offered $66,500 by the White Sox. His mother again refused to agree. Gardner felt that she was persuaded by Dedeaux that he should stay in college and obtain a degree.[6]

Pitching was only one of Gardner's varied talents. Legendary Fairfax High School basketball coach and NBA official Marty Biegel, who was one of Gardner's teachers and delivered the eulogy at his funeral, described him as an young man who was "charming in his enthusiasm, cultured, smart, an outstanding student, who may have been less than realistic in his ambitions involving baseball and unable to accept not playing in the majors.[7]

"His first love—his only love—was baseball," said his mother, Mrs. Betty Gardner (Gardner's father had died when he was three). "He was always looking back, wondering what would have happened if he had gone into baseball right out of high school, wondering what would have happened if he hadn't hurt his arm, or if he hadn't tried to throw too soon after the accident."[8]

But to Gardner, his mother's interference regarding his wishes to play professional baseball out of high school was a cruel disregard of his life's ambitions. From the age of ten, the sport consumed him. In 1950, aged twelve, he wrote, "Ever since I have been playing baseball, it has been my ambition to one day be in the major leagues."[9]

After his career ended, his mother, sensing his loneliness and isolation in a life devoid of his obsession, wrote a letter to Fresco Thompson of the Dodgers asking if the organization had some position for her son. After receiving a negative answer from Thompson, Gardner discovered the letter and bitterly wrote in his scrapbook:

> Now my career is over. Eight years late and now my mother is concerned. My mother's philosophy is to get concerned when it is too late. But create the predicament by not using reason beforehand. She says a scout reneged. I guess because I didn't sign. He didn't renege. She shouted 'NO,' at me. I'm afraid the shadows of Rod Dedeaux in the wings made her unable to move in any direction.
>
> Quit bothering the wrong man, Mother. Looking back, I don't see what I could have done differently except to quit baseball earlier. My life was taken away.[10]

Gardner's meticulously maintained scrapbooks included pictures next to which Gardner wrote various thoughts. They provide some insight about what this disturbed young man went through. One page carries a photo of him when he signed his professional contract. He was smiling in the picture, but wrote that he was unhappy.

> I cried that night. I had thrown away three baseball seasons. I had thrown away a very important amount of money. And though I had a college degree, I couldn't see its importance. I was older, and there was something wrong with my arm. It took me a long time to warm up the last few games at USC.[11]

The entry near another photo, taken in 1958, indicated that he had been unhappy ever since his mother had not allowed him to sign a pro contract after he graduated from high school. The photo pictured a smiling Gardner with three USC teammates, but he later wrote:

> I look happy on the outside, but I'm thinking, 'What am I doing here? I should be in professional ball by now, establishing my credentials.'"[12]

Rod Dedeaux, the highly successful USC baseball coach, portrayed Gardner as a very happy athlete during his 40-5 varsity career, which included eighteen wins in 1960. Dedeaux recounted, "He was totally happy with college, yet he could have signed at any time while he was at USC, like Ron Fairly and Len Gabrielson did. There was no restriction whatsoever on keeping kids from signing in those days."[13]

But Gardner, at least near the end, saw things very differently. His suicide note blamed his coach for most of his sorrows.

> Let my blood be the pathetic proof to those who have heard Rod Dedeaux say that a college education is worth $100,000 more in a man's lifetime. Because it is so deceitfully true. The man who starts at $800 a month versus the one who starts at $600 a month will wind up, after 40 years, with $100,000 more.
>
> And isn't that enough reason to shatter the hopes and dreams of an 18-year-old boy who has the opportunity to sign into professional baseball with offers high in five figures?
>
> To keep him in college, don't let him believe that he could do anything with that kind of money but squander it. Don't ask what it is the boy wants to accomplish. Because he might tell you that he would like to go into professional baseball, especially in light of the fact that many who know baseball have regarded him very highly. And that it's his love.

Then don't look too carefully at the facts. Don't think that a good student—president of Bancroft Junior High and Fairfax High—with the determination of a winning miler, captain and three-year cross-country runner, and the excellence of an All-City pitcher, could possibly have the wherewithal to make decisions concerning his own life.

Since he is too young to sign for himself, scare his mother. It's even easier, because his father passed away when the son was three. Let the mother feel that her boy will be wandering skid row if he leaves college. So that when he begs her to let him sign, she has nothing but shouts of 'no.' Do all these things carefully, Rod Dedeaux, and you will have an All-American. And his mother will get her vicarious college degree. Don't let any of his advantages get in the way of your National Championship.

He'll have graduated before your half-truths become the realities of his place in the world. And then he'll wonder where is the magic in the education you don't seek, and why so much energy is compulsively wasted in containing his bitterness and moving one foot in front of the other to get to each day's meaningless job. Where his $800 a month won't buy the home he's never had, meet the friends he's never entertained, nor call the mother he never wants to see. To what direction have the fragments of his broken heart discarded his ability to give and receive love?

But given another 32 years in retirement he'll be able to look back with that overpowering joyful knowledge that some people in their work-a-day world jobs didn't earn the $100,000 more that he did in his. And that's when he'll hug his diploma and die of unhappiness. But somehow I don't need to wait anymore for that day. I reached it years and years ago.

I saw no value in my college education. I saw life going downhill every day and it shaped my attitude toward everything and everybody. Everything and every feeling that I visualized with my earned and rightful start in baseball was the focal point of continuous failure. No pride of accomplishment, no money, no home, no sense of fulfillment, no leverage, no attraction. A bitter past, blocking any accomplishment of a future except age.

I brought it to a halt tonight at 32.

6-6-71[14]

After drinking the equivalent of four highballs on June 7, and leaving a will in the roller of his typewriter, he drove to the USC campus. The bulk of his $3,000 estate was left to a friend and he gave his mother just one dollar.[15] By his own account he had been dead since leaving professional baseball.

Notes

1. *Daily Trojan*, November 14, 1985.
2. Ibid.
3. Los Angeles *Times*, June 10, 1971.
4. *Daily Trojan*, November 14, 1985.
5. Ibid.
6. *Los Angeles Magazine*, June 6, 1986.
7. Marty Biegel, personal interview, June 1, 1998.
8. Los Angeles *Times*, June 10, 1971.
9. Ibid.
10. *Daily Trojan*, November 14, 1985.
11. *Daily Trojan*, November 14, 1985.
12. Ibid.
13. San Francisco *Examiner*, June 19, 1971.
14. *Daily Trojan*, November 14, 1985.
15. *Daily Trojan*, November 14, 1985.

Bibb Falk

Charles Kaufman

In 1920, about the time Judge Kenesaw Mountain Landis wound up and fired a blistering ban ball at the heads of eight ball players in Chicago, the White Sox were battling for another American League flag and accelerating their search for new talent. One prospect was Bibb Augustus Falk (1899-1989), a young college pitcher from Texas, who was summoned to hop a train to Chicago in June. He mostly watched as the soon-to-become Black Sox were building another championship season. That is, until Landis issued his edict, rendering the Sox as Samson without locks. The White Sox were en route to St. Louis when Falk got the news that he was starting that day in left field, filling the shoes of Shoeless Joe Jackson.

Undefeated in three years as a starting lefthanded pitcher at the University of Texas at Austin—he also played outfield and first base, and hit .360, .460, and .400—Falk brought his tools to a team that was primed to win its second consecutive American League pennant. Then, with Cicotte, Felsch, Gandil and company exiled, the White Sox lost two of their last three games. Cleveland, boosted by its own Texas slugger, Tris Speaker, took the flag.

That fall day in Chicago, the first game of his career, Falk batted fifth and collected three of the team's eleven hits, going three-for-five. The Sox lost, 8-6—that was a game with fourteen runs, played in one hour and forty minutes. During his seventeen at-bats in seven games at the end of the 1920 season, Falk showed

power. Of his five hits, one was a double, another a triple.

Over twelve seasons with the Clean Sox and the Cleveland Indians, Falk registered statistics that were reasonably close to those of his predecessor. His lifetime .314 average is among the highest of any eligible player who is not in the Hall of Fame. He hit more home runs and almost as many doubles as Jackson, in 331 fewer career at bats. Falk's fielding average was better than Jackson's, .967 to .962. From 1923 to 1927, Falk hit .328. In 1924, he finished third in the batting race to Babe Ruth and Charlie Jamieson, with a .352 mark.

In 1923, Falk was selected to tour with a dozen other Americans in Japan, China, and Korea. He hit third on a team that included Herb Pennock, George Kelly, Luke Sewell, Casey Stengel, Waite Hoyt, Amos Strunk, Emil Meusel, Riggs Stephenson, Bart Griffith, Bullet Joe Bush, and Fred Hofmann. He hit for the cycle in each of the Americans' first two games and consistently registered multiple-hit games.

Back home, baseball was changing right before Falk's eyes. Jackson and the Black Sox were banned. So was the spitball and "emery ball" in 1921. Ruth emerged. Two years later Yankee Stadium was built. It was definitely a hitter's era

Some things did not change, however—like salaries in Chicago. Falk received a $1,000 bonus and a $2,500 rookie salary, but over the next eight seasons, he experienced Charles Comiskey's frugality and made known his discontent. Falk showed characteristic guts by being the only player who demanded and got two-year contracts. After his big .352 season in 1924 he wrote

Charles Kaufman *is president of Kaufman Communications, a media and communications consulting firm in Austin, Texas. He played baseball at the University of Texas in 1971-72.*

Bib Falk
CHICAGO, A.L.

Mike Falk

The young Bibb Falk's swing made him a feared line drive hitter, averaging .314 during his twelve-year career. His name appeared in print—and in his own accommodating autographs—as both Bib and Bibb.

the White Sox asking if they thought he deserved a bonus. "They wrote back," Falk recalled, "that they didn't, saying they'd never heard of a player giving them a refund after he had a bad year."

As the team lay mired in the second division during the twenties, Falk's dissatisfaction with his salary soared. After the 1928 season, he was shipped off to Cleveland for catcher Martin "Chick" Autry and $30,000. Connie Mack wanted Falk for his rebuilding A's, but he wouldn't give up Rube Walberg, whom

Comiskey demanded. The Yankees, it was rumored, wanted Falk and Eddie Collins for Bob Meusel, Aaron Ward, and a third player the teams could never agree on.

Cleveland would make a suitable home. Indians fans remembered how Falk had stolen three games as a member of the Sox with sensational catches at League Park. They also figured that many of his line drives would ricochet off the right field wall for extra base hits. In his first year as an Indian, he hit four homers in a six-day span, a colossal feat for anyone who wasn't a barrel-chested Yankee.

Indians manager Roger Peckinpaugh said he considered Falk one of "the truly great outfielders of the game's history—strong hitter, and great thrower and a marvelous fielder. Why, I've seen that fellow make catches that no other outfielder has duplicated in my time. He is the only man I ever saw who could leave his feet in a dive after a fly ball and make the catch, while actually in midair. Other fielders will lunge after a ball so that they are off balance and slide on their rears after they make the catch, but they have a foot on the ground when they stick out their mitt. This guy just sails through the air and grabs the ball while both feet are off the ground. As far as his throwing, there are mighty few men in the game who can whip the ball around as swiftly and as accurately as Falk."

That accuracy and strength harked back to his days as a pitcher. In fact, Falk typically warmed up for big league games in the bullpen. Old habit, mostly, but he once said he did it just to stay trim. Anyway, in his mind he never was sure when he might be called on to pitch. (In a 1919 semipro game in Donna, Texas, Falk struck out thirty players in a sixteen-inning game, winning, 2-1. He threw a fastball, a curve, and a "mysterious" knuckler.)

Falk's defensive play impressed others beside Peckinpaugh. Willie Kamm, whose thirteen-year career with the White Sox and Indians almost paralleled Falk's, told New York *Evening Journal* reporter Ford Frick that "the greatest individual play" he ever saw was in Yankee Stadium by Bibb Falk on a screaming line drive by Bob Meusel. "Bob swung viciously," Kamm said. "The ball sailed on a dead line over third and down the left field foul line. It looked a sure double at the least.

Falk, left, and George Kelly pose with a Korean during the 1923 tour. The caption in Falk's album reads: "Some hat."

Mike Falk

"But Bibb was away at the crack of the bat and he came in fast. No one thought he could possibly get there. I don't think he thought so himself. But he kept coming. And when it seemed the ball would surely hit the ground he left his feet in an old-fashioned football dive. Watching him from third it seemed to me he slid full twenty feet, and then he stretched out his hand and took the ball. His head and shoulders were on the ground, his feet in the air, and he was only inches from the concrete stand. But he held on—and came up with the ball.

"The stands rocked with applause as he walked to the bench. Even the Yankees rushed out of their dugout to pat him on the back. I've seen a lot of great plays, but that one, to my mind, was the greatest I ever saw."

Falk had twenty-six assists in 1924. In 1926 he topped all outfielders with a .992 fielding average, making only three errors in more than 350 chances.

Falk did more on the field than any box score or mass of career statistics would ever reveal. He didn't earn the nickname "Jockey" for nothing. He rode players unmercifully from the bench, and he wasn't afraid of tossing a few verbal darts at the plate. In later years he remembered facing the Yankees, batting with men on base. The count was full. Just as the pitcher began winding up to deliver a 3-2 pitch, Falk stepped out of the batter's box. After calling time, he turned to umpire Tom Connolly to explain that a gust of wind had blown sand in his eyes.

"It's funny to me," Connolly told him, "that you players are always getting sand in your eyes and we umpires never do."

"That's because you guys keep your eyes closed," Falk said.

"You'd better swing at the next one, son," the future Hall of Fame ump fired back. "It's going to be a strike."

One of Bibb's favorite targets was Babe Ruth. Bibb called him a "gooney bird" because Babe was, well, a big goon and had those twig legs. In one game when they were both playing left field, Falk spotted a dead sparrow on the ground. He stuffed it into the mitt that the Babe had tossed aside at the end of an inning. When he jogged back to the outfield Ruth had a hard time jamming his fingers in the mitt and soon discovered the feathered mess that was inside. He instantly knew who the culprit was, boomed Falk's name, and sprinted toward the Sox bench. Bibb escaped through the tunnel, shut the door, and brought down a crossbar that served as a lock. Bibb said Babe was so big and strong that when he slammed into the metal door he nearly knocked it down.

Falk retired as a player after the 1931 season, then drew a managing assignment with the Indians' Toledo club. He moved back to Cleveland as a coach before taking a similar position with the Red Sox in 1934. He scouted for Boston between 1935 and 1940, when he returned to Austin to attend to family members and coach at his alma mater. He even donned a uniform for Uncle Sam at age 43 and oversaw the athletic program for the Army Air Force in San Antonio. After the war he resumed his post with the University of Texas Longhorns.

Riggs Stephenson, Falk, Casey Stengel, and Luke Sewell toast their successes during the tour. "Not soda water either!"notes the scrapbook.

While everything Falk frowned on was "bush league" or "semipro," from politicians and boxers to movie actresses, everything about Bibb Falk was "big league," bat, arm, even his acid-laced tongue. Players he coached said his vocabulary was "rough" and "starchy." Everybody was either "lefty"—even right handers—or a "mullet." He was always direct and to the point. "Goddam you lefthander, get that ball over the plate." When people eyed him curiously for the foul language, he reminded them that he was a coach, not a preacher.

Falk paid attention to baseball detail. He stole signs. He recognized opposing players' weaknesses and tendencies. He knew and talked about every conceivable baseball nuance. He would never argue balls or strikes, but no one beat him on a rules violation. When he walked toward an umpire, reaching in his back pocket for his rule book, umpires knew they were in for a test. During practice sessions, Falk was legendary as a master of that arcane baseball skill, hitting fungos.

He also mastered staying unmarried fir his entire life and the stock market. He made his fortune buying and holding General Motors and Sun Ray Oil, among other stocks, but he never flaunted his wealth, living in a bungalow in an old Austin neighborhood. A tough guy on the outside, Falk frequently played Santa for his family and often came through financially for friends in need.

When he was asked to be Texas coach Billy Disch's assistant, he was told that while the department couldn't afford all of the $2,400 head coach's salary, it could find $1,200 for him. Falk took the job, but not the money. "Let me tell you one damn thing," he said. "As long as that ol' man is alive, he gets every penny of it." Eventually succeeding his old coach, Falk won back-to-back NCAA national championships in 1949 and 1950 and two decades worth of conference titles. Players from Bobby Layne to Max Alvis describe a man with a diamond-hard exterior and an interior as soft as pudding.

Baseball Mascots in the Nineteenth Century

Larry G. Bowman

Men would never be superstitious, if they could govern all their circumstances set by rules, or if they were always favored by fortune: but being driven into straits where the rules are useless, and being often kept fluctuating pitiably between hope and fear by the uncertainty of fortune's greedily coveted favors, they are prone to credulity."
    —Spinoza, Tractus-Theologica Politicus[1]

The culture of baseball in the late nineteenth century exhibited a fascination with the impact of superstitions upon the outcome of games. Fans, players, managers, and owners all paid a good deal more attention than we do to the effects of such matters as mascots, "hoodoos," and other forms of supernatural intervention in the daily outcome of games. Historians and novelists of the early days of the game often mention mascots, and normally attribute their presence to ignorance and racism. But the existence of mascots may have been more complicated than simply products of primitive thought.

An article in the Chicago *Tribune* dated April 6, 1890, asserted that the early years of baseball witnessed many superstitious practices which were foolish and senseless. The unsigned item speculated that the primary reason for such widespread practices arose from the fact that most of the players came from lower-class, poorly-educated elements of American society, and that the athletes and the managers brought their eccentric beliefs with them to organized baseball.[2] But, the *Tribune* article went on to emphasize, the game changed in the late 1880s and a new breed of better-educated,

more genteel players banished the more egregious practices from the game.

One habit the *Tribune* castigated was the use of mascots by professional teams. According to the article, mascots were: "...generally chosen for some hideous peculiarity, such as a dwarfed figure, hump-back, or crossed eyes. If a little negro, black as the ace of spades, dwarfed in every limb, and with crossed eyes could have been secured the ideal mascot would have been presented to the gaze of the base-ball world."[3]

The questions are, first, why did the ideal mascot need to be misshapen, preferably African American, and diminutive in stature, and second, was the *Tribune* correct in its assertion that superstitions were the legacies of ignorant ballplayers?

On the matter of the persuasiveness of superstitious practices, many scholars argue that superstition is not solely the province of poorly educated people. Gustav Johoda, the author of *The Psychology of Superstition*, points out that Sigmund Freud and C. C. Jung agree that:

> "... superstitious beliefs and practices are deeply rooted in man's unconscious mental processes; both held that superstition is not a thing of the past, or confined to the less educated—in fact it is regarded as a part of everybody's mental makeup liable to come to the surface under certain circumstances."[4]

Arguing that mascots were simply a product of lower-class, poorly educated minds may well have been

Larry G. Bowman *lives in Denton, Texas.*

inaccurate. Late-nineteenth-century ballplayers may have largely been drawn from lower-class rungs in American society, but many psychologists argue that the players' sense of superstition arose from a primeval essence within mankind, not their ignorance.

Why did mascots need to be misshapen or dwarfs? According to C. J. S. Thompson, one possible answer may stem from beliefs found among all races from earliest times that hunchbacks, dwarfs, and deformed people with squinting or different colored eyes possessed powers to protect people from misfortune.[5] Perhaps the earliest historical example of such a figure to parry evil appeared in ancient Egypt in the form of a household god known as "Bes" or "Bishu." Bes has been described as a dwarf or embryo-like god with a tail, a broad flat nose, the ears of a cat, long arms, and crooked legs. His image was that of a talisman against sorcery, and he was placed on or near beds to keep evil spirits away from sleepers.[6] Evidence indicates he was probably imported by the Egyptians from Nubia. Modern-day archaeologists have found scores of clay figurines of Bes in the detritus of excavated Egyptian sites which indicates that Bes apparently had a pervasive presence in the daily lives of early Egyptian society.

After Alexander the Great conquered Egypt, the Phoenicians adopted Bes and introduced him to other parts of the Mediterranean world.[7] That led to the introduction of the god to the emerging western European societies' lore of superstitions where eventually the concept rooted itself. The term "mascot," according to Marian Leach, derives from the Provençal word "masco" which means little magician.[8] As a consequence, a Nubian god adopted by the Egyptians eventually penetrated western European culture and then came to America as a part of our forefathers' cultural baggage. Bes was lost in the haze of centuries of travel and metamorphosis, but he, or his descendant, re-emerged in late nineteenth century baseball parks.

Modern-day baseball fans are accustomed to seeing the Phillie Phanatic, the San Diego Chicken, or some other contemporary mascot cavorting about a ballpark and simply entertaining the spectators, leading cheers, and generally behaving foolishly. While turn-of-the-century mascots also led cheers and entertained the fans, they had a more important function. Their principal duty was to fend off the "hoodoo" placed upon their teams by opposing mascots or cranks. Hoodoo, as defined by Marian Leach in the *Dictionary of Folklore, Mythology and Legend*, is:

"A category of magic in the beliefs found among Negroes of the southern United States. The derivation of the word may come from the

Haitian *Vodun* that in turn comes from the identical Dhomean word that means deity. The meaning found in the customary American speech, whereby hoodoo signifies bad luck."[9]

Originally then, the mascots' roles were to take a prominent place among the members of a team, and to serve as lightning rods against misfortune.

In the early days of baseball, when a team was on the road the players dressed in their hotel and then went to the ballpark by carriage or public conveyance. The parade gave the team an opportunity to advertise the game, draw attendance, heap scorn on the local cranks, and deride their loyalty to their local heroes.

During the parade, the mascot was prominently displayed to discourage any of the pedestrians from placing a hoodoo on the team as it journeyed to the game site. Once in the park, the mascot usually glared at the opposing team and its mascot (if it featured one), extended his arms, and shook his fingers and hands at them. That served the double purpose of throwing the hoodoo at the opposition and fending one off in return. During the game the mascot served as a batboy, chattered to his team while it was on the field, entertained the cranks, and kept a vigilant watch for evil spirits that could have an untoward effect on the game's outcome. Mascots were entertainment, but they were the talismen against misfortune. Certainly, many of the spectators and players did not take the mascots too seriously, but until the 1890s the diminutive charmmakers were a common sight in dugouts.[10] In the 1880s, the prime example of a mascot emerged in the person of Clarence Duval, whose name became associated with Albert Goodwill Spalding's Chicago White Stockings.

Clarence Duval served as a mascot to the Chicago White Stockings in 1888 and 1889. Not much is known about him prior to his brief stint with the team, and after his brief association with the White Stockings, he slipped away into obscurity. But in 1888 and 1889, Duval became something of a celebrity in baseball circles.

Early in the 1888 season, Adrian Constantine "Cap" Anson, the redoubtable leader of Albert Goodwill Spalding's Chicago White Stockings, discovered Duval[11] in Philadelphia. Anson was intrigued by the diminutive African American's skills and appearance. Although not a dwarf, Duval was quite small and he could sing, dance, and twirl a baton with great artistry. In the racist language common in that era, Anson later wrote of Duval that Clarence was, "…a little darkey…a singer and a dancer of no mean ability, and a little coon whose skill in handling a baton would have put to the blush many a bandmaster of national reputation."[12]

While serving as mascot for the White Stockings during a vital series with New York, Duval attracted a good deal of attention. He led the team to the Polo Grounds, coped with potential hoodoos, served as a batboy and comrade for the White Stockings, and sang and danced for the fans and the players. Duval, who became the epitome of a mascot in the eyes of baseball fans, fascinated Verona Jarbeau, a French actress touring the United States with a troupe of vaudevillians.[13] Sensing that he might have some box-office appeal, Mademoiselle Jarbeau invited Duval to join her company and tour with it. The glamour of the stage proved too much for Clarence. He left the White Stockings. Or, in the eyes of Anson and several of the White Stockings, he deserted the team. The players had bought him new clothing, pampered him, and generally, they thought, promoted his interests, only to be unkindly repaid when he joined Jarbeau's troupe.

After the 1888 season, the White Stockings embarked on a series of postseason exhibition games. The extended road show started in Chicago and was first billed as the "Australian Tour." The "tour" was Spalding's notion of a means to showcase major league baseball in parts of the United States where it was something of a novelty, and to take the game to New Zealand and Australia where he hoped to popularize it and, coincidentally, to serve his interests as a sporting-goods tycoon. The White Stockings were accompanied by a handpicked roster of major league all-stars (headlined by John Montgomery Ward of the New York Giants) who were billed as the All Americas. The teams were scheduled to play a long series of exhibition games in the United States, the Sandwich Islands, New Zealand, and Australia. Once on the road the tour proved so successful financially that Spalding decided to return home by way of the Suez Canal, making stops in Asia, Africa, and Western Europe. Consequently, it became a "World Tour."

Duval unexpectedly became a part of Spalding's traveling baseball show. He appeared when the White Stockings and the All Americas arrived in Omaha, Nebraska, on October 25 for one of their exhibition dates. The teams made the usual parade by carriage from the railway depot to the playing field. En route, several of the players noticed Duval standing among the spectators. According to the account in the Chicago *Times*: "…The boys were a little surprised upon starting their parade to see the little son of Ham among the crowd. He was lifted into one of the carriages and warmly welcomed."[14] Although some of the players were glad to see Duval, Anson was not among them. He at first refused to reinstate Clarence as mascot. Later in the day, he relented and declared he would permit Duval to accompany the teams to Hastings, Nebraska, where they were booked for an appearance the next day.[15]

Duval's benefactors, Anson reluctantly among them, thereupon contributed to a purse, purchased new clothing for Clarence, gave him a bath he did not want, and got him ready for the game. When the White Stockings and the All Americas arrived in Hastings the next day, the spiffy Duval led the teams to the field from the railway. Decked out in his new outfit, he strutted ahead of the players and obviously pleased the crowd with his antics. Al Spalding, who had just rejoined the tour after a business trip to Kansas City, quickly recognized that the mascot added a good deal to the excitement of the afternoon's festivities. After the game, Spalding invited Duval to travel with the teams and to serve as the official mascot of the tour.[16] Clarence became a minor celebrity.

This was partially the doing of Harry Clay Palmer. He represented the New York *Herald*, Boston *Herald*, Chicago *Tribune*, and the *Sporting Life* on the tour, and regularly filed reports about the tour's progress and the day-to-day events of the players and their companions. Palmer also published *Athletic Sports in America, England and Australia* in 1889, which was his detailed account of the world-girdling tour, and Duval played a prominent part in his narrative of the teams and their activities.

Clarence's showmanship was his greatest asset. He always led the players to the ball park, and you can imagine what a sight he must have been to the spectators in New Zealand, Australia, and in Western Europe. Dressed in a fine suit of clothes, strutting magnificently, and twirling a baton, Duval cut quite a figure. He was a sight to behold.

Once the teams arrived in the ball park, Clarence strode up and down the bench, keeping a wary eye open for evil spirts. His vigilant watch for harbingers of misfortune intrigued spectators. Second, he served as bat boy. And finally, Clarence chattered with the players on the field, danced about in the bench area, and generally amused the patrons during lulls in the game.

Duval's antics made him famous with the fans who witnessed his show, and with the baseball fans in the United States who followed the tour in the accounts Palmer filed. Duval and Palmer unconsciously set the standard for mascots to come.

Off the field, Clarence amused his companions. He sang, danced, served tables, and often gambled with the players as they whiled away the long hours on trains and steamships, but he was not a social equal. Class and race lines were clearly drawn in Spalding's entourage, and Clarence, of course, was at the bottom of the social scale. Nevertheless, even though he was frequently the butt of jokes and pranks, Clarence apparently enjoyed his role, and he was not overtly abused.

When the tour returned to the United States in April, 1889, the fans in New York City organized a raucous welcome for the teams which, among other things, featured a banquet at Delmonico's attended by such luminaries as Mark Twain, Theodore Roosevelt, actor DeWolf Hopper, Chauncey Depew, the mayors of Jersey City, Brooklyn, and Hartford, Connecticut, and others.[17] About 300 people attended the banquet to honor Spalding and his players.

Duval's name does not appear in any of the accounts of the festivities in New York City or in the accounts of the teams' last days on the road. Either he again jumped ship or he simply was not newsworthy enough to draw attention once the teams were back in the United States.

Clarence Duval is one of those shadowy figures who decorate historical events but prove elusive in later times. The model mascot disappeared from public notice, and died as the result of injuries he sustained when he was run over by a train in Bloomington, Illinois, in the summer of 1892.[18]

Notes:

1. Benedict de Spinoza, *A Theological-Political Treatise and A Political Treatise*, R. H. M. Elwes, trans. (New York: Dover Publications, 1951), 3.

2. Chicago *Tribune*, April 6, 1890, 36.

3. Ibid. Crossed eyes especially concerned ballplayers, fans, and other sportsmen patronizing racetracks or other sporting events. See "Queered by Cross-Eyes," Chicago *Daily News*, August 14, 1886, 5. Jim Hart, the manager of the National League Boston team, knew that Jim Mutrie, manager of the New York Giants, had a particular phobia about crossed eyes. Iin 1889 a rumor emerged that Hart planned to hire a score of cross-eyed men to sit behind the Giants dugout at the Polo Grounds to unnerve Mutrie during a series with Boston. The bizarre hoodoo effort did not occur, but many people put some credence in the rumor. *The Sporting News*, July 20, 1889.

4. Gustav Johoda, *The Psychology of Superstition* (London: The Penguin Press, 1969), 69.

5. C. J. S. Thompson, *The Hand of Destiny: The Folk-Lore and Superstition of Everyday Life* (Detroit: The Singing Tree Press, 1970), 67.

6. Ibid. Gertrude Jobes, ed., *Dictionary of Mythology, Folklore and Symbols* (New York: Scarecrow Press, 1961), I, 205-06.

7. Walter Addison Jayne, *The Healing Gods of Ancient Civilizations* (New York: University Books, 1962), 32.

8. Marian L. Leach, *Dictionary of Folklore, Mythology and Legend* (New York: Funk and Wagnalls, 1949), I, 502.

9. Ibid.

10. *The Sporting News*, July 30 and August 10, 1889.

11. Harry Clay Palmer, *Athletic Sports in America, England and Australia* (Philadelphia: Hubbard Brothers Publishers, 1889), 168.

12. Adrian C. Anson, *A Ball Player's Career* (Chicago: Era Publishing Company, 1900), 148. (Chicago *Times*, October 26, 1888, 2.

13. Anson, *A Ball Player's Career*, 148. Palmer, *Athletic Sports*, 168. (Chicago *Times*, October 26, 1888, 2.)

14. Chicago *Times*, October 26, 1888.

15. Rocky Mountain *News*, October 28, 1888, 3.

16. Palmer, *Athletic Sports*, 141.

17. Ibid., 444-49. *The Sporting News*, April 13, 1889. Peter Levine, *A. G. Spalding and the Rise of Baseball: The Promise of American Sport* (New York: Oxford University Press, 1985), 107. New York *Tribune*, April 9, 1889.

18. Chicago *Tribune*, July 22, 1892, 7. Jerry Malloy, an indefatigable researcher as most SABR members know, supplied me the note on Duval's fate, and I gratefully acknowledge his assistance.

Ouch! A Hit in his only at bat

On September 11, 1955 Fred Van Dusen of the Phillies accomplished a feat probably unique in major league history when he was hit by a pitch in his only major league plate appearance. In the second game of a doubleheader that day at Milwaukee's County Stadium, Van Dusen made his major league debut in the ninth inning as a pinch hitter for relief pitcher Lynn Lovenguth when he was hit by a pitch from Braves pitcher Humberto Robinson. Van Dusen thus compiled a lifetime on base percentage of 1.000 while having no lifetime batting average without the benefit of a base on balls.

—Charlie Bevis

The Six Degrees of Rogers Hornsby

Tom Remes

In 1997, when the Baseball Writers Association of America voted on its all-time team, it voted Rogers Hornsby its starting second baseman.

And why not. Seven batting titles. Highest single-season batting average in the twentieth century (.424 in 1924). Second-highest career batting average (behind Ty Cobb). Along with Ted Williams, the only man to win two Triple Crowns. World Series champ. Hall of Famer.

But there's another reason Hornsby belongs on the all-time team that the writers couldn't possibly have known, and that nobody knew until now: The baseball universe revolves around Rogers Hornsby.

The same way the movie universe revolves around Kevin Bacon.

Thus, the Six Degrees of Rogers Hornsby.

To introduce this baseball game, I've connected a current player from each major league team, as of the end of the 1998 season, back to the Rajah in six steps.

And to make it more challenging, I set up these conditions: a.) each current major leaguer used must have played for someone other than his current team (that's why you won't find Tony Gwynn, Ken Griffey, Jr., Barry Larkin or Chuck Finley); b.) the current team (franchise) of each current major leaguer cannot be used during his run; c.) no team used more than twice in any particular run, with the two uses having to be consecutive and separated by at least ten years; d.) no player used more than once.

Tom Remes' *connection to Rogers Hornsby is that he too spent his best years living and working in St. Louis.*

(If you want to try playing the Six Degrees of Rogers Hornsby yourself, you're going to need either Bob Costas or the *Baseball Encyclopedia*. I went with the book even though it weighs more.)

It's too bad Rogers Hornsby isn't around to appreciate this renewed fame. But given that he shunned reading to save his batting eye, he probably wouldn't have seen it anyway.

Arizona Diamondbacks
Matt Williams was on the 1990 San Francisco Giants with
Rick Reuschel who was on the 1973 Chicago Cubs with
Billy Williams who was on the 1961 Chicago Cubs with
Richie Ashburn who was on the 1949 Philadelphia Phillies with
Schoolboy Rowe who was on the 1936 Detroit Tigers with
Jack Burns who was on the 1934 St. Louis Browns with
Rogers Hornsby

Atlanta Braves
Greg Maddux was on the 1987 Chicago Cubs with
Andre Dawson who was on the 1977 Montreal Expos with
Tony Perez who was on the 1965 Cincinnati Reds with
Joe Nuxhall who was on the 1944 Cincinnati Reds with
Woody Williams who was on the 1938 Brooklyn Dodgers with
Leo Durocher who was on the 1933 St. Louis Cardinals with

Rogers Hornsby

Chicago Cubs
Sammy Sosa was on the 1990 Chicago White Sox with
Carlton Fisk who was on the 1972 Boston Red Sox with
Luis Tiant who was on the 1966 Cleveland Indians with
Rocky Colavito who was on the 1956 Cleveland Indians with
Cal McLish who was on the 1944 Brooklyn Dodgers with
Johnny Cooney who was on the 1928 Boston Braves with

Rogers Hornsby

Cincinnati Reds
Bret Boone was on the 1992 Seattle Mariners with
Pete O'Brien who was on the 1985 Texas Rangers with
Buddy Bell who was on the 1974 Cleveland Indians with
Jim Perry who was on the 1959 Cleveland Indians with
Elmer Valo who was on the 1942 Philadelphia Athletics with
Bill Knickerbocker who was on the 1937 St. Louis Browns with

Rogers Hornsby

Colorado Rockies
Larry Walker was on the 1989 Montreal Expos with
Hubie Brooks who was on the 1980 New York Mets with
Elliott Maddox who was on the 1970 Detroit Tigers with
Al Kaline who was on the 1956 Detroit Tigers with
Bob Kennedy who was on the 1940 Chicago White Sox with
Jack Knott who was on the 1934 St. Louis Browns with

Rogers Hornsby

Florida Marlins
Gregg Zaun was on the 1995 Baltimore Orioles with
Kevin Bass who was on the 1985 Houston Astros with
Joe Niekro who was on the 1967 Chicago Cubs with
Curt Simmons who was on the 1949 Philadelphia Phillies with
Eddie Miller who was on the 1936 Cincinnati Reds with
Bill Hallahan who was on the 1926 St. Louis Cardinals with

Rogers Hornsby

Houston Astros
Randy Johnson was on the 1988 Montreal Expos with
Andy McGaffigan who was on the 1985 Cincinnati Reds with
Pete Rose who was on the 1963 Cincinnati Reds with
Charlie Neal who was on the 1956 Brooklyn Dodgers with
Pee Wee Reese who was on the 1940 Brooklyn Dodgers with
Joe Medwick who was on the 1933 St. Louis Cardinals with

Rogers Hornsby

Los Angeles Dodgers
Gary Sheffield was on the 1991 Milwaukee Brewers with
Robin Yount who was on the 1975 Milwaukee Brewers with
Hank Aaron who was on the 1954 Milwaukee Braves with
Lew Burdette who was on the 1950 New York Yankees with
Johnny Mize who was on the 1936 St. Louis Cardinals with
Jesse Haines who was on the 1924 St. Louis Cardinals with

Rogers Hornsby

Milwaukee Brewers
Jeromy Burnitz was on the 1993 New York Mets with
Frank Tanana who was on the 1980 California Angels with
Freddie Patek who was on the 1975 Kansas City Royals with
Harmon Killebrew who was on the 1954 Washington Senators with
Mickey Vernon who was on the 1943 Washington Senators with
Tony Guiliani who was on the 1936 St. Louis Browns with

Rogers Hornsby

Montreal Expos
Dustin Hermanson was on the 1995 San Diego Padres with
Fernando Valenzuela who was on the 1982 Los Angeles Dodgers with
Rick Monday who was on the 1966 Kansas City Athletics with
Mike Hershberger who was on the 1962 Chicago White Sox with
Early Wynn who was on the 1942 Washington Senators with
Bobo Newsom who was on the 1934 St. Louis Browns with

Rogers Hornsby

New York Mets

John Olerud was on the 1992 Toronto Blue Jays with
Pat Tabler who was on the 1986 Cleveland Indians with
Phil Niekro who was on the 1966 Atlanta Braves with
Eddie Mathews who was on the 1953 Milwaukee
Braves with
Andy Pafko who was on the 1945 Chicago Cubs with
Stan Hack who was on the 1932 Chicago Cubs with
Rogers Hornsby

Philadelphia Phillies

Curt Schilling was on the 1990 Baltimore Orioles with
Mickey Tettleton who was on the 1987 Oakland Athletics with
Carney Lansford who was on the 1978 California Angels with
Ron Fairly who was on the 1959 Los Angeles Dodgers with
Gil Hodges who was on the 1943 Brooklyn Dodgers with
Billy Herman who was on the 1932 Chicago Cubs with
Rogers Hornsby

Pittsburgh Pirates

Turner Ward was on the 1994 Milwaukee Brewers with
Brian Harper who was on the 1979 California Angels with
Nolan Ryan who was on the 1966 New York Mets with
Ken Boyer who was on the 1956 St. Louis Cardinals with
Whitey Lockman who was on the 1945 New York Giants with
Mel Ott who was on the 1927 New York Giants with
Rogers Hornsby

St. Louis Cardinals

Mark McGwire was on the 1987 Oakland Athletics with
Reggie Jackson who was on the 1970 Oakland Athletics with
Felipe Alou who was on the 1958 San Francisco Giants with
Hank Sauer who was on the 1948 Cincinnati Reds with
Ken Raffensberger who was on the 1940 Chicago Cubs with
Gabby Hartnett who was on the 1929 Chicago Cubs with
Rogers Hornsby

San Diego Padres

Ken Caminiti was on the 1987 Houston Astros with
Jose Cruz who was on the 1974 St. Louis Cardinals with
Bob Gibson who was on the 1963 St. Louis Cardinals with
Bobby Shantz who was on the 1949 Philadelphia Athletics with
Eddie Joost who was on the 1936 Cincinnati Reds with
Kiki Cuyler who was on the 1929 Chicago Cubs with
Rogers Hornsby

San Francisco Giants

Barry Bonds was on the 1986 Pittsburgh Pirates with
Jim Morrison who was on the 1980 Chicago White Sox with
Minnie Minoso who was on the 1951 Chicago White Sox with
Hank Majeski who was on the 1939 Boston Braves with
Al Lopez who was on the 1932 Brooklyn Dodgers with
Hack Wilson who was on the 1929 Chicago Cubs with
Rogers Hornsby

Anaheim Angels

Ken Hill was on the 1995 St. Louis Cardinals with
Ozzie Smith who was on the 1982 St. Louis Cardinals with
Jim Kaat who was on the 1961 Minnesota Twins with
Billy Martin who was on the 1950 New York Yankees with
Joe DiMaggio who was on the 1936 New York Yankees with
Pat Malone who was on the 1929 Chicago Cubs with
Rogers Hornsby

Baltimore Orioles

Roberto Alomar was on the 1992 Toronto Blue Jays with
Dave Winfield who was on the 1979 San Diego Padres with
Gaylord Perry who was on the 1964 San Francisco Giants with
Duke Snider who was on the 1947 Brooklyn Dodgers with
Arky Vaughan who was on the 1932 Pittsburgh Pirates with
Tommy Thevenow who was on the 1926 St. Louis Cardinals with
Rogers Hornsby

Boston Red Sox

Pedro Martinez was on the 1993 Los Angeles Dodgers with
Tim Wallach who was on the 1982 Montreal Expos with
Woodie Fryman who was on the 1966 Pittsburgh Pirates with
Billy O'Dell who was on the 1954 Baltimore Orioles with
Vern Stephens who was on the 1944 St. Louis Browns with
Mike Kreevich who was on the 1931 Chicago Cubs with

Rogers Hornsby

Chicago White Sox

Albert Belle was on the 1994 Cleveland Indians with
Jack Morris who was on the 1984 Detroit Tigers with
Darrell Evans who was on the 1975 Atlanta Braves with
Ray Sadecki who was on the 1963 St. Louis Cardinals with
Stan Musial who was on the 1942 St. Louis Cardinals with
Lon Warneke who was on the 1932 Chicago Cubs with
Rogers Hornsby

Cleveland Indians

David Justice was on the 1991 Atlanta Braves with
Lonnie Smith who was on the 1980 Philadelphia Phillies with
Tug McGraw who was on the 1965 New York Mets with
Roy McMillan who was on the 1951 Cincinnati Reds with
Connie Ryan who was on the 1942 New York Giants with
Bill Jurges who was on the 1931 Chicago Cubs with
Rogers Hornsby

Detroit Tigers

Damion Easley was on the 1992 California Angels with
Bert Blyleven who was on the 1971 Minnesota Twins with
Leo Cardenas who was on the 1960 Cincinnati Reds with
Gus Bell who was on the 1950 Pittsburgh Pirates with
Clyde McCullough who was on the 1940 Chicago Cubs with
Dizzy Dean who was on the 1933 St. Louis Cardinals with

Rogers Hornsby

Kansas City Royals

Dean Palmer was on the 1989 Texas Rangers with
Charlie Hough who was on the 1973 Los Angeles Dodgers with
Al Downing who was on the 1967 New York Yankees with
Bill Monbouquette who was on the 1960 Boston Red Sox with
Ted Williams who was on the 1939 Boston Red Sox with
Joe Vosmik who was on the 1937 St. Louis Browns with
Rogers Hornsby

Minnesota Twins

Paul Molitor was on the 1978 Milwaukee Brewers with
Cecil Cooper who was on the 1975 Boston Red Sox with
Carl Yastrzemski who was on the 1962 Boston Red Sox with
Dave Philley who was on the 1947 Chicago White Sox with
Luke Appling who was on the 1930 Chicago White Sox with
Dutch Henry who was on the 1927 New York Giants with

Rogers Hornsby

New York Yankees

David Cone was on the 1993 Kansas City Royals with
George Brett who was on the 1975 Kansas City Royals with
Vada Pinson who was on the 1962 Cincinnati Reds with
Johnny Klippstein who was on the 1950 Chicago Cubs with
Phil Cavarretta who was on the 1935 Chicago Cubs with
Freddie Lindstrom who was on the 1927 New York Giants with

Rogers Hornsby

Oakland Athletics

Dave Magadan was on the 1987 New York Mets with
Keith Hernandez who was on the 1974 St. Louis Cardinals with
Joe Torre who was on the 1961 Milwaukee Braves with
Warren Spahn who was on the 1948 Boston Braves with
Frank McCormick who was on the 1934 Cincinnati Reds with
Jim Bottomley who was on the 1936 St. Louis Browns with

Rogers Hornsby

Seattle Mariners

Jeff Fassero was on the 1992 Montreal Expos with
Gary Carter who was on the 1978 Montreal Expos with
Dave Cash who was on the 1971 Pittsburgh Pirates with
Roberto Clemente who was on the 1956 Pittsburgh Pirates with
George Munger who was on the 1943 St. Louis Cardinals with
Debs Garms who was on the 1933 St. Louis Browns with

Rogers Hornsby

Tampa Bay Devil Rays

Fred McGriff was on the 1992 San Diego Padres with
Craig Lefferts who was on the 1983 Chicago Cubs with
Jay Johnstone who was on the 1969 California Angels with
Hoyt Wilhelm who was on the 1952 New York Giants with
Max Lanier who was on the 1938 St. Louis Cardinals with
Bob Weiland who was on the 1935 St. Louis Browns with

Rogers Hornsby

Texas Rangers

Will Clark was on the 1986 San Francisco Giants with
Vida Blue who was on the 1972 Oakland Athletics with
Ken Holtzman who was on the 1966 Chicago Cubs with
Ernie Banks who was on the 1953 Chicago Cubs with
Dutch Leonard who was on the 1939 Washington Senators with
Sammy West who was on the 1936 St. Louis Browns with

Rogers Hornsby

Toronto Blue Jays

Roger Clemens was on the 1986 Boston Red Sox with
Tom Seaver who was on the 1973 New York Mets with
Willie Mays who was on the 1951 New York Giants with
Eddie Stanky who was on the 1944 Brooklyn Dodgers with
Augie Galan who was on the 1936 Chicago Cubs with
Charlie Grimm who was on the 1918 St. Louis Cardinals with

Rogers Hornsby

If you forget about my conditions you can stay with one team:
Ron Gant was on the 1996 Cardinals with
Ozzie Smith who was on the 1982 Cardinals with
Keith Hernandez who was on the 1974 Cardinals with
Bob Gibson who was on the 1963 Cardinals with
Stan Musial who was on the 1947 Cardinals with
Joe Medwick who was on the 1933 Cardinals with

Rogers Hornsby

And to prove that Hornsby really is the center of the baseball universe, here's his connection to one of baseball's first stars:
Rogers Hornsby
was on the 1919 St. Louis Cardinals with
Walton Cruise who was on the 1919 Boston Braves with
Jim Thorpe who was on the 1914 New York Giants with
Christy Mathewson who was on the 1905 New York Giants with
Bill Dahlen who was on the 1896 Chicago White Sox with
Cap Anson who was on the 1876 Chicago White Sox with

Ross Barnes

Research in Baseball Index (RBI)

An Electronic Index to Baseball Literature
www.baldeagle.com/bibcomm rbi.htm

What is RBI?

RBI is an electronic index to baseball literature encompassing books, pamphlets, magazine and feature newspaper articles, recordings, scores, films - in other words, nearly *everything* - about baseball. Currently, we have cataloged over 120,000 items (over 17,000 books, 93,000 articles, and 12,000 book sections) and are adding thousands more each year.

RBI is now by far the largest resource available on baseball literature and provides an excellent starting point for any baseball research project.

- *Are you writing a book about Cal Ripken?*
- *Are you interested in the Black Sox Scandal?*
- *Are you looking for some books on how to throw a curveball?*
- *Are you working on a bibliography to baseball poetry?*
- *Are you researching aluminum vs. wood bats?*

RBI will list many sources on these subjects.

Individual records include:

- Author
- Title
- Copyright date
- Statistical and graphical information
- Material type
- Named persons (significant detail)
- Topics
- Full bibliographic data

All types of information are searchable.

How can I get it?

RBI is available to anyone as a data file on CD-ROM. A free **demo download** is available at:

**www.baldeagle.com/bibcomm/
rbicdrom.htm**

The CD-ROM includes the **RBI** database, a subject term directory, an index to RBI's Bibliographic Coding system, and a printed manual with searching tips (manual and coding system are included as electronic text files).

Available formats are:
- MS Access 2.0+
- Paradox 5.0+
- dBase
- MS FoxPro
- MS Excel 97
- Lotus 1-2-3
- FileMaker Pro 3.0+ (only Mac format available)

Minimum Requirements:
- **486/50, 8mbs RAM or higher (PC)**
- **68040, 8mbs RAM of higher (Mac)**
- **30 mbs of hard disk space**

Simply copy the RBI database to your computer's hard disk and search it the way you would any other file using your computer's commercial database program (see available formats listed above).

When placing your order, be sure to Include the computer and software types you require.

RBI on CD-ROM

(Full Database)
Includes Manual and Coding Key

tion	One-Time Purchase	One-Year* Subscrip-
SABR members	$70	$90
Non-Members	$105	$130

Note: Institutional and Network orders are available. Please contact us at the one of the addresses below.

* - *Includes first copy plus two updates (one every six months). Subscriptions are renewable at half the first year price.*

MN Residents add 6 1/2% sales tax

International customers, please pay in US dollars.

Payment can be made with check or money order.

Institutions: Please include purchase order number.

Orders are filled within 3 weeks upon receipt of payment or purchase order.

Mail your order to:
RBI
3536 Orchard Lane
Minnetonka MN 55305

Questions? Please write to us at the address above or at:

sabrrbi@baldeagle.com

Want to use RBI's resource without buying the whole database? Try the…

RBI Data Service

www.baldeagle.com/bibcomm/
dataserv.htm

This is a Fee-Based research service. There is no charge for initial inquiries, but a fee will be charged for obtaining literature references.

The RBI Data Service will allow you to access the RBI Database and gather information on any baseball topic, *other than statistical data*. Think carefully about your research topic before submitting your request.

Once you have decided on your research request, send your request to via post or email to the address above.

Requests normally take 3-5 days to process.   You will be notified via email or post as to the results of your research request. The results will relate the number of sources found, along with a fee statement for obtaining the information. You are charged only if you decide that you want to see the list of sources found in the search.

RBI Data Service Pricing
for SABR Members*

# of Citations	Via Email	Via Post
1-25 Citations	$2	$3
26-50 Citations	$4	$6
51-100 Citations	$6	$8
101-200 Citations	$8	$12
201-300 Citations	$12	$16
301-400 Citations	$15	$20
401-500 Citations	$20	$25
501-600 Citations	$25	$30
601-750 Citations	$35	$45
Over 750	Negotiable	Negotiable

* - *Pricing for non-members is higher - Please review our Web site for further information.*